Grace Moore
and Her Many Worlds

Also by ROWENA RUTHERFORD FARRAR:

Bend Your Heads All
A Wondrous Moment Then

Grace Moore
and Her Many Worlds

Rowena Rutherford Farrar

New York ● *Cornwall Books* ● *London*

Cornwall Books
4 Cornwall Drive
East Brunswick, New Jersey 08816

Cornwall Books
27 Chancery Lane
London WC2A 1NS, England

Cornwall Books
Toronto M5E 1A7, Canada

Library of Congress Cataloging in Publication Data

Farrar, Rowena Rutherford.
  Grace Moore and her many worlds.

  Bibliography: p.
  Includes index.
  1. Moore, Grace, 1898–1947.   2. Singers—United States
—Biography.   I. Title.
ML420.M57F4   782.1′092′4   [B]   81-67955
ISBN 0-8453-4723-3   AACR2

Printed in the United States of America

For
Jimmy, Gina, Sally, and Suzy

Contents

List of Illustrations   9
Foreword   11
Preface   13
Acknowledgments   19

Part I: Running Wild in the Sun

1   The Sparks Would Fly   27
2   Born to Sing   34
3   The Quality of Obsession   44
4   The Thirsty Sponge   49

Part II: Her Guardian Angels

5   Glorious Adventures   63
6   New Worlds to Conquer   74
7   Star Quality   85
8   A Heady Hilltop   94

Part III: To Keep a Dream

9   Now or Never   101
10   Mimi   107
11   A Bitter Dose   117
12   Dreaming a New Dream   127

Part IV: Another World

13   In and out of Hollywood   135
14   Music between Them   144
15   Comeback   155
16   Busiest Girl in the World   165
17   Her Melodic Grace   175
18   War with Hollywood   180
19   Somewhat of a Goddess   188
20   "A Damn Good Buy"   194

Part V: War Clouds

21	Louise	207
22	Far Away Meadows	222
23	Without Her Balance Wheel	231
24	Tosca	238

Part VI: War Years

25	Ravishing Prima Donna	247
26	"Talons, Great Wings, and a Strong Heart"	254
27	Final Curtain	263

Part VII: The Magic Quality

Epilogue: The Whole World Grieved	279
Appendix: Metropolitan Opera Appearances, 1928–1946	283
Grace Moore Discography	284
Notes	292
Bibliography	296
Index	303

List of Illustrations

Bride and Groom, 1897	28
Early Family Portrait	38
Four on a Donkey	40
Musical-Comedy Star	91
Colonel Richard L. Moore	110
Mimi in *La Bohème*	113
Gustave Charpentier and Grace Moore	123
Her First Movie Role	138
New Moon	140
Romance and Marriage	148
One Night of Love	161
Honored by the Society of Arts and Sciences	168
Royal Command Performance	173
The Valentin Pareras	178
Grace Moore in the Prime of Her Beauty and Success	183
The Pareras at Casa Lauretta	189
Grace Moore and Sweden's Prince Carl	191
Grace Moore as Massenet's Manon	195
Grace Moore—Singing Star of Radio	199
Grace Moore Proudly Displays Medals	201
Grace Moore as Fiora	208
The Two-Hundred-Year-Old Saltbox	209
Mary Garden and Protégée	215
Louise—Her Favorite Opera	217
Far Away Meadows Farm	224
Homegrown and Home-Cooked	226
As Tosca	233
Soldiers' Favorite	249
Celebrating the Liberation of Paris	255
One of Her Last Photos in the United States	261
Arrival for Last Concert	264
A Grace Moore Bow	266

Foreword

The only party I ever crashed was a reception for Grace Moore after her first recital in Nashville. I was a freshman at Vanderbilt University and an usher at Ryman Auditorium, where she sang. I could hardly be expected to have been on the list. No matter. I had to be there.

The night before I caught a glimpse of her, radiant in the May night, in the doorway of the Governor's Mansion opposite the campus where she was a house guest. She was all magic and glamour. It was a Sunday night so there was not too much interference from traffic, but the vibrations would have penetrated a barrage of tank fire.

She had made her Metropolitan Opera debut only three months before and had come with the company to Atlanta for its annual week there. Immediately after that she returned to her native Tennessee for three homecoming concerts—in Chattanooga, Johnson City, and Nashville.

As Rowena Rutherford Farrar relates, Nashville was far from sold out. Nevertheless, it was a great and glorious evening. Grace was rounder than she later became, but she looked lovely in silver lamé—short, according to the fashion of the day—but with two longer bands of the material falling from her shoulders down her back. Her hair was still brushed with a suggestion of red, so beautifully described hereinafter.

The concert over, we all repaired to the mezzanine of the Andrew Jackson Hotel, then only three years old and now gone. My eyes could no more have left her than I could have stopped breathing.

Years later I got to know her. "She was a handful and she knew it," Claudia Cassidy wrote in the *Chicago Tribune* after her death. She could be maddening, outrageous, but you would have been willing to stand in line for more. As Alfred Lunt said in *Idiot's Delight* of the character played by Lynn Fontanne, there was something about her that was indelible.

The manager in Atlanta was Marvin McDonald. He wasn't just a Georgia cracker; he was a Florida cracker. He had the worst accent I ever heard and the loudest and most raucous laugh. He controlled about ten dates in that territory and could therefore exact better terms from his artists by block booking. He treated them like field hands. In his entire career I don't think more than a half dozen rated a greeting backstage or on arrival; but when Grace Moore returned to Atlanta for the first time after the smash of *One Night of Love*, the film that rescued her from galloping oblivion, Marvin was down at the station bright and early.

"Miss Moore," he said, in an accent that would make Billy Carter sound like the late Leslie Howard, "*One Night of Love* did wonders for you."

"Doesn't it," Grace shot back without batting an eye, "for us all?"

This is the girl who comes glamorously back to life in this book, not only Grace Moore but her supercharged times—plural, as in the title, which happily puts it, her "many worlds."

We will ever be in Mrs. Farrar's debt.

FRANCIS ROBINSON

Preface

A few years after Grace Moore's tragic death in 1947, one of her sisters-in-law, Nancy Moore, was waiting for an appointment in a Paris beauty salon. She turned to an elderly woman in a chic tailored suit, who looked vaguely familiar, to ask directions to a certain shop. Nancy's soft southern drawl caused the other's eyes to fill with tears. "Where are you from, my dear," she exclaimed, "and what is your name?"

"Chattanooga, Tennessee," Nancy answered. "Mrs. Richard L. Moore."

The Chattanooga housewife and mother was suddenly enfolded in a warm embrace, and an internationally famous prima donna said between sobs, "Oh my dear! I am Mary Garden."

The two women spent an hour or more sharing tears and laughter over some of Grace Moore's audacious escapades and glittering triumphs.

Although this happened more than a quarter of a century ago, similar incidents occur with surprising frequency whenever two or more of the millions still alive who knew and loved Grace Moore cross paths. Once you had met her, or heard her warm and joyful singing, you would never be the same again, and you would never forget her. There was something electric in her looks, personality, and voice. You would be charmed, aroused, perhaps even shocked into renewed eagerness and determination to rise above all obstacles, as she had done, to climb *your* highest mountains.

"I shall never forget a concert she gave at a woman's club in Westchester," one woman said to me, when we talked of Grace's remarkable showmanship. "Despite speeding from an earlier commitment behind a motorcycle escort with sirens screaming, she arrived almost an hour late. The audience was furious. When at last she strode on stage, breathless, stunning in a vivid blue lace concert gown that matched her eyes, exuding eagerness and good will from every pore, instead of the warm applause she usually received, we remained coldly silent.

"She flashed a dazzling smile at us, lifted her long, full skirt, and with an exaggerated pirouette exclaimed gaily, 'Ladies, you just must see these darling panties I have on!'

"A famous couturier had designed the tight-fitting, knee-length panties of the same blue lace as the gown. Her quick wit and daring brought instant laughter and applause. Before she had sung a note she had shocked us, delighted us, and won our forgiveness."

When I first told Francis Robinson that I was considering writing a biography of our fellow Tennessean Grace Moore, his sunburst smile, vast store of fond memories, and willingness to cooperate were encouraging. His "Musical Biography of Grace Moore" was one of the first of the series he broadcast during the popular Saturday afternoon matinees at the Met. "I was her number-one fan," he said. "I adored her and her voice."

Long ago I lost count of the number of persons with whom I have talked or corresponded who also claimed to be her "number-one fan."

David Harkness, an enthusiastic promoter and historian of Southern artists of all kinds, grew up in Jellico, Tennessee, Grace's home town. He loved all the Moores and as a little boy was often in and out of their house. Mrs. Moore would hand him a long letter she had just received from her famous daughter and say, "Please read it to me, honey, while I just lie down here and rest my heart." Before her death, Mrs. Moore destroyed all the letters Grace had written to her over three decades. Fortunately this number-one fan was able to recall many revealing bits and pieces of them.

Emily Coleman, another number-one fan, as well as one of Grace's closest personal friends, responded to my first letter of inquiry by calling me long distance from her home in Griswoldville, Massachusetts, to suggest that we meet at Far Away Meadows, the 200-year-old saltbox house in Connecticut that was the prima donna's beloved permanent home. Subsequently, we met at the Old Newtown Inn to have lunch and get acquainted before our appointment with Mrs. John A. Hindrum, the present owner of the old place.

During the tour, Mrs. Hindrum paused as we crossed a second-floor hallway to indicate a huge, somewhat battered wicker trunk standing there. "I found that old thing in the attic," she said casually. "It is filled with cards and papers and stuff. I brought it down to go through it, but so far haven't had time."

We exchanged excited glances. We had found the "little brown trunk," filled with papers, that Grace had mentioned in her auto-biography, *You're Only Human Once.*

During the days we spent together going over the contents of that trunk, Emily's eyes were rarely ever dry. She was one of the many whose lives were profoundly influenced by knowing Grace Moore. She considers their friendship the high point of her life.

In the world of opera, Grace Moore made what Quaintance Eaton, well-known writer about the Met, called "quite a splash." She listed Grace among the last of the tempestuous prima donnas, between Geraldine Farrar and Maria Callas. Grace made quite a splash in an amazing number of worlds other than opera, but opera was always her first love. She rose to the top in six categories—musical comedy, opera, concerts, motion pictures, radio, and records.

Despite her many attributes, accomplishments, and trailblazing contributions, in almost every article I have read about her since her death in 1947 the writer emphasized one or more of the worst facets of her many-faceted character. Although the pieces are all based on truth and make fascinating reading, they tend to leave a distorted impression of one of the most beautiful, dynamic, and successful American women of this century.

"In every human heart," wrote Ambrose Bierce, "are a tiger, a pig, an ass and a nightingale. Diversity of character is due to their unequal activity."

Grace Moore's tiger was powerful, ferocious, and equipped with razor-sharp claws. Whenever she felt threatened, her tiger would leap to her defense. Her pig would never stop squealing for more—more fame, fortune, medals, houses, paintings, clothes, jewels, books, plays, sports, travel, friends, lovers—*everything.* She had a fantastic greed for life. Frequently, and always at inauspicious moments, she would balk, or do asinine things—such as indulging in stingy and stuffy spells and temper tantrums over trivial annoyances.

Although her tiger, pig, and ass would sometimes provoke friends and promote enemies, sooner or later her nightingale, with its incredibly strong wings, great heart, and golden throat would soar ahead of her three demons and redeem her so gloriously almost everyone she had dismayed, shocked, or wounded would gladly forgive her and love her more than ever.

Grace Moore was unique in that all four of those competitors for first place in her character were too strong for any known bars or locks and were almost equally active. She would vow to thwart her demons, but whenever she let her guard down for a moment they would escape, catch up with her nightingale, and plunge full speed ahead. The race was swift, relentless, and never ending.

"My neighbors have told me that Grace Moore had many wild parties here," Mrs. Hindrum said to me at our last meeting at Far Away Meadows. "What kind of woman was she?"

Countless relatives, friends, enemies, colleagues, critics, lovers, and number-one fans have tried to answer that question. Although it is impossible to pin her down in a few words, some have come close:

"She was ravishing, preposterous, a law unto herself." (Francis Robinson)

"She was a complicated mixture of pure vision and hard practicality. She really *liked* to sing—and few singers I have known can say the same." (Emily Coleman)

"Grace was a golden whirlwind." (Lily Pons)

"Here was tremendous flash, dash and excitement gloriously rolled into one woman. Where she is there is a current of suppressed passion. Her entrance is a fillip, her stay stimulating. She's no one-track career creature, but a resplendent woman of the world." (Gladys Swarthout)

"She was always a good friend and we had lovely times together. I miss her. When everything was copacetic she could really sing. Sometimes her performances stank. Her technique was very poor, but she had flair, stage excitement—an electric something—and audiences loved her." (Doris Doe)

"A good friend and a great woman." (Dorothy Kirsten)

"She was warm with great star quality; she matured into a very fine artist, and a very fine woman." (Jean Dalrymple)

"An incredible creature, with superhuman energy, extraordinary business genius, unlimited curiosity, a monumental restlessness." (Frederick C. Schang)

"She was a very sexy and great singing actress." (Maurice Chevalier)

"Grace Moore always radiated sexuality; every man longed to lay her." (Virgil Thomson)

"She was a woman of sublime contradictions." (Vincent Sheean)

Others have called her, among other things, twin sister to the spring, America's Darling, an animated swizzle stick, a lovebird who sings in full-throated gladness, Crown Princess of Song, a pioneer, a trailblazer, and a free spirit.

Her life was filled with amazing contrasts, contradictions, and excesses. She is a vivid symbol of many of the extremes of the first half of twentieth-century America, from the harshest realities of those turbulent years to the loftiest dreams. She is also a symbol of how high a talented and ambitious woman can climb if she has *all* her freedoms, and of how many dangers those freedoms can generate. She was both the Ugly American and the supremely Beautiful American.

She made shambles of many myths, including the one about the woman who is liberated, brainy, talented, successful, and aggressive turning men off. Grace turned so many men on that she not only had lovers galore but received proposals of marriage by the dozens, including some from titled Europeans and at least three of the richest men in the world. She took keen delight in her power over men. One perceptive male admirer said of her, "She stimulated every man's urge to escape the commonplace."

She also had many women friends, and almost all of her friendships, male and female, lasted her lifetime.

During her brief splash in the world of motion pictures, Ruth Geri, a Hollywood critic, wrote that one could pick away at a typewriter until your fingers ached, or string together many pages of fine writing, without coming close to putting on paper the illusive personality of Grace Moore—the real person of that excitable, sentimental, determined, whimsical figure.

This book is my attempt to answer Mrs. Hindrum's question, and to meet the challenge of that Hollywood critic. Grace Moore's story deserves and needs to be remembered. I agree with Eric Sevareid, that a society that loses its symbols can lose its identity, and become a stranger to itself. If we do not recognize the symbols of a vanished era, and try to see them whole, how can we possibly make intelligent judgments about yesterday, today, and tomorrow?

Acknowledgments

This first biography of Grace Moore could not have been written without the generous cooperation of Valentin Parera, of Madrid, Spain, her one husband, and of her only living brother, Richard L. Moore, Jr., and his wife, Nancy, of Chattanooga. On my first visit to their home on Lookout Mountain the Moores showed me their Grace Moore room and the many pictures of her on their walls, allowed me to bring home about twenty enormous scrapbooks which Grace and her mother had kept of her career, and about sixty priceless original recordings to listen to and tape, some taken from live performances. Grace's only sister, Emily, Mrs. Kenneth M. Wright of Chicago, was most helpful with reminiscences of their childhood in Jellico.

I am also deeply indebted to Francis Robinson, tour director and consultant of the Metropolitan Opera Association, who shared his Grace Moore memorabilia and vast store of memories with me; introduced me to opera officials and close friends of the prima donna; read, criticized, and corrected errors in both the first and last drafts of the manuscript, and wrote the Foreword.

Invaluable help was given to me by Mrs. John H. DeWitt Peltz, former art editor of *Opera News* and archivist of the Met; Edmund Fenech, former art director, and Ilene Roth, former assistant art director of *Opera News;* Frederick C. Schang, former head of the Metropolitan Musical Bureau, Division of Columbia Concerts Corporation of the Columbia Broadcasting System, and his wife, Emily; Jean Dalrymple, Grace Moore's publicist, personal representative, fan, and close friend, now executive director of the American National Theater and Academy; Emily Coleman, former music editor of *Newsweek,* who shared her Grace Moore papers and memories with me, and Terry Ferrer, former educational editor of the *New York Herald Tribune.*

Others who have helped immeasurably are David Harkness, director of Library Services, Division of Continuing Education,

University of Tennessee, Knoxville, who not only introduced me to many of Grace Moore's childhood friends from Jellico, but spread the word of my research needs throughout the South; James Hayden Siler, of Oak Park, Illinois, who grew up in Jellico, wrote me many letters filled with revealing anecdotes and information; Dr. Alfred H. Guthe, former director and Dr. Paul Parmalee, director, of the Frank H. McClung Museum, University of Tennessee, where the largest collection of Grace Moore memorabilia is preserved, set up a special exhibit for me of her costumes, wigs, medals, pictures, posters, and programs and other papers.

Others in Chattanooga to whom I am greatly indebted are Mr. and Mrs. Robert H. Baker, Louise Holdam, Doris Doe, former prima donna of the Met, and Helen Huff Johnson, a Grace Moore protégée, who brought her scrapbook and other material to my hotel and wrote me many letters. Bill Park of Athens, Texas who made many long-distance calls and spent many hours working up an up-to-date and authentic Grace Moore discography; Miss Goldie Garber of Jellico lent me the Grace Moore scrapbook James Hayden Siler had given to her and answered many questions both in conversations and letters. Others in Jellico who were of great help were Mrs. Homer Hackney, Mrs. Hugh Finley, Mrs. Mabel Tramell Jones, Mr. and Mrs. Herman Tramell, Mr. and Mrs. Ray Ellison, Mrs. Sam C. Baird, Mrs. Robert Clemens and Mayor Paul W. Harp. Also helpful were Guilford Dudley, Jr., former U.S. Ambassador to Denmark, and Mr. and Mrs. Arthur Terrell Jones, of Nashville; A. Stenver of Statens Luftfartsvaesen, Copenhagen; Maurice Chevalier, Milton Cross, Virgil Thomson, Constance Hope, Mrs. Gilbert W. Chapman, Wilma Dykeman and James Stokely, of Newport, Tennessee and Bruce Kellner, of Norman, Oklahoma.

I wish also to thank Mrs. S. F. Kimbrough, Mrs. Bert Vincent, Mrs. Chattie Rainwater, a Grace Moore cousin who lives in Nough; Mrs. Lillian Brown, Mrs. Charles Burgin, Mr. and Mrs. Noland Wells, Mrs. Karl Bahret, John A. Parker, Mrs. Joseph B. Baker, Mrs. Charles E. Dexter, Mrs. John A. Hindrum, Mr. and Mrs. Irving J. Rand, Mr. and Mrs. William P. Molette; and Mrs. Florence Traylor, whose patience and typing skill were extraordinary.

Grateful thanks go to librarians in Chattanooga, Newport, Jellico, Nashville, Knoxville, Richmond, Washington, D.C., New

York City, Chicago, London, Paris, Cannes, Nice, Monte Carlo, Bordeaux, Madrid, Barcelona, Venice, and Vienna.

And, as always, I am grateful to my husband, Monty, who promptly fell in love with Grace Moore and her voice, accompanied me on research trips in this country and abroad, taped interviews, cleaned, patched, taped and filed phonograph recordings, took pictures, spent many hours working on the discography with Bill Park, and gave daily doses of encouragement and professional editorial assistance.

Grace Moore
and Her Many Worlds

Part I
Running Wild in the Sun

Whether people feel hatred or love toward me, I want
them, in either case, to know me as I am.

1 The Sparks Would Fly

At the turn of the century, the Stokelys and Huffs of Cocke County, Tennessee, were in a tizzy. Instead of choosing a mate among the descendants of local pioneer farmers who had for more than a hundred years loved and tilled the land, seventeen-year-old Tessie Jane Stokely had fallen in love at first sight with a smooth-talking "foreigner," an "upstart North Carolina peddler," and married him without her parents' consent.

The young husband, Richard Lawson Moore, had only recently stepped off a train at the tiny Del Rio railroad station to become a clerk in the commissary operated by a lumber company in Nough, a foothill cove town of the Great Smoky Mountains, four miles west of Del Rio. Often called Slabtown, it consisted of little more than a sawmill, the commissary, a church, a few primitive houses, and huge piles of slabs and sawdust. The young couple set up housekeeping in a three-room slab shack attached to the commissary. The bride's dowry was a hope chest of sheets and blankets and a coop of chickens.

Despite winter isolation, first pregnancy, and the dire predictions of her numerous relatives, the young wife celebrated their first wedding anniversary with a glow on her face and a hum in her throat. Although she still considered Richard, or "Dick," far superior to any of the local young men she could have married, the crowning reason for her joy in such bleak surroundings was her lusty baby daughter, Mary Willie Grace, born at her parents' farm on 5 December 1898.

In pleasing ways, Grace resembled her handsome, dark-eyed father, as well as the best looking of the blue- and gray-eyed Stokelys and Huffs. She had thick auburn hair, a delicate peach-petal complexion, and enormous curly-lashed eyes of a deep dazzling blue.

One day, when she was still crawling about the bare pine floor of the station shack, the commissary manager absconded, leaving

BRIDE AND GROOM, 1897. Tessie Jane Stokely and Richard Lawson Moore were married in 1897. Their first child was christened Mary Willie Grace. *Courtesy of Richard L. Moore, Jr.*

the young husband in danger of being indicted for misappropriation of funds. The child was too young to be upset by this first of many crises in her small world; but she was, no doubt, aware of the sudden intrusion of tension. Eventually, the most obliging of the Stokelys helped "Tess's man" straighten things out and start a small dry-goods and notions store.

Grace was two years old when a brother, Herbert Briscoe, was born, and four when Tessie Jane gave birth to Martin Stokely. It was her duty to keep an eye on Herbert and the baby while her mother cooked, cleaned, and washed diapers. The moment her brothers would fall asleep, she would rush away on what she called "glorious adventures." She loved the hills and mountains and the pure open sky. She would listen with delight to the cluck of hens and the crow of roosters, to the castanets of crickets and to the symphonic rush of wind in the trees. In the spring she would welcome the hundreds of birds—meadow larks, flicks, thrushes— that flew into the cove to trill mating calls, establish boundaries, and build nests. The piercing whine of the huge saw slicing through logs and the grunts and gurgles of the old mill wheel in the nearby creek would arouse her sense of wonder and eager curiosity. Sometimes she would venture across the road to explore the forbidden territory of sun-warmed sawdust piles, sift the particles through her fingers and toes, and climb to the top of the highest pile and roll or tumble all the way to the bottom.

Her father was the parent who spoke sternly to her when she was disobedient. If she could not disarm him with a smile, a pert remark, or a shrewd question, she would sharpen her wits and temper by defying him. Then the sparks would fly between the hot-tempered Irishman and his equally hot-tempered daughter.

She loved to peek through the store window to watch him at work, and all her life she would remember the hollow "thump-flap" the cloth made when he released it from its folds, and the "swish-snip" of his scissors as he cut off a few yards. Whenever a sale appeared doubtful, he would turn on all the charm he possessed, which was considerable. This was a daily lesson in salesmanship that she would use in future years with brilliant results.

On warm days the young mother would gather up her three children, cross the creek, and hike down the four miles through the woods and open fields to spend the day at the farm. A narrow dirt road, the trains of the Southern Railroad, and the French Broad River connected Del Rio to the outer world. Foothills referred to affectionately as "Jeff's Knoll," "Stokely's Peak," and "Netty Kizzie Knoll" defined and scalloped the town's horizon; winter sunsets, often veiled in thin blue smoke, left an afterglow behind "Tater Hill."

Regardless of the season, the farm house on Big Creek, built of sturdy logs, weatherboarded, and sealed, would give off welcoming odors of burning wood, open-fire cooking, and pipe tobacco, and every window would frame a vista of such serene and lofty beauty no member of the family would feel a need for man-made art.

After Grandma Stokely had welcomed them, Grace would rush to the open fire to peer into the big iron pot. Grabbing a long-handled wooden spoon, she would stir and sniff the fragrant stew, or beans, or greens, then help set the table on the porch and ring the dinner bell. The hearty midday meal would be spiced with good-natured teasing and laughter, often ending in spirited arguments over politics, religion, and the Civil War. There would be talk of President McKinley's assassination and of the awesome energy and forceful personality of the new crusading president, Theodore Roosevelt.

The few local citizens who had journeyed to Nashville in the summer of 1897 to attend Tennessee's centennial celebration would never tire of telling those unable to go about that once-in-a-lifetime experience. Some had heard William Jennings Bryan, the "silver tongued orator," speak; all had seen the replicas of the Parthenon, the Rialto Bridge, and the Blue Grotto, listened to the famous Bellstedt Ballenberg Band, eaten at the Lion's Roof Garden Restaurant, and watched the fabulous display of fireworks.

They had visited hundreds of exhibits, including those in the Woman's Building, modeled after Andrew Jackson's Hermitage. Here, Tennessee women were proclaimed "the ideal blending of strength and grace"; their exhibits were dedicated "to stimulating women to higher education." The Cocke County men weren't particularly impressed by such new-fangled ideas, by the thousands of books on display written by women, or by the special editions of the *Nashville American* and the *Knoxville Tribune* written and edited solely by women. Exhibits attempting to prove that a woman was as capable as a man were dangerous propaganda. Their women had plenty to do at home—having babies, taking care of their families and farms, waiting on them. Book learning made a woman uppity and more difficult to keep in her place.

This was a sore subject to some of the local women, but they rarely ever made an issue of it.

Grace's maternal grandfather, William Russell Stokely, was Scotch-Irish and proud of it; proud also of the land he had inherited and accumulated, and of his record as one of the youngest lieutenants in the Confederate Army. He always held himself as straight as a fencepost, wore a handsome, militarily correct goatee, and looked askance at foreigners and damn yankees. The latter included anyone, kin or not, guilty of fighting on the "wrong" side.

Grace's maternal grandmother, Emma Huff Stokely, came from a pioneer family of German ancestry. Huff descendants, considered the cream of the local families, had intermarried with Stokelys, Burnetts, Joneses, Nichols, and McMahons to such an extent that almost everyone Grace knew and loved during the first five years of her life was related by blood, or marriage, or both.

These families had acquired their land with blood and hard work and had helped build the country from scratch. Most of them had little formal education or polish, but they were amply endowed with courage, resourcefulness, and vision. These traits, plus a sense of humor and a love of home, country, freedom, and God, were ingrained in their bones and in the bones of their numerous offspring.

Tessie Jane's husband was called a "foreigner" not only because he was a newcomer, from Murphy, North Carolina, but because he owned no land, no livestock, and no crops and had no desire to settle permanently in their beloved valley. Furthermore, he expected his wife to do without everything except the barest necessities so he could accumulate a nest egg and move on.

Grace's favorite among the many Huffs and Stokelys in the county was Aunt Laura, her mother's youngest sister. Bright, gregarious, fun-loving, and only five years her senior, Laura would play hide-and-seek with the children in the smelly old barn, take them wading or fishing in Big Creek, and help them gather herbs and wild flowers and catch butterflies. Barefooted, brown as the little Cherokee Indians who once had roamed freely there, hair sun bleached and stringy, bodies clothed in as little as their mothers would allow, the youngsters would spend long happy days running wild in the sun.

At dusk they would struggle home, weary, disheveled, and sometimes covered with berry stains, or stick-me-tights, or chigger bites, or all three. "Lord of Mercy, honey," Tessie Jane would worry, "Your Pa's apt to skin us all alive." When Grandma Stokely would scold her for saying "Lord of Mercy" so much lately, especially in front of all the "young-uns," Tessie Jane would exclaim contritely, "Lord of Mercy, Ma, did I say Lord of Mercy again?"

After the crops were laid by, the best fiddlers in the county would gather on the Stokely porch, tune up their homemade instruments, and saw away for hours. The roots of country music destined to become so popular in the South and all over the world and establish its core of activities in Nashville, now known as "Music City, U.S.A.," can be traced back to England, Ireland, and

European countries and to the farming communities in Tennessee, Kentucky, North Carolina, Virginia, and Georgia, where they flourished among people who lived close to the soil.

The grown-ups would choose partners and whirl around in intricate square dances and reels. Grace's eyes would sparkle and her feet would tap to the beat of the singable and danceable tunes. Uncle Estel Stokely taught her to call out the dance steps, and Grandpa Stokely taught her to sing "The Cherokee Girl," and "The Last Indian." Sometimes she would show off her square-dance calling and foot-stomping or sing her two solos without waiting to be asked.

Whenever Richard Moore would appear at these annual harvest celebrations, he would, instead of joining in the fun, demonstrate his stern disapproval by grabbing his oldest child by the hand and yanking her around with him while he collected the other members of his family. Then he would march them all home. A hard-shell Baptist, drilled from childhood to believe that dancing and singing anything other than hymns and gospel songs was a sin, Richard would arouse his wife's ire—his daughter's too—by muttering grim warnings. Unless her kinfolk mended their ways, they were all headed for hellfire and damnation.

With emancipation still in its infancy, and the term "male chauvinist pig" far in the future, a woman kept a civil tongue in her head and got her way, if at all, by manipulating her men with calculated feminine wiles. On the surface, most of the women were as straitlaced as Richard Moore, but many of them would fulfill some of their suppressed longings vicariously by reading romantic fiction in secret. Except for prostitutes, fallen women, and a few brave rebels, sex was a taboo subject. A nice woman did not enjoy sex or have orgasms. A pregnant single girl was ruined for life. A wife submitted and endured as a duty to her husband. She gave birth to from six to a dozen children, remained as inconspicuous as possible during her many pregnancies, and died young.

The tight corsets, prim shirtwaists, long full skirts, and many petticoats were serious handicaps to any freedom of body, and freedom of mind and spirit were almost unheard of in small Bible Belt towns.

Sometimes Tessie Jane would dare to talk back to her husband; at other times she would sulk or retreat into one of her many ailments. Hypochrondia was her refuge. It was the refuge of millions of women of her era, women who were expected to know

their place and abide in it contentedly, but who often felt oppressed and rebellious and didn't know why—or else lacked the
necessary courage and training to dare to rebel against their sec-
ond-class status and demand equal rights as human beings.

2 Born to Sing

Grace was five years old when her father accepted a job as traveling salesman for the Daniel Briscoe Company and moved his family to Knoxville. Living in the city was exciting and although the house he rented had ample space for the choice rose cuttings Tessie Jane had brought from Slabtown, she found it difficult to adjust. Tied down to pregnancy, baby tending, and watching every penny, and too far away to be able to spend frequent days at the farm, she would often fume, nag, or take to her bed.

Grace, too, missed her relatives and the farm. Every weekday she would have to put on stockings, new tight-fitting shoes, and a clean, stiffly starched dress with a big sash bow tied primly in the back and go to kindergarten. The imprisonment indoors for endless hours with strange city children staring at her, exchanging whispers and snickers, and calling her a backwoods freak did considerable damage to her ego. The exuberant child began to feel left out, different, inferior.

The teacher, a frail lavender-and-old-lace spinster, fascinated the new pupil and inspired a series of romantic fantasies that made the hours of imprisonment pass less slowly. Her sudden death was a shock, and Grace grieved as if for a close relative.

Richard uprooted his family within a few months to move to Jellico. Now thirty-one years old, he had shrewdly sized up the little coal-mining town located on the Tennessee-Kentucky border, near the divide between the watersheds of the Cumberland and Tennessee rivers, in the heart of the heavily timbered Cumberland Mountain range, and at the junction of two railroads, as an ideal distribution point. Although he moved there as a new partner in the Baird Dry Goods Company, he began to save and scheme to start a wholesale business of his own. He put his family on a stringent budget and himself on a work schedule that would have broken a less strongly motivated man. Perhaps because he loved them so much, he was never as successful in disciplining his children as he was in running a business. Considering his rigid rules unnecessary and tyrannical, Grace would blithely go her own way; her brothers would tag along.

Next door to the modest frame house the Moores rented on Fifth Street lived the Tramells, substantial citizens of the community. Little Tramells and Moores would play and fight every day. Herman Tramell, a friendly, long-legged boy, would become Grace's favorite playmate, first sweetheart, and possibly her first lover. The surrounding hills and mountains would soon become as familiar to her as the foothills of the Smokies, and serve as a refuge whenever solitude and breathing space became imperative.

When school started, the children in the first grade vied for her friendship; one little girl refused to stop howling until she was permitted to share a desk with the new girl. Although Grace introduced new games during recess, she sometimes led her classmates into adventures that brought them low grades in deportment and severe punishment at home. Some Jellico parents forbade their children to play with her.

Despite the deaths of Tessie Jane's father in 1907 and her mother a year later, she and her children spent a dozen summers at the farm in Del Rio. All summer long Richard would work early and late, going home at least twice a day to an empty, lonely house.

To Grace, life at the farm was a constant joy and challenge. She loved to linger at the big table on the porch, talking, laughing, and feasting, or climb on the bare back of a mule and help round up the cows. She loved to milk, churn, and mold butter or to wring off a chicken's neck, and pluck, singe, and cut the meat into individual portions which she would then fry. Singing happily, she would rush from household chores to outdoor play, a mother's helper one day, a tomboy the next.

On Monday mornings the women and children would gather at the creek to do the wash. The toddlers would be allowed to strip naked and splash in the shallows; the older children would help scoop gobs of homemade soap from a wooden bucket, lay soiled garments on a rock, swab, beat, and rinse them in clear water, then wring them and spread them on sunny bushes to dry. Then they would rush away to search the hills for Indian arrowheads, or fish in Big Creek, or peel off outer garments and plunge into their favorite swimming hole. Sometimes the water would be too cold for the other children, but never for Grace. She would spend the afternoon energetically practicing her strokes and diving off a tree root or any available male shoulder.

She loved to go visiting with her mother, especially when their destination was the Burnetts', because there was a piano in their parlor. On one such visit, after Grace had sung "Maggie" and "Where the River Shannon Flows," Mrs. Burnett said, "Tess, if you don't have that child's voice cultivated, it'll be a shame. She was born to sing."

Since few of her kin could carry a tune, Grace's mother did nothing more than smile and nod. The compliment sounded sweet to the little girl.

Sometimes Richard would arrive unexpectedly, pause for a brief visit, then take one or two of his children by train to Frog Pond, North Carolina, to see his relatives. On these trips Grace would come to know and love her Moore kinfolk and explore another world of coves, mountains, and streams.

Grandma Moore, a Martin, had died when Grace was three years old, but Grandpa Moore had married again and was siring a second family. Some of the women she met in the hill country of North Carolina thought nothing of giving birth to eight or ten "young-uns" without ever "so much as layin' eyes on a doctor." Asked why he rarely ever left his isolated hollow, one uncle answered philosophically, "Aw, shucks! Me and my wife, we jes' stay put here at home 'cause then we always know whar we're at."

During Richard's childhood, lack of money and lack of transportation were serious handicaps. Wanting far more than Frog Pond, Hayesville, or Murphy had to offer, he had managed to spend a year at the nearby Baptist Mission School and had kept in touch with the "out-county" world by reading the *Raleigh News and Observer*, the *Atlanta Constitution*, and the *Toledo Blade*. These weekly newspapers would be dropped off a train, and the natives who were hungry for knowledge would gather at the country store to be read aloud to by one of the three best readers in the community. In summers the ambitious boy would work for the railroad, or for a local hardware or dry-goods merchant.

Falling in love, getting married, and having children so much earlier than he had originally planned had handicapped him severely, and he often chafed at the slowness of his progress. His many responsibilities and frustrations only served to harden his determination, spur him on. He burned with ambition to show his mercurial wife and all her land-loving relatives, as well as all the Moores who still clung to their hills and snake-infested hollows with almost nothing to show for their long years of hard work, just how far a shrewd, hard-working, God-fearing Baptist Moore could climb.

Grace looked after Herbert and Martin when her mother gave birth, in July 1906, to twin babies. The boy was named Estel Carver, for Tessie Jane's brother, and the girl, Emily Huff, for her mother. Emily resembled Grace, yet she was so different, so utterly feminine and quiet in her cradle, that she reminded her mother of a contented hen perched on a setting of eggs. Tessie Jane called her baby girl "Little Settin." Richard, Grace, and her brothers called her "Em," adored her, and always catered to her slightest wish.

On Saturdays, the farmers and miners would bring their families to Jellico to visit and shop. One Saturday, a neighbor glancing out a window saw Grace free every horse, mule, and donkey hitched to the pickets along Main Street. She watched them scamper away, many dragging wagons or buggies behind them. For hours the town was in an uproar, but the neighbor did not tell. She, as well as Grace, enjoyed the commotion and the knowledge that the animals were running free, however briefly.

A few weeks before Grace's eighth birthday, six-year-old Herbert died suddenly of what the doctor diagnosed as acute indigestion. The family suffered shock, grief, and months of agonizing friction. The parents released long-pent-up grudges in explosive quarrels, each blaming the other for Herbert's death, and for every other disappointment they had suffered since their marriage.

Grace would weep one day and feel anger and rebellion the next, often putting the *hells* and *damns* she had heard all her life to blistering use. Sometimes she would skip school; occasionally she would indulge in what the town gossips called "that Grace's taking ways."

The phase of kleptomania she went through appalled her parents and neighbors. There were no specialists in Jellico to help the father and mother understand and ease their own tensions, much less those of a high-strung, rebellious eight-year-old, or to help Grace understand herself. Before attempting to discipline her, Richard would fortify himself with a stiff drink. The whiskey he would consume and the lectures he would deliver to his wife and daughter would serve to relieve his tensions momentarily, but aggravate theirs.

One day Grace stood outside her parents' closed bedroom door listening to one of their fiercest quarrels. She did not realize they

EARLY FAMILY PORTRAIT. *Left to right:* Richard L. Moore; son Estel, a twin who died young; Mrs. Moore; Emily, the other twin, now Mrs. Kenneth M. Wright, of Chicago; Grace; and her brother Martin. *Courtesy of Richard L. Moore, Jr.*

were quarreling about her until she heard her father call her impudent, a willful liar, and a thief. As she stood immobilized, vowing to reform, join the church, and somehow redeem herself and make her father proud of her, the door was suddenly yanked open. The furious man paused long enough to blast her with another stern lecture, adding eavesdropping to the long list of crimes already heavy on her conscience.

The scrappy Moores fascinated Jellico, and they became a favorite topic of gossip and conjecture. Some claimed Richard Moore was entirely too ambitious, unscrupulous, and money-loving. Because of his friendly business relations with blacks, Jews and Catholics, at a time when there was strong anti-black, anti-Jew, and anti-Catholic sentiment in small Southern towns, he was

branded by some as a "nigger, Jew and Pope lover." The mother
was flighty, gruff, and so busy pining for Del Rio that she neglected her children.

Others, including Goldie Garber, the daughter of a prosperous
Jewish merchant, always spoke highly of the Moores. She described Richard's passion as "making money; he was close with a
dollar, but liked to entertain in style. He had a temper, was stern
and strict, but undeniably a fine man. Much more suave than
Grace."

Despite fanning the flames of racial prejudice and bigotry, the
Moores and Garbers prospered from mutual respect, friendship,
and doing business with each other. The Moore children grew up
free of racial prejudice; Grace once spent a week at a Jewish resort,
eating kosher food three times a day, without realizing that she
was the only Gentile there until a friend mentioned it.

Another son, Richard Lawson Moore, Jr., was born in 1909.
Two years later Estel Carver died of bronchial pneumonia. This
time the family's grief was tempered by the birth of still another
boy, James Leslie, the following December. Now thirteen, Grace
called Jim her "baby," and always adored him. The last child,
Anna Catherine, was born in October 1915; but she, too, died
young, of pernicious anemia. In those days of limited medical skill
and lack of sanitary precautions, having eight children and losing
three of them during early childhood was not unusual.

By adding to his savings the $500 his wife inherited from the sale
at the farm of a cow and a sewing machine, Richard was able to
establish his own business and to buy the large white McComb
house across Fifth Street, opposite the Methodist church. His
wholesale dry-goods business prospered, and gradually he devoted
more and more of his time to town, county, and state politics.
Among the many influential friends he made was Cordell Hull, a
few years his senior, born a poor boy in nearby Pickett County,
and a fellow Democrat, who would become a United States
senator, the secretary of state under President Franklin D.
Roosevelt, the "father of the United Nations," and in 1945, winner
of the Nobel Peace Prize.

Governor Tom C. Rye rewarded Richard Moore for his support
during a heated campaign by appointing him an honorary Tennessee colonel. Henceforth he was known in the South as Colonel
Richard Lawson Moore, a man of title and substance, one of the
pillars of his church, his town, and the state of Tennessee.

With the move across the street to the more spacious Victorian

FOUR ON A DONKEY. With teenager Grace holding the reins, sister Emily and brothers Richard and Martin ride the animal acquired by their father as payment for a bill at his thriving store in Jellico. *Courtesy of Richard L. Moore, Jr.*

house, and Laura's arrival to work for her brother-in-law, Tessie Jane began to feel more at home in Jellico and less in need of spending long summer months in Del Rio. She subscribed to the *Ladies' Home Journal,* studied its articles and pictures, and with enthusiasm and natural aptitude decorated her new home and planted her garden. From early spring until late fall her rose garden was one of the town's beauty spots. She kept arrangements of pink roses, her favorite flower, on top of the new piano that now stood in the front parlor, and often gave bouquets and cuttings to friends.

Grace inherited her shrewdness, sales ability, and fierce drive to achieve from her father. Her flair for the dramatic, her tendency to sulk and exaggerate, and her love of all things creative and beautiful came from her mother's genes.

The family went regularly to the First Baptist Church. The children would sit primly erect with a parent guarding each end of the pew. Sometimes the father would be asked to read the lesson from the pulpit. The sermon would be long and filled with big words;

the children would squirm, their mother would doze. Richard would keep one stern eye on his offspring and the other on his wife, who might snore.

There were several Welsh miners in the choir with excellent voices and a love of singing. Grace would always sing along with them, and she eventually joined the children's choir. At the eleven o'clock service one Sunday morning she stood in the choir stall, clad in her first store-bought dress, a simple muslin, her hair hanging in pigtails tied with a huge bow of blue ribbon, and sang her first solo, "Rock of Ages." The experience did so much for her self-esteem that she began to spend more time in the front parlor practicing her music lessons and Sunday School songs and browsing through the musical magazine that had become her favorite— *The Etude.*

After Colonel Moore bought the family a phonograph, Grace invested her allowance in records, and she played her favorites— Mary Garden's "Annie Laurie" and "Comin' through the Rye"— over and over.

When he purchased a car, the first Cadillac in Jellico, she promptly took to the wheel. She would fill the big touring car with thrilled youngsters and take off on the narrow dirt road bound for High Cliff, never slowing down on sharp curves or stopping when horses reared up in fright or when she hit a mud puddle, a fowl, or a cow. Indignant farmers would rush to the wholesale merchant's office to demand reimbursement; the embarrassed father would pay, then hurry home to lecture his irrepressible daughter.

Occasionally, when he was out of town on business, Tessie Jane would take a sudden notion to give away all the new household furnishings she had recently acquired, then plunge into another orgy of decorating. While she was absorbed in this fascinating project, Grace and the boys would gleefully skip school, roam the hills, and sometimes camp out overnight.

Inevitably, when the colonel returned, there would be a violent reckoning. Mrs. Moore would remind her angry husband that some of the money he had invested in his business belonged to her and she could spend her part of the profits any damn way she pleased. If this did not quiet him, she would moan a few "Lord of Mercys," and retreat into a blinding headache or a palpitating heart and take to her bed.

Since the boys were afraid of the colonel, and Grace was not, she would take all the blame and receive all the punishment.

Some of her energy went into the game of basketball, a high

school activity her father frowned upon at first as unladylike and much too strenuous for a girl. Furthermore, he didn't want his daughter wearing bloomers and socks. Outvoted by every other member of his family, he finally gave in, and eventually began to enjoy the game.

Grace became a forward on the Jellico High Bear-Cats, the star dribbler and goal shooter, and in her senior year was elected captain of the team. But within minutes after Miss Mabel McSween's whistle sounded for the opening of her first big game as captain, a red-headed Irish girl on the opposing team knocked her down and tickled her. Grabbing a fist full of red hair, Jellico's Bear-Cat captain, suddenly turned tiger, yanked and pulled until her enemy hit the floor. The two girls rolled over and over, clawing, snarling, and kicking. Soon the teams were locked in a savage free-for-all, with the spectators taking angry sides.

A series of shrill blasts from the teacher's whistle eventually ended the bedlam. Because of the disgraceful conduct of the captain of the home team, Miss McSween announced severely, with reproachful glances at Grace, that the game was called off. With many disappointed onlookers shaking angry fists at their daughter, the shamed and speechless Moores got up to leave. During the savage fracas the captain had lost her dark blue bloomers; after she had managed to pull them back on, she stood up with eyes glaring, hands on hips, yelling defiantly, "Well, if the game's over, it's not my fault, and to hell with it!"[1]

One of the hundreds of Christmas cards stored away in a folder in that costume trunk at Far Away Meadows was sent in 1936 by Mabel McSween, of Newport, Tennessee, to "Miss Grace Moore" in Hollywood, California: "I owe you an apology—I knew very little of artistic temperament. What a foolish teacher I was. . . . And what a dear original character she [Grace's mother] is!" On the margin of that card, in her large-lettered, free-swinging handwriting (her capital letters are an inch tall—the others three-eighths of an inch), Grace scratched a note to her secretary: "Keep—too wonderful!"

One fine day a motion picture theater opened its doors on Jellico's Main Street—admission five cents. Twice a week thereafter Grace went to the movies. Her favorite star was Mary Pickford, not because of her golden curls or the Victorian purity and innocence which she symbolized to millions, but because she would, in some pictures, show determination and spunk. As did so many young girls of her day, Grace began to fantasize about becoming a glamorous motion picture star.

Although almost everyone in Jellico enjoyed silent pictures, the unfolding live drama of an audacious local girl who was plagued by too many as-yet-unrecognized and contradictory drives, talents, and dreams, and cramped into a mold too narrow and soul pinching to be passively endured, would become far more attention-grabbing to them than *The Perils of Pauline* or any other fictional cliff-hanger. The stormy battles Grace would wage to be free to hitch her wagon to stars of her own choosing, and the photo-finish race her demons would run against her nightingale, would keep the town shocked, titillated, and in delicious suspense for several decades.

3 The Quality of Obsession

Almost every boy in Jellico competed for the favors of the high-spirited Moore girl. Even the younger boys, the ages of Rich and Jim, sought her company. She was not only exceptionally pretty, she was talkative, gregarious, adventure loving, and more fun to be with than anyone else in town. Her legs had grown long and slim, her bustline nicely rounded, her waist narrow and supple. Her dazzling blue eyes and smiling mouth were set in a peach-blossom face. Her auburn hair was rich, thick, and long.

At first she served as Laura's official chaperone, but soon Laura was chaperoning her. Sometimes the aunt and niece would double date. To guard his eldest daughter's reputation and virginity, Colonel Moore tried to police her every thought and move. He forbade her to play cards, to dance, to read trashy novels, to sing suggestive songs, to wear low-necked, short-sleeved dresses, to paint her cheeks and lips, to have dates with boys who smoked or drank, to stay out after nine o'clock, to ride alone with a boy in an automobile, or to go out alone with a boy beyond the front gate.

Mrs. Moore would try to mediate the fierce clashes that more and more frequently occurred between her strict husband and her popular daughter, but she was rarely successful. On some Sundays—or so the town whispered—she would actually help Grace outwit her father. After checking to make sure he was asleep, she would greet her daughter's second date at the back door and entertain him in the kitchen while Grace said goodby at the front door to her early date.

Grace's mother enjoyed being with young people and they loved her. She was different, tolerant, and young in heart. The town understood the mutual attraction, but this new mother-daughter teamwork, the gossips agreed, was going too far.

Sometimes Grace would say goodnight and retire to the room she shared with Emily. As soon as the family was asleep, she

44

would climb out the window, slide down the drainpipe, and rejoin her beau in the rose garden.

One day, Mabel Tramell, Herman's cousin, showed a group of friends a new ring she had on, which belonged to her brother-in-law. The ring passed from hand to hand and was greatly admired. When it was Grace's turn, she tried it on, promptly fell in love with it, and persuaded Mabel to let her keep it overnight. Two days passed without a word from Grace about the ring. When Mable finally asked her for it, Grace said that she had lost it, or else someone had walked off with it. The others suspected her of stealing it and lying to cover up her crime. Mabel refused to believe Grace would do such a thing. No matter how shocked and indignant her peers might be, or what they accused her of behind her back or to her face, Grace stubbornly stuck to her story. She had lost the damn ring, and to hell with them for not believing her.

Years later on her first visit to Jellico after her debut at the Met, she went to see Mabel, who had married one of Grace's old beaux and worked at the post office. Mabel Tramell Jones was behind the grilled counter, sorting mail, a job she would keep for thirty years. After exchanging greetings, Grace shoved a check through the opening, "to pay for the ring I lost."

"You don't need to do this, Grace," Mabel said, looking at a check made out to her for $100. "The ring was forgotten long ago. Besides, this is far more than it was worth."

"Oh, but I want to, honey," said Grace, with a grin and a farewell wave of her hand.

When in trouble, Grace would climb the steep hill behind the house and on up beyond the tiny new Negro Baptist church to her favorite retreat. At the highest point, on a ledge of rock, she would sit for hours nursing her wounds, pondering her misdeeds, wrestling with her conscience, asking herself why she did such damnable things, and wishing that she were more like her little sister.

Sweet, gray-eyed Emily had a will of her own and almost always got whatever she wanted, but without losing the approval of her father or the town and without causing friction. Grace would reflect upon her sister's iron-fist-in-a-velvet-glove approach and wonder what was wrong with herself. In her need to ease her guilt, remorse, and unnamed yearnings she would gaze heavenward, pray, and make solemn vows.

Grace was always blessed, and cursed, with the quality of obsession. Whatever challenged her received her full attention—that is, until she was challenged in some other direction. After the ring incident, she joined the church and became a passionate Christian, almost a religious fanatic. She taught a Sunday School class, took her pupils on picnics, rehearsed them in new songs, and led the children's choir. She sang in the church choir at both morning and evening services. Eventually, she was elected president of the Baptist Young People's Union, and presided over the meetings.

Occasionally "Aunt" Willie, the Moore's day help, would take her to the Negro Baptist Church, or to a baptizing in a creek near Newcomb. Brother Johnson's prayed spirituals and the worshippers' rich, velvety voices lifted in shouts, amens, and praise-the-Lords would stir her deeply. Often when she was on her way to her refuge, she would pause outside the little hillside church to listen to homegrown spirituals and hymns about the devil, King Jesus, heaven and hell, the Bible, angels, and Judgment Day. The simple melodies, sung from the depths of oppressed hearts, would inspire fresh hope and joy in the souls of the black people of Jellico, and in Grace Moore's soul, too. "Steal Away to Jesus" and "Ain't Gonna Study War No More" would always move her to tears. The songs and prayers of her black friends would add a new dimension to her own singing and to her own faith. She found religion through music, and music through religion.

The director of the local Methodist choir, Homer Rodeheaver, a devout young man who would become world-famous as musical assistant to evangelist Billy Sunday, would frequently compliment her singing and urge her to train her voice and use it to the glory of God. Later he would try to persuade her to join the Billy Sunday crusading team.

The interlude of ardent religious dedication lasted several months. Relieved and proud, her father relaxed his anxious vigil. But one day, soon after Laura's wedding and departure from Jellico, Grace began to backslide. On that Sunday morning the Sunday School superintendent paused outside the door of her classroom to check on her teaching methods. Instead of focusing on the Bible lesson, she was exuberantly recounting her latest glorious adventure to a fascinated audience. Shocked and furious, the superintendent marched in and scolded her in the presence of her pupils.

She was still smarting from this humiliation on the day she attended a party in Williamsburg, Kentucky. One of her admirers dared her to dance with him. Never one to pass up a dare, she moved swiftly into his arms and waltzed gaily around the room. Dancing, she discovered, was almost as exciting as singing. But a few minutes later someone called out a warning reminder of her father and Brother Martin, the stern Baptist preacher who had begun his ministry in Jellico in 1912 and would continue there until 1927. Grace broke away and fled home.

News of her "outrageous" conduct had preceded her. The colonel stood at the front door armed with righteous wrath and several swigs of whiskey. The clash was loud, bitter, and seemingly endless. He accused her of committing a mortal sin against God Almighty. Grace insisted that she had done nothing wrong.

An editorial appeared in the *Jellico Sentinel* condemning a certain young church member for taking her first steps on the road to perdition. Brother Martin called an emergency meeting of the church brethren; a grave decision was reached, the distressed father concurring. Unless she confessed her sin before the preacher and the congregation, humbly pleaded for forgiveness, and vowed never again to dance, her name would be stricken from the membership roll and she would suffer eternal damnation.

At first Grace indignantly refused to consider such harsh punishment. But after a few days of being whispered about, lectured to, and ostracized, she reluctantly capitulated. The church was packed for the next prayer-meeting service. Her friends had come to offer moral support, her enemies to witness her public humiliation. The Moores arrived early and sat in stony silence in their regular pew. Lined up between them were Grace, Emily, Martin, Rich, and Jim. The little sister was close to tears. The boys were in a state of anxious suspense, half hoping and half fearing that Gracie would do something catastrophic—perhaps tell Brother Martin to go straight to hell.

The service over, the preacher spoke of a grave matter he must bring before the congregation. At his signal and a nudge from her father, Grace numbly rose, humbly confessed her sin, and asked for the forgiveness of God and the church. It was her dearest wish, she added, warming to her subject, to carry His message to the farthest corner of heathen China. She hoped soon to win her qualification certificate and devote her life to serving God as a Baptist missionary.

"Amen!" cried the congregation. "Amen." Amid much smiling and shaking of hands, she was forgiven and reinstated.

The ordeal was over, but she felt no catharsis. She fled from the church and shut herself in her room. When Emily returned, Grace pretended to be asleep. Later she slipped out of bed, dressed, tied a few things in a bandana, and ran away—to her hilltop refuge.

There, in bright moonlight, she flung herself on her rock and let the sobs explode from her throat.

She would never forget the torture and humiliation of that service. Neither would her family nor the town. More than fifty years later, when Emily was asked about Brother Martin, she said shortly, "I don't want to talk about him." The traumatic experience would leave a scar and mark a sharp turning point in Grace Moore's personality development. Since she felt no guilt and knew she would dance again, she berated herself for giving in, for being untrue to her own half-formed beliefs, ambitions, and needs. Dancing, like singing, was one of the pleasures of living. She wanted to live joyously, not in constant fear of gossip, reprisals, and humiliation. That night she began consciously to free herself, shape her own philosophy, grasp hold of her own destiny.

In casting about for a means of escape she considered marriage, but quickly rejected that idea. Running the risk of being tied down in Jellico for the rest of her life was as unthinkable to her in 1916 as remaining in the hills and hollows of North Carolina had been to her father in 1897. Becoming a missionary to China still appealed to her sense of adventure, and to her genuine desire to serve others and win approval—but with a different approach. Her God was a joyous God, not a stern disciplinarian. In order to qualify as a singing missionary and carry that message to far off heathens, she would need to go away somewhere for special training. Getting away from Jellico was vital to her well-being. By dawn she had worked out a plan that was designed to please her father, heal her wounded ego, and open exciting new doors.

4 The Thirsty Sponge

During the train trip to Nashville in September 1916, despite the hot cinder- and soot-laden air pouring through the open windows, father and daughter enjoyed a few hours of rare understanding and companionship. Grace was resplendent in a new dress and matching hair ribbon; her trunk was filled with fine new clothes and going-away-to-school presents. She was enraptured by victory, excitement, and eager anticipation, and lavish with love, gratitude, and promises to work hard and stay out of trouble.

Although Colonel Moore discounted her singing-missionary talk, her desire to go to Ward-Belmont School for Girls, and the prestigious Nashville school's prompt acceptance of her, had lifted a load from his mind and made him proud. The two well-to-do Jellico families who had sent daughters to the school had frequently spoken of its music department as the finest in the South. If she learned nothing more than how to be a lady, sing properly in church choirs, and perhaps give music lessons, he would consider his money well spent. He hoped some nice young man, preferably a dedicated Baptist, would transform her soon into a loving and dutiful housewife and mother.

As always in September, Nashville lay in her natural saucer edged with hills, limply resigned to the tyranny of a merciless sun and high humidity. But the huge railroad station, blackened by soot spouting from smokestacks of countless soft-coal-burning engines, the busy flow of traffic on Broad Street, the handsome business establishments, churches, and brick homes Grace saw from the streetcar window on the ride to Ward-Belmont kept her emotions at high pitch.

Both Moores were awed by the magnificence of Belmont, or Acklen Hall, the mansion used as a school building. Long famous as one of the country's outstanding examples of Italian-inspired architecture, it stood amid the splendor of formal gardens. Flower-

49

bordered walkways led to octagonal iron-lace gazebos scattered among the boxwood, urns, and pieces of sculpture of biblical and mythological themes. Here carefully chosen teachers were preserving and passing on to thousands of young ladies from the finest families in the country, mostly from southern states, the most cherished traditions of the Old South.

The father and daughter entered the reception room and stood open-mouthed and wide-eyed, staring at the elaborately carved marble mantel, the large gold leaf mirror above it with its fruit motif, the handsome gasolier and plaster medallion, the intricate crown moldings, and the windows of ruby red Venetian glass.

Mrs. Rose, the dean of girls, a tall, gray-haired, sharp-featured woman clad in a severe black dress, was as awe-inspiring as the setting. As soon as Colonel Moore had met her and paid the tuition, he excused himself and hurried away to visit friends on Capitol Hill and at the Hermitage Hotel.

At that time, President Woodrow Wilson was running for a second term, riding high on the slogan "He Kept Us Out of War." But with the Huns destroying Europe and sinking American as well as British ships, many Democrats, including Grace's father, feared the president would soon be advocating war. Other political worries included the increasing demand for national prohibition and suffrage for women. A woman in Montana, Jeanette Rankin, was running for election to the U.S. House of Representatives, while hundreds of other females were parading and going on hunger strikes in their fight to win the vote. If Wilson and the state of New York surrendered to their demands, other states might fall in line. But not, the Colonel had vowed, *his* state—and not the other Southern states. Although a few Southern women and their husbands had joined the Woman's Suffrage Movement, he was pressuring all his friends in the solid Democratic South to hold firm. Times were changing too rapidly to suit him. Being a good Baptist, he was strongly against change.

Left to cope with Mrs. Rose alone, unaccustomed to such grandeur and to being questioned so thoroughly in such a cultured voice, Grace became aware, perhaps for the first time, of her hillbilly accent. In her eagerness to make a good first impression on her roommates, she spoke too naively of going to China as a singing missionary and laughed too gustily at the wrong things. They stared at her with hostile eyes, then turned away and began to chatter about going shopping in New York City, making debuts, and acquiring rich husbands. Every subject they gushed about bespoke a way of life totally foreign to her experience.

Although Grace tried to make friends, to belong, she continued to feel different and left out. The culture shock that she suffered at Ward-Belmont was a repetition of her Knoxville kindergarten experience, only much more damaging to her self-esteem. She learned by painful experience that it is far more difficult to overcome prejudice and snobbery than it is to acquire knowledge.

Sometimes, when her classmates would be especially snobbish or cruel, she would release long-pent-up emotions in hot-tempered explosions that would shock both students and teachers. The dean would summon her to the office and give her a stern lecture on the proper behavior of a lady. Holding defiant retorts in check, Grace would apologize, promise to refrain in the future from using "gutter language," and make another conscientious effort to conform.

The school offered many extracurricular activities, but she participated in only one: as a forward on the Panther basketball team. The sport relieved some of her tensions—at least for a few weeks. Her courses included English, French, piano, voice, history of music, ear training, and practice. The teachers were excellent in their specialties, but none was trained to guide a wounded girl safely through the dangerous psychological shoals upon which she was floundering.

Only one teacher, Professor Charles Campbell Washburn, dean of the Voice Department, a graduate of the Cincinnati College of Music and Vanderbilt University, showed any awareness of her potential. After a few vocal lessons, he added special instructions in piano, harmony, and sight-reading to her schedule, and urged her to devote her study periods to French and English literature.

On the day he first played back a recording he had made of her clear, sweet notes, she glanced up at him in stunned disbelief. He smiled and nodded. It was true. She had a voice, a God-given talent. Her spirits lifted. No wonder she liked to sing—needed to sing to feel truly alive and loved. Perhaps that was the moment when Grace first began to dream of a bright future in the entertainment world, though certainly her dream was not yet clearly defined.

Professor Washburn tried to keep her energies constructively channeled, with the result that she concentrated so passionately on his courses she neglected others. Her indignation continued to mount over the school's tough and clear-cut rules, which she considered stupid and pointless, over the dean's stern lectures, and over her loneliness and rage against her snobbish classmates.

One morning in January, after a happy Christmas in Jellico and a quick trip to Del Rio to sing "I Love You Truly" at a cousin's wedding, she was again summoned to the dean's office. Mrs. Rose believed, as did Colonel Moore and Brother Martin, that a girl's conduct was either right or wrong, black or white. She recognized no gray areas. Very sternly she informed Grace that she had neglected some of her most important studies and failed in French; she had been impudent and hostile; she had used language unbecoming a Ward-Belmont girl; she had slipped out at night to attend a dance at Vanderbilt; and she had not only helped herself to a few items of apparel that did not belong to her, she had denied it when accused.

Grace could neither explain nor defend her conduct. She was as stunned and confused as the dean was appalled. Today her lapses into kleptomania would be diagnosed as desperate cries for acceptance, for enlightened guidance, for space in which her spirit could expand. In January 1917 she was given another stern lecture and expelled.

Her sudden downfall shocked and shamed the Moores and put Jellico in another tizzy. After a tongue-lashing from her father, Grace fled to her hilltop refuge. There, in freezing solitude, she scourged herself, deplored her crimes, and wallowed in remorse. Then came calming prayers and shrewd thinking.

Although her four months at school had come high, both financially and emotionally, Professor Washburn had alerted her to the natural beauty and range of her voice and also to the years of proper training she would need to achieve any kind of singing career. Singing would be her life, she knew by now, but no longer did she dream of becoming a singing missionary to China. She had peered through that door only as a possible means of escape, with approval, from small-town narrowness, prejudice, and bigotry. The brief exposure to wealth and gracious surroundings had wakened in her a fierce thirst for all the beautiful things an ambitious girl with a voice could acquire, *if* she applied herself. She was eager to apply herself, if for no other reason than to catch up with all those snobs at Ward-Belmont and pass them by. There were other schools of music.

A few days later the Moore front parlor was the scene of another clash of strong wills. Grace had waited until almost train time to reveal her plans to her father. The other members of the family were anxiously huddled in the back parlor, prayerfully rooting for her. She had been in correspondence with the Wilson-Greene School of Music in Washington, D.C., she told him, her trunk was packed, and with money borrowed from a friend—probably Goldie's father—she was ready to say goodby. Would he please give her his blessings?

The shocked and angry man informed her that *he* would make any decisions concerning where she would or would not go. Her diplomacy and shrewd salesmanship failed to break down his resistance, so she switched to more drastic measures. When he lost his temper, she lost hers. When he threatened to lock her in her room, she retorted that her brothers would help her escape.

Since he could not budge the obstinate female from her steely purpose, Colonel Moore suddenly changed tactics. He would return the borrowed money, he informed her, accompany her to Washington, and personally check the credentials of the Wilson-Greene School.

"Lord of Mercy!" exclaimed Mrs. Moore. "She's won!"

Emily and the boys were overjoyed.

Aghast, the town berated that fool father for taking that hard-headed girl all the way to Washington to enroll her in another expensive school.

As they emerged from the Union Station, Grace caught her first glimpse of the nation's capitol through swirls and drifts of snow. The many white government buildings topped with waving flags, the handsome store windows, and the heavily trafficked circles she observed from the streetcar they boarded kept her in a state of joyous excitement. They walked the last few blocks, the colonel carrying her suitcase.

After the magnificence of Acklen Hall, the modest building at 2601 Connecticut Avenue was an unexpected letdown. As they waited in an unpretentious hallway to be received, the unmistakable click of billiard balls, interspersed with girlish laughter, aroused the father's smoldering ire. This was no music school, he snorted, and with a few caustic words about not squandering his money to send her away to learn to play pool, headed for the door.

Before he could reach it, Kate Wilson Greene appeared, shrewdly sized up the situation, maneuvered him into her office, and sent for her partner-husband. She was a handsome woman, in her fifties, a native of Washington and a former singer. Both she and Thomas Evans Greene were highly respected teachers and recognized musical leaders of the city; her chief passion was engaging the world's greatest artists to perform in the nation's capital. She mentioned Caruso, Paderewski, and the Chicago Civic and Metropolitan Opera companies.

Within a short time she had Colonel Moore mollified, even impressed. Eventually he departed in a better humor, but not without admonishing his daughter to study hard, behave like a lady, and prepare herself for marriage and homemaking.

Now at last Grace was in her element, a "thirsty sponge," as she called herself, free to make new friends and soak up new experiences.[1] The long-cramped buds of her voice and personality began to open wide, to blossom as lushly as did her mother's properly tended roses. She exuded a radiance the teachers admired, her classmates envied, and the few young men she met under careful chaperonage found irresistible.

The other students were intelligent, attractive, and, to her delight, congenial. Her favorite among them was Blanche LeGarde, a lively blonde from Norfolk, Virginia, who secretly dreamed of some day dancing on Broadway. In those days a girl from a good family did not dare divulge her career dreams to her parents.

Grace's new schedule included seven hours of daily studies in French, voice, dramatic art, sight-reading, and piano for practice; also frequent trips to libraries and museums, and attendance at all operas, concerts, and plays the city had to offer. Eventually she earned ten dollars a week, her first salary, singing in the choir of the Calvary Baptist Church.

Mrs. Greene, the dominant member of the Wilson-Greene teaching team, deserves more credit than she has been given for helping Grace Moore find herself. She set an example of dynamic dedication to work, of high standards, of courage and daring under the stress of an ambitious goal. She gambled all she possessed on her concerts—and won. She is said to have been the only woman who ever conducted the Marine Band through an entire opera— *Samson and Delilah*. The new student admired and respected her; in turn, the teacher was known to be "crazy about Grace."

Mrs. Greene made sure that her students met every artist she brought to Washington. During her first year there Grace met Mary Garden, the internationally famous prima donna who was destined profoundly to influence her future. A concert by Mary Garden was indeed a special event. At that time the leading soprano of the Chicago Civic Opera Company and approaching the height of her career, she created a furor of excitement, adoration, and controversy wherever she appeared.

Garden arrived in Washington fresh from a benefit performance of *Carmen* in Paris to raise funds for the wounded soldiers of France. When she came on stage, clad in a stunning Parisian gown, glittering jewels, and a flaming red wig, and began to sing, Grace became so enthralled by the radiance and mystic quality of her beauty, personality, and voice that long before the last dazzling smile and low, sweeping bow her dreams had soared far beyond the vague "some kind of singing career" to a definite high goal. She knew at last what she wanted to do with her life and talent— become a dynamic opera prima donna, another Mary Garden.

As always when Mrs. Greene escorted her students backstage to meet an artist, she cautioned them to be very quiet and not to crowd too close. The others hung back, but Grace rushed eagerly forward, fell on her knees, kissed the prima donna's hands, called her a goddess, and announced that she was going to be a singer, too.

The embarrassed teacher hurried her students out of the dressing room. Grace walked back to the school on air, aglow with new purpose.

During the summer vacation at home she longed to share her dream with her family, but dared not. Her mother was absorbed in tending her beloved roses and indulging in another splurge of redecorating; Martin was engrossed in his plans to go to the University of Tennessee in the fall; Emily, Rich, and Jim were still children. Grandpa Moore had died recently, and Colonel Moore was still grieving; he was also harassed with trying to cope with the demands and shortages brought on by the United States' declaration of war against Germany on 6 April 1917.

Strangely enough, Grace had been so preoccupied with her dream that she had not realized until her return home how totally involved her country had become in a world war. Not far from Jellico, in Kentucky, an army camp had been hastily built. Some Jellico girls were working there, or in factories and offices, making good money and enjoying a little freedom and independence for the first time in their lives. Many of her local beaux were in uniform and far away. War talk was on every tongue. There would soon be meatless Tuesdays and wheatless Mondays and Thursdays, hours of bandage rolling, War Bond rallies, bands and parades. Grace sang "Danny Boy," "Kiss Me Again," "Let Me Call You Sweetheart," and other popular songs at military gatherings and bond rallies, and met many new men. The town gossips became skeptical about the many proposals of marriage she would reject, and felt sorry for her hard-working father, who still hoped that soon she would find the right man, get married, and settle down to raising a family.

In the fall of 1918 she complained to Mrs. Greene about the slowness of her progress. The teacher promised her the coveted role of assistant artist at the school's annual concert, starring Giovanni Martinelli, provided she could win the approval of the opera tenor's manager, Charles Wagner. Martinelli had made his debut at the Met as Rodolfo in *La Bohème* in 1913–14, and although he was overshadowed by Caruso, he was one of the company's leading tenors.

Excited and challenged over the prospect of singing on the same program with a famous tenor of the Met, Grace chose to sing the difficult aria "Ritorna vincitor" from *Aïda,* the first opera she had attended in Washington. She passed the audition, and on 20 February 1919, made her debut at the National Theater.

As she stood in the wings awaiting her cue, listening to Martinelli's soaring high notes, and noting the enthusiastic applause and many curtain calls he received, she suffered her first full-fledged siege of stage fright. Lips dry, knees quaking, throat tied in knots, she made an awkward entrance and began in a light nervous soprano. She managed somehow to steady her nerves, to will her voice to rise true and clear. To the sweet roar of approval she bowed low in the Garden manner, and all but pranced off stage.

One Washington critic wrote: "Yesterday at the National Theater a concert was given by a lion and a mouse. The lion was the famous tenor, Giovanni Martinelli—the mouse, a young lyric soprano from Tennessee who showed promise."[2]

Those last three words convinced the eager, impatient girl that she was ready for the big time, but Mrs. Greene began to have second thoughts. There was Colonel Moore's strong objection to his daughter undertaking any kind of stage career. A maid had recently brought her an ardent love poem sent to Grace by Fisher Hepburn, a major on assignment in Washington from Cleveland, Ohio. The conscientious teacher decided it was her duty to send for the Jellico merchant.

The previous November, Grace had celebrated the capitulation of the Kaiser and the end of World War I with Major Hepburn and Blanche LeGarde in a Connecticut Avenue restaurant. Outside there was wild joy, but she was preoccupied with her new dream and her new beau. Major Hepburn possessed all of the qualities that had become important to her—especially solvency, gallantry, and sophistication. Although she was flattered by the ardent attention of an army officer several years her senior and strongly attracted to him, she would not allow herself to become too involved emotionally. Mary Garden had never married. Neither would Grace Moore—at least not until she had kept her dream.

Once again the father and daughter waged a fierce battle. Colonel Moore accused her of seeking romance instead of an education. She was furious at the sneaky maid, at her teacher, and at him. She was old enough to choose her own friends, she informed him, to receive love poems, and to write them if she felt so inclined. She was a free human being and no man, not even her own father, could control every tick of her heart.

Not only was she man-crazy, he persisted angrily, she was secretly plotting to go on the stage. She was hell-bent on shaming her family again, breaking her mother's heart, inviting ruination and eternal damnation.

The shouted accusations and retorts, generously sprinkled with *hells* and *damns* toward the last, resounded throughout the school, shocking both students and teachers. To calm herself and her angry father, Grace suddenly switched tactics—another feint she had learned from him. She agreed to remain in school until the end of the term, to see no more of Major Hepburn unless she intended to marry him, and to entertain no more plans for a stage career until they could discuss the matter more thoroughly and quietly at home.

The moment he was out of sight, however, she coolly informed Blanche that she had no intention of keeping that promise. Breaking a promise made under tyrannical pressure was just a small sample of what she was prepared to do, if necessary, to be free to shape her life to her own needs. She'd had a bellyful of Papa's lectures, of worrying about what Jellico would say. Furthermore, she'd learned all that the Wilson-Greene School could teach her.

Her more cautious and tradition-oriented friend advised her to stick it out until the end of the school term, but Grace was adamant.

The telegram the Moores received from the Greenes a few days later informed them that Grace had run away. They had hired a detective, but so far she had not been found. Word spread quickly. Goldie rushed to comfort the weeping mother and the frightened sister and brothers. The local gossips hung on telephones and over back fences. The father stalked about in a state of anxious fury, hired another detective, and kept in close touch with Mr. and Mrs. Greene.

After two weeks of waiting, praying, and imagining all kinds of horrors, a letter arrived from the runaway, postmarked New York City. Grace gave the family her new address, the Martha Washington Hotel, on Twenty-ninth Street, asked forgiveness for causing them so much worry and expense, informed them of her desire to seek a career in opera, and pled for time and for their belief in her.

Mrs. Moore tried to persuade her husband to forgive Grace and encourage her ambitions, but he would not listen. Instead he packed his bag and boarded another eastbound train, vowing to bring that stage-struck, man-crazy, mule-headed troublemaker home where she belonged and never let her out of his sight again.

One morning Grace was summoned by a frightened porter to the hotel desk. There stood the colonel, dark eyes flashing, mouth grim, temper on a short leash. To avoid shocking the elderly residents scattered about the lobby, she rushed him out the street door and into a nearby Childs restaurant, where they sat over coffee and doughnuts eyeing each other warily. Soon, in lowered voices, they waged their last fierce battle.

At his command, she briefly filled him in on the past two weeks. She had simply packed her bag, walked out the front door of the school on a rainy Sunday evening, and spent a week hidden in a tiny back room of Washington's Ponciana Hotel, registered as Genevieve Morena. There she had awaited a call from Blanche, who had promised to win her release from the school and meet her in New York City. Blanche knew the big city; Grace had been reluctant to tackle it alone.

The day after she had registered at the New York hotel, she had applied for a job at the Packard Agency, had been given an audition, and was expecting a call about a singing job at any moment. She had postponed writing, she concluded, until she was reasonably sure that she could pay her own way.

Colonel Moore listened without expression or comment. Suddenly he picked up the check, rose, and stalked to the cash register. Once outside, he demanded to know what she had been using for money. When she told him she had borrowed three hundred dollars from Major Hepburn, he sternly ordered her to go pack her bags, he was taking her home.

Grace was just as stern in her determination to stay in New

York. As they walked up and down Fifth Avenue she again reminded him that she was twenty-one years old and assured him that her prospects were bright and that she was gloriously happy. If he would forgive her, trust her, try to understand, she would never ask him for another cent.

The unhappy father had no choice but to accept defeat. He made one stipulation—that she perform only in ladylike classical plays. Although Grace quickly acquiesced, the moment she bade him good-bye she dismissed that promise, too, as impractical and tyrannical.

Part II
Her Guardian Angels

I was probably the most naive person in the world. Nothing had really touched me. I wanted to open my arms and clasp life to my heart. Yet I drew back, distrustful and afraid. Its perils and pitfalls had been dinned into my ears since childhood and my imagination had exaggerated them. I was hungry for friendship yet distrustful of people.

5 Glorious Adventures

Grace was in the vanguard of young women of the postwar era who would stream into New York City by the thousands in the next few years in search of freedom and a more meaningful identity. Some would go overboard before they got their bearings, and become lost to themselves and their families. Others would enjoy an exciting change of pace, but soon return home to assume their traditional roles as housewives and mothers. Only a few would possess the motivation, talent, and guts needed to survive and reach their dream goals. But all would have had the satisfaction of at least a whirl at freedom, challenge, and life.

Soon most of those who remained at home or school would join their more daring sisters in adopting the symbols of the emancipated woman—bobbed hair, plucked brows, loose-fitting girdles or none at all, knee-length stockings and skirts, spiked heels, rouge, lipstick. They would smoke cigarettes, drink illegal liquor, pet, and boldly reject the double standard. The fallen woman was out; the flapper was in.

A beautiful and talented young couple, F. Scott Fitzgerald and his bride, Zelda, the daughter of an assistant justice of the Alabama Supreme Court, called by critic Edmund Wilson (Fitzgerald's roommate at Princeton) "a barbarian princess of the soul,"[1] would get married in New York City as soon as his first novel, *This Side of Paradise*, was accepted by a publisher, gaily pick up the candle that the poet Edna St. Vincent Millay had been burning so brightly at both ends, and unfurl the new era—the "Jazz Age."

Fitzgerald's first novel, published in 1920, would become instantly successful and would set a new tone and pace. To celebrate her husband's sudden success, her freewheeling popularity at parties, and especially her retinue of gay young blades, Zelda of the wild hair, strange eyes, and vivacious self-destructive personality would perform such antics as jumping into the fountain at Union

Square fully clothed, or with her husband, spend a joyous half hour whirling around in the revolving door of their hotel. For a tragically brief while, this golden couple would reign supreme, she as Queen of the Flappers, and he as the brilliant interpreter of their generation. In the Hollywood of silent pictures, the Dutch-bobbed Colleen Moore and the "It" girl, Clara Bow, would pick up the torch of Flaming Youth and carry it to the farthest hinterlands.

The 1919 vanguard of the merry, nonsensical era just ahead would sail a stormy, uncharted sea, with tempting lanes luring them off in dangerous directions. Grace, so free and eager for adventure, for life, would try them all. Fortunately, her guardian angels—her voice and her dream—would prevent her from going too far out or down. She would quickly embrace New York City as a world of excitement, stimulation, and opportunity. Its pace suited her perfectly. She called herself a child of the speed age, always in a hurry.

Every day she would sally forth to meet new challenges. It was a thrill just to ride up and down Fifth Avenue on a double-decker bus, or to come upon Times Square at night with all its light blazing, or to read the many fat metropolitan newspapers. It was a joy to be living within a few blocks of the Met, and in the same city as Millay, whose "Renascence" had created such a sensation, and the violinist genius, Jascha Heifetz, whose first concert at Carnegie Hall had astonished critics.

In 1919 the more than two million doughboys returning from overseas were welcomed home with hysterical acclaim. Flags flew, bands played, ticker tape snowed down from high windows. When General Pershing named Corporal Alvin C. York, of Fentress County, Tennessee, the greatest hero of the war, the Tennessee Society of New York staged a tremendous celebration in his honor, and Grace's Tennessee hillbilly heart almost burst with pride.

In France's Argonne Forest in 1918 this young mountaineer, whose hometown, Pall Mall, was not many miles over the mountains from Jellico, killed twenty German soldiers, and captured 132 others and a fortified hill. Once a heavy drinker, gambler, and hell-raiser, he had reformed and become a conscientious objector. Not until his captain had convinced him of his duty to his country by quoting the Bible—"Blessed are the peacemakers"—did he fight his remarkable one-man-against-many battle.

Although the girl from Jellico was having what she often referred to as a "happy, wacky time," the going was far from
smooth. It was raining the day Blanche met her at the Pennsylvania
Station. Nevertheless, Grace insisted on going immediately to see
the Metropolitan Opera House. They stood outside the locked
doors of the old yellow brick building in awed silence. She said
finally, with fierce dedication, "Someday I'll be starred here."[2]

After checking in at the hotel she called Ruth Obre, the sister of
Arthur Obre, a midshipman she had met in Washington. The three
girls had lunch together at Schraffts and then Grace and Blanche
went to a musical matinee, starring an actor who would eventually
become one of her close friends—Clifton Webb.

Ruth Obre, beautiful, talented, vivacious, with a job on Wall
Street, was afflicted with the urge to write. Since Grace had frequent attacks of that incurable disease, they recognized each other
at once as kindred spirits. Ruth advised her to try to see the manager of the Packard Agency, and if she made it as far as his inner
office to invent a bit of experience—otherwise she wouldn't have a
chance.

After waiting in the agency's reception room for several hours
every day for a week, Grace was finally admitted. When she told
the cigar-chewing man behind the desk that she had been touring
on the West Coast in the opera *The Lilac Domino,* he called her a
liar, adding that he should know—it was his company. Un-
daunted, she quickly switched to her more effective Southern
"line," which won her a grudging audition. He told his secretary
to take her name and telephone number. Grace jumped to the
conclusion that he would call her within a few days. She waited
with eager expectation for a call that never came.

Soon the three girls and a would-be sculptress named Lillian,
whose weakness was a yen for men of the sea, pooled resources
and rented a cheap walk-up apartment in Gramercy Park. Ruth
gave up her job in favor of a typewriter. At the foursome's parties
the guests would sit on the floor, nibble cheese and crackers, drink
whatever they could scrounge, and share experiences, advice, and
dreams.

One day, after hours of making the rounds of casting offices
with no luck, Grace, Blanche, and Ruth spent almost their last
dollars eating in a cheap Greenwich Village restaurant. Then they
joined the sidewalk strollers and window shoppers. At one open
doorway, they paused to glance wistfully inside. It was a night-

club, the Black Cat Café. The master of ceremonies was announcing a singing contest, with prizes of a vanity case and perhaps a job.

Catapulted through the open door by her need, with the help of a few swift pushes and shoves, Grace was soon standing in the spotlight singing Victor Herbert's "Kiss Me Again." At the last sentimentally rendered "Kiss me, kiss me," an attractive young man rushed forward and kissed her. Grace blushed, then laughed. The customers howled. The manager offered her a week's trial at thirty-five dollars and supper. Within a short while she was the "Toast of the Village," earning seventy-five dollars a week with dinner as well as a late supper included, and saving money.

The young man, Walter Dean Goldbeck, a talented portrait painter who also had an excellent singing voice, recommended his Italian voice teacher to her as good and cheap and became her steady beau. She spent her days taking vocal lessons, practicing scales, and going to matinees, and her evenings singing at the cafe and late-dating with Goldbeck.

He was brilliant, articulate, ardent. His talk of symbolism, complexes, significance of one's childhood relationships, and of analyzing one's dreams often baffled and upset her. She dipped into Freud's books and was soon talking as sophisticatedly as any of her new friends about the ego, the unconscious mind, and the important role that sex plays in one's life.

At one party, Goldbeck introduced her to Morris Gest, son-in-law of the great playwright, director, and producer David Belasco. Without Gest's knowledge, Grace used his name to gain an audition with the great man. Then in his seventies, with thirty-five years of theatrical triumphs to his credit, Belasco received her graciously and permitted her to read the balcony scene from *Romeo and Juliet*. Since he had auditioned hundreds of girls, and had transformed a few with the necessary talent and temperament into great actresses, he knew instantly that she was not right for the part of Juliet. If anything, he told her, she was a potential singer rather than actress, and suggested that she approach Shakespeare through her music.

Stimulated rather than depressed by his slight encouragement, Grace studied the role of Juliette in Gounod's opera based on Shakespeare's play. Despite many weeks of hard work, she made little or no progress. The high and low ranges of her voice had become stronger and surer, but she had almost no middle register. Although she suspected that she had the wrong job, the wrong teacher, and the wrong beau, she was too enraptured with her new world to make any drastic changes. Her procrastination almost cost her her career.

A young Southern girl, Mary Watkins Reeves, who would later become Emily's college classmate and another number-one fan, ran into Grace one day at the water fountain in Washington Square. Her offer to hold down the pedal while Grace drank was accepted, and soon the two homesick girls sat down on a park bench to munch on stale gumdrops and get acquainted. Grace announced that the shopkeeper had vowed the gumdrops were fresh. Being cheated like that made her so mad she could spit. It wasn't the dime that infuriated her, it was the principle involved.

Reeves recalled that Grace looked no more than eighteen, with dull but rather pretty hair, her body somewhat plump, little or no makeup, a wonderfully clear skin and wide smile. Her dress could have come from a store or been made at home. Her stubby-toed shoes were of blond kid; her matching stockings were rolled.

The girl described is a far cry from the Grace Moore of a few years later.

One morning, shortly after this encounter, Grace opened her mouth to sing for her teacher and found she could not make a sound. Singing the same songs night after night in a cheap smoke-filled cafe, sometimes when she was suffering from a bad cold, studying with a second-rate teacher who had her bellowing her scales to increase the volume of her voice instead of letting it develop naturally, and dating an ardent young man who was draining her emotionally had caused "terrific vocal fatigue."[3]

Appalled, furious at herself, at her teacher and at her boyfriend, Grace became hysterical. Goldbeck appeared in time to calm her, beg her to forget her ambitions, and marry him. Holding her throat, she kept mutely, stubbornly, shaking her head.

Blanche advised her to go home to Jellico until she was well, but again she shook her head. She had heard of Dr. P. Mario Marafioti, who had served for several years as throat specialist and physician for many Met stars, including Caruso. In desperation, she went to see him at his office on Fifty-ninth Street, and waited many hours before he would take the time to see her.

A handsome man in his forties, with brilliant dark eyes that reflected his enthusiasm for the different and controversial method of voice care and training that he had devised, this graduate in medicine from the University of Naples was to play an important role in her rise to stardom, but their first meeting was brief and hope-shattering. He diagnosed her trouble as acute laryngitis and strain. Her voice was seriously damaged; she might never sing again. Recovery, if it came at all, would depend upon many months of rest in absolute silence. Every word she uttered would endanger or delay her chances. She should go away, rest, avoid speaking aloud for at least three months, and then return for another examination.

As she was leaving, in utter despair, he handed her a copy of *Jean-Christophe* by Romain Rolland, and suggested that she take the book with her. It would give her courage, he said, adding, "Music is a hard road."[4]

She was soon absorbed in reading a masterpiece of fiction dealing with art, love, death, and the purpose of life, written by a genius who drew much of his material from the life of Beethoven.

> Music is not enough for the present day musician, not thus will he dominate his age and raise his head above the stream of time. Life! All life! To see everything, to know everything, to feel everything. To love, to seek, to grasp Truth. . . . Art for art's sake. That's a fine faith. But it is the faith of the strong. Art. To grasp life as the eagle claws its prey, to bear it up into the air, to rise with it into the serenity of space. For that you need talons, great wings and a strong heart.[5]

In one of the last essays André Maurois wrote before his death in 1967, the famous French biographer, novelist, and essayist discussed his debt to Romain Rolland: "The novels which most surely affect and instruct the young generation are those that describe years of apprenticeship that paint the passage from an abstract and naive vision of the world to a concrete knowledge of the hard realities of life. We discover in . . . Jean Christophe our hopes, anguish, sighs and tears of joy. . . . Few Frenchmen have had such a universal and attentive audience throughout the entire world."[6]

Reading such eloquent passages at such a critical moment inspired Grace to swift action. She called an old friend, Orme Campbell of Atlanta, who happened to be in New York. His parents once owned a summer home near Jellico, but now spent their summers on a lake island in the St. Lawrence River. Since his family was now abroad, he offered her the use of their cabin for as long as she would need it, but warned her that she would become lonely and depressed living there alone. Grace thanked him, quit her job, and within hours was on her way to Canada. For fear she might weaken, she left without saying goodby to Goldbeck. Ruth

Obre took her place on a dinner date with him, and within a year became his wife. Later she would become Countess de Vallombrossa, and still later Mrs. André Dubonnet, and an internationally noted connoisseur of good food.

During those weeks of restful solitude Grace read the books she had brought along and others she found at the cabin, studied French and Italian, and wrote long letters to her mother and to Mary Garden. She fished, rowed, swam, and took long walks. She communicated with the caretaker and the few neighbors she met by signals and notes. Her meals were simple; by sundown she would be in bed "amid such stillness," she wrote her mother, "my own heartbeats sound like drums."

She spent many hours taking stock of herself, acknowledging the inferiority complex that had plagued her ever since her kindergarten and Ward-Belmont experiences. She vowed to subdue her hot Irish temper and lust for life, to find the proper balance between work and play, and never again allow herself to overcompensate or plunge overboard in either direction. Freedom, she had discovered, was also a hard road.

Singing at the Black Cat Café had given her experience and professional status, taught her which popular songs were surefire, and how to project her personality as well as her voice. Those weeks of silence, solitude, and soul-searching had thrust her nightingale far out in front—but she knew that if she failed to remain on guard, her demons would break free, catch up again, and vie for the lead.

"One does not amount to much," Grace would often say, in advising young people, "until one has spent a great deal of time alone."

Upon her return to New York City she lived a solitary life in a one-room apartment near Dr. Marafioti's studio, and read poetry to him every day in his soft native tongue, which he called a "vocal massage."[7] Desperate for money, she ate most of her meals with Clara and Mario Marafioti. Their cook, Maria, kept her appetite assuaged with generous servings of spaghetti, which Grace thought was the best in the world. Maria gave her the recipe, one of the first of hundreds she would collect and use over the years.

Although many musicians call Marafioti a charlatan, he was in vogue at that time and he did help Grace save her voice. From him she learned, among other things, to take care of her vocal chords, to breathe properly, and to concentrate on the color and flavor of the lyrics and their meaning apart from the music. In turn, Grace eventually became as important to his career as he was to hers, and to the end of her life defended his teaching methods.

On the first annual celebration of Armistice Day, 11 November 1919, she made her debut in vaudeville as part of a special program at the Palace Theater. One of Dr. Marafioti's friends, F. C. Whitney, manager of *The Chocolate Soldier,* heard her sing at the Palace, and, at the doctor's suggestion that she was ready, came to the studio to audition her. He offered her the ingenue lead in *Suite Sixteen* at $75 a week, with rehearsals to begin the next day.

On opening night, in Syracuse, the ingenue was told to do her own makeup and select her costume from the store of leftovers from *The Chocolate Soldier.* When she appeared in the wings to await her cue, the manager's wife took one horrified glimpse of the overpainted and overdressed ingenue, clad in high heels and an ermine coat of ancient vintage, whisked her into a dressing room, scrubbed her face, and replaced the old fur with her own simple wrap.

After a thirty-five-minute delay, with the other members of the cast fuming and the audience waiting impatiently for the curtain to rise, the ingenue at last rushed on stage, upset, awkward, and obviously inexperienced. Her one song, "First You Wiggle—Then You Waggle," at first aroused little response. In her determination to win her listeners somehow, Grace belted out the words more saucily and illustrated them with exaggerated wiggles and waggles. Immediately the audience perked up; her exit waggle brought down the house.

Grace was too excited over being in a musical comedy to mind the drafty dressing rooms and stages, the wretched food, the cheap cold hotel rooms, and the practical jokes, jealousies, and intrigues that almost always prevail among members of the cast of a show doing one-night stands. Every evening she would sing her one song, do her wiggles and waggles, and be rewarded, especially in college towns, with roars of applause. She liked having Blanche LeGarde in the cast as one of the dancers. But the show was failing. One reviewer called it a mistake to have Grace Moore disappear in the beginning of the play. He considered her the only member of the cast who could really sing; her one song apparently revealed a voice that was rare and charming.

She was learning to control and project her voice without damaging it, to devise means of communicating with an audience however apathetic or supercritical, and to value publicity. With gaiety and enthusiasm, she cherished every experience of the tour—until the morning she awoke to a North Dakota blizzard and was told that the Whitneys, having lost heavily in the stock market, had departed suddenly, leaving the cast stranded. Eventually the Actors' Equity Association sent each member train fare and twenty-five dollars. The young troupers arrived in New York City on 23 December, weary, hungry, and almost broke. Desperately homesick and reluctant to spend her first Christmas away from home in another cheap hotel room, Grace talked Blanche and Lillian, who met the train fresh from a failed romance with the captain of a tramp steamer, into signing a six-month lease at two hundred dollars a month on a furnished apartment on West Sixty-seventh Street, in the famous Artists Studio Row.

The three girls pooled resources to make up the necessary one-hundred-dollar deposit and blithely moved in. Shocked at their daring, they soon began to wonder where they would get the money to stock their empty icebox and pay the rent at the end of the month.

Blanche remembered a friend named Ginsberg who lived nearby. She called him to announce her return to the city, and he came through with an invitation to all three of them for a turkey dinner especially prepared by Reuben. Since Grace was not interested in spending Christmas with strangers and the other two were lukewarm, she called Arnold Reuben at his nearby restaurant, introduced herself as a newcomer to the neighborhood and a friend of Mr. Ginsberg, mentioned the fact that the banks were closed and she was short of cash, and ordered a turkey dinner for three sent in—on credit. Her apartment mates thought she had lost her mind. The restauranteur knew at once that the girl with the honey-sweet voice was handing him a Southern "line," but he kindheartedly honored the order. Amid giggles, what-ifs, and optimistic predictions, they ate their fill and had enough food left over to keep them smiling and self-confident for almost a week. Arnold Reuben would never regret his Good Samaritan act.

By 1920, musical comedies and musical extravaganzas had become extremely popular. *The Ziegfeld Follies,* with Irving Berlin music, Jerome Kern's *Sally,* and George White's *Scandals* were all smash hits. Many other shows were drawing full houses every night. Beautiful showgirls were in demand. Grace could have qualified, but she stubbornly held out for a singing part.

One day after Grace had auditioned for a part in George White's *Scandals* with Kreisler's "When You Are Free" from *Apple Blos-*

som Time the young man who had accompanied her on the piano quietly introduced himself. He was George Gershwin. She did not get the part, but in future years whenever they met at parties they would go to the piano and restage that audition. She sang "When You Are Free" and Gershwin accompanied her at one of Elsa Maxwell's parties just a year before his death in 1937.

Grace eventually won a singing part in John Cort's *Just a Minute* but it closed in Pittsburgh after only three weeks. She went to see Charles Dillingham, the always gracious, and at that time highly successful, Broadway producer. The first to take an interest in her career, he sent her to Boston to try out for a show he was producing, *Hitchy Koo,* starring Julia Sanderson and Raymond Hitchcock.

As she hurried across the rehearsal stage at a Boston theater to keep an appointment with Hitchcock, she stepped on the cloth-of-gold train of one of the showgirls. The girl moved and the train ripped off. With blue eyes blazing and lace panties exposed, the angry female whirled around, called Grace a greenhorn, and asked why in hell she couldn't lift her club feet.

Grace was too intent upon reaching and impressing the famous actor to pause for an apology or a savage retort. Hitchcock arranged for her to sing for Jerome Kern, who was writing songs for the show. Apparently impressed with the fresh beauty of her face, figure, and voice, Kern gave her a small part, singing a specialty number called "Oh Moon of Love." A performer with years of experience and a lovely singing voice, Julia Sanderson, indignantly demanded to be given the new song. The demand was ignored, but another specialty number which Grace had hoped to sing was commandeered by the determined prima donna.

Nette Thomas, or Jane Thomas, the beautiful and angry girl with the pretty lace panties, whom Grace described as "quick-tongued, savvy and generous,"[8] comforted the newcomer by castigating the prima donna in vivid language.

Despite the hostility of their first encounter, Grace and Jane soon became friends. Almost the same height, stature, and age, each was attracted by the other's marvelous sense of humor, complete naturalness, and zest for living. When Grace went to Hollywood, she wore Jane's fur coat. Later she would lend clothes to Jane for special occasions. They would tour Europe together and frequently fall in love with the same man.

Years later Jane Thomas recalled that first meeting with Grace and described their stay together at the Copley Plaza. They spent their entire salaries on their room and clothes. Grace was always the center of attention; she was also a hard worker with rigid rules for self-improvement. Jane was still astonished at the way Grace starved herself to keep her figure, and the effort she made to have both a good marriage and a successful career.

On one trip to Europe they fell in love with the same man. One night Jane returned from a date with him to find that Grace had checked out and sailed for home. She followed on the next ship. They ran into each other at their favorite tearoom on Fifth Avenue. After smiling tentatively at each other, they burst out laughing.

6 New Worlds to Conquer

When *Hitchy Koo* opened at the new Amsterdam Theater in New York, Grace served as stand-in, in addition to singing "Oh Moon of Love" in front of a line of showgirls who interjected a series of satirical questions and comments in counterpoint to her conventional rendition of the song. The number was a hit, but she was not. One critic mentioned her slim part and her slim figure and predicted she would have a slim future. The negative criticisms, and others to come over the years, only increased her determination to succeed—to prove the critics wrong about her potential. Always conscious of being only two blocks from her ultimate goal—the Met—she would sometimes walk by the building and renew her dedication to her dream.

After the Thanksgiving Day matinee, and only a few hours before curtain time, she was told that Julia Sanderson had been stricken with indigestion and she would play the lead that evening. Grace rushed to the telephone to spread the word. Friends notified friends, thus enabling her to sing her first lead on Broadway to a packed house that was prejudiced in her favor.

One of the front seat occupants, a multimillionaire playboy, T. Markoe ("Tommy") Robertson, invited all the girls in *Hitchy Koo* to a supper party at a famous nightclub, where champagne and risqué repartee flowed freely. Sluffing off the bothersome remnants of her smalltown Baptist inhibitions, Grace let herself go. One of the wealthy men at that party, Whitney Warren, Sr., architect of New York's Grand Central Station, many large hotels, and other buildings, took her under his wing. Years later, his son, Whitney Warren, Jr., a member of the board of directors of the San Francisco Opera and the owner of a highly successful peach ranch, would take her under *his* wing, and whenever she sang in San Francisco he would give a supper party in her honor, and see that she met everyone in this city worth knowing.

Through her blossoming romance with gay blade Tommy Robertson, she began to sample New York nightlife in all its glittering aspects. Attending late supper parties would soon become her favorite way of unwinding and celebrating after a performance. He escorted her to many social gatherings and introduced her to some of the celebrities she had read about and admired from afar. Among them were Alma Gluck, whom she had heard sing in Washington, and her husband, the famous violinist Efrem Zimbalist; the John McCormacks; Jascha Heifetz; the Samuel Chotzinoffs, he a pianist (and later her accompanist), teacher, and critic whose wife, Pauline, was Jascha Heifetz's sister; and Mischa Levitski, who won Grace's heart briefly by playing Chopin for her while looking romantically melancholy.

One night, at a party in Alma Gluck's salon, Robertson introduced her to George Biddle, a talented Philadelphia painter, sculptor, and member of one of the most prestigious main-line families. They were instantly attracted to each other.

George Biddle was brilliant, distinguished, and different. Since Grace had acquired a chic new wardrobe and could now dress appropriately for every occasion, she had become so clothes-conscious that she would refuse to go out with a man who arrived at her door after six o'clock wearing brown shoes. Biddle's nonconformist attitude toward clothes, especially his addiction to threadbare strawberry tweeds, and his love of cats kept her from going completely overboard.

Biddle was a serious and cynical product of Haverford School, Groton, and Harvard Law, where he had graduated cum laude. After living in California and Paris, he served as an infantry lieutenant during the war. A sensitive and sophisticated rebel, he was divorced and was about fifteen years her senior. He became interested in what he considered "the dark potential of [her] mind," and opened many new worlds to her.[1] She met his many friends, went with him to all the museums, and gradually became a knowledgeable art buff.

During this phase of her growth Grace's native intelligence, good memory, and eagerness to learn served her well, as did her beauty, disarming frankness, and remarkable gift for making and keeping influential friends. From every friend she clasped to her heart, from every book she devoured, from every scintillating conversation she listened to, she absorbed know-how for herself as a singer on the rise and as a human being out to conquer worlds.

Biddle and Robertson were both Walter Pater enthusiasts. Often in letters she wrote to her mother Grace would quote Walter Pater as well as Romain Rolland. Pater's writing would also become a part of her credo; she would quote him all the rest of her life:

> The service of philosophy toward the human spirit is to rouse, to startle it to a life of constant and eager observation. . . . Not the fruit of experience, but experience itself, is the end. . . . A counted number of pulses only is given to us of a variegated dramatic life. How shall we pass most swiftly from point to point, and be present always at the focus where the greatest number of vital forces unite in their purest energy? . . . To burn always with this hard, gemlike flame, to maintain this ecstasy, is success in life. . . . All art constantly aspires toward the condition of music.[2]

The young singer and the nonconformist artist were soon considering marriage. Loving him, and feeling the need of an anchor, she was torn between wanting to become his wife and wanting to remain free to pursue her high goal.

When the show reached Cincinnati her family arrived to see her for the first time on a professional stage. Fascinated by all the activity behind the scenes, they crowded into her dressing room, watched her don a provocative silver gown, comfortable shoes—she knew better now than to stumble around on spiked heels—and just enough makeup to bring out her vivid natural coloring and the glint of red in her dark hair.

Grace's mother was not her usual talkative self, due to the recent loss by fire of her family's farmhouse in Del Rio, but her father had much to say. So intent was he upon convincing her that she was degrading herself and her name that he caused her to be late for her cue. Hitchcock had just ordered her number scratched when Grace rushed onstage, exclaiming that she *had* to sing because her family had come all the way from Jellico to hear her. Her plea and a roar of laughter and applause from the audience won her a reprieve.

By the end of the show, Colonel Moore's fundamentalist rigidity had been shaken. Her voice had shown remarkable improvement; her song was a hit. She not only looked radiantly happy, she had communicated some of her radiance to the audience—even to him. Furthermore, Raymond Hitchcock was not an ogre, as he had suspected, but a clever ad-libber, an interesting human being, and a great artist.

By 1921, the attitudes that had prevailed in the South for many years had undergone rapid change. The ambitions and talents of young women in small towns were no longer completely bogged down in quagmires of prejudice, bigotry, and rigid tradition. Girls were still brought up to know their place, and when a girl stepped out of line she was still branded by men, and alas, by a large majority of women, as a wanton, a traitor to her sex. But a few enlightened and courageous Southerners of both sexes had begun to challenge the status quo. More and more suffragists in the South had joined their Northern and Western sisters in the long fight to win the vote. This first step toward equality had ended successfully in Nashville, Tennessee, in August 1920.

From all over the country, prominent pros and antis had gathered at the state capitol to try to influence, by fair means or foul, the votes of the Tennessee legislators. On that memorable day, Grace's state by a margin of one vote became the thirty-sixth and final needed to ratify the Nineteenth Amendment.

This important right finally won, the suffragists were too exhausted to do much more than cast their votes (for Warren G. Harding, alas) and rest on their laurels. They looked to younger women to carry on their crusade for women's rights in the League of Women Voters. They had thought, mistakenly, that the vote would unshackle all women and put an end to oppression and war.

Grace was too busy pursuing her dream to be active in the women's suffrage movement or in the League of Women Voters, but as one of the few women of her generation to free herself in body, mind, and spirit, she helped the woman's movement tremendously. She was a shining example of the new woman, self-willed, ambitious, a tradition-smashing trailblazer, a woman equal to any man alive and superior to many, a patriot, a fighter, an adventurer, a free spirit.

Although in 1921 women of the streets still euphemistically called themselves "actresses," performing on a stage was no longer unthinkable in small Bible Belt towns. The intelligent citizens had begun to appreciate, however grudgingly, the amount of talent, courage, and sheer hard work required before a stagestruck girl could become successful in any role behind the footlights.

Grace's father was too shrewd and successful in business and politics, and too aware of his daughter's ambitious dreams, talents, forceful personality, and staying power to remain forever out of tune with the changing times. Also, he was impressed that a Biddle wanted to marry her. Long before the final curtain, he had begun to relax and enjoy the show.

By the time *Hitchy Koo* closed, both the Jellico Moores and the

Philadelphia Biddles had become more or less resigned to the contemplated marriage. Though tempted, Grace continued to be plagued with doubts. Was she truly in love, or was she merely dazzled by her fiancé's name, talents, and background? What if marriage should rob her of her hard-won freedom to pursue her own goals? Would a successful artist husband from a distinguished social register family and a home and children be enough? Would she feel frustrated, resort to ailments, ruin his career as well as her own?

In his autobiography, Biddle admitted to similar doubts. Could he bother to dress to please her, lead the busy social life she enjoyed, help further the career she insisted upon, and still become and remain a first-rank artist? Was their love strong enough to overcome the vast differences in their ages, backgrounds, and temperaments?

Grace tackled her pressing heart problem with the calculated shrewdness she always used effectively. She invested her savings, $865, in a chaperone–secretary–traveling companion and a two-month Mediterranean cruise and sailed away in May 1921, accompanied by her fiancé and Jessie Harrison, a charming though somewhat austere white-haired New Englander in her early fifties. If their love could survive sixty-two days of continuous togetherness cruising and sight-seeing, she would risk marriage. If not, she would have saved herself from marrying the wrong man at the wrong time and enjoyed her first trip abroad with a most competent guide and escort.

At their first stop, Ponta Delgada in the Azores, Grace fell in love with the villa where Wagner had once lived and tried to buy it on the installment plan. Since she did not have the necessary down payment, one of the men in the party, Murray Nelson, a noted Chicago criminal lawyer, offered to buy it for her. She was gratefully considering accepting his offer and leaving the ship to complete the purchase when she learned that Ponta Delgada was a place noted for its frequent epidemics of boils. The sale was called off.

After the trip was over, Grace summed up her first experiences abroad in these words, "George Biddle taught me to appreciate what was the best in art and architecture, putting me under his serious tutelage on tour and, with the help of a Baedeker, dinning into my head every known fact about church, gargoyle, or steeple. . . . He dragged me through the mistral heat to see the murals of Puvis de Chavannes, the paintings of Poussin, and the Chateau d'if. . . . After Marseilles we motored to Bandol, where at the Grand Hotel I first tasted the paradise *en pension* of the Riviera which could be had for two dollars a day. We motored up the Riviera through a coast line like our own Chamber-of-Commerce California; eternal sun, palms, lush vegetation, and semitropical trees, with always the henna-colored rocks jutting over the cobalt Mediterranean."[3]

When the cruise ended, Grace and Jessie Harrison spent two weeks in Jellico visiting her family. Her gray-haired chaperone charmed, impressed, and disarmed the family and the town. Harrison, in turn, was fascinated by Jellico, and its front-porch way of life. Grace picnicked with old friends at Sandy Beach, and climbed to her hilltop rock to meditate on past mistakes, current progress, and future glory.

Still a long, long way from keeping her dream, she was almost sure now she would never marry George Biddle. They had both tried, but love was not enough. Long before they had reached Marseilles, they had got on each other's nerves and quarreled frequently. Perhaps their first fight was over her asinine conduct at Ponta Delgada—not only her eagerness to buy a villa she could not afford, but her willingness to permit a rich man she scarcely knew to pay for it!

Two careers in one family would be one too many. Her freedom was too hard won and too precious to risk losing it before she had realized her dream. Furthermore, her visit to Mediterranean shores had awakened her to the wide gaps in her education, intoxicated her senses, and aroused new thirsts. Since she had barely scratched the surface of all the cultural riches across the sea, she was eager to go back as soon as possible, especially to Paris, the artistic capital of the world. Mary Garden's talent had flowered in Paris; surely hers would, too.

Town Gossip, with Grace singing the lead, opened in the remodeled Ford's Opera House in Baltimore, in September 1921. The *Baltimore Evening Star* critic praised her performance as having "a great deal of quiet elegance and a real distinction."[4] One night during its brief run, the pianist, Edythe Baker, whose act required her to play on stage with all the cast listening, angrily accused Grace of deliberately distracting the audience by flirting with the bald-headed men in the front row. Grace indignantly denied it, claiming the front row had been occupied by Harvard boys, and if she had smiled at them and they at her, so what? There was certainly no intent of upstaging anyone. The two soon came to strong words and actual blows and the argument began to resemble a high school basketball fight. More than once they were pulled apart.

The cast was both amused and shocked to see how quickly a pretty young singer "of quiet elegance and a real distinction," could become a clawing tiger.

Thus began the reputation Grace would earn on her way up, as a temperamental terror who would give no quarter verbally or physically when her career was in any way threatened.

Years later, the pianist and the prima donna met again on the French Riviera and laughed over their savage encounter, attributing it to nervous tension. There is great tension when a show is succeeding, but when it is failing the strain sometimes becomes almost unbearable, especially when one's whole future is at stake.

Although her performance was an improvement over previous efforts, Grace was not yet experienced enough to carry a musical comedy. The show closed suddenly, a painful moment for her and for the forty showgirls in the cast left stranded without train fare or eating money. Grace goodheartedly took it upon herself to raise the money that they would need to get back to New York. By this time her father could have afforded a considerable loan, but she was too proud and stubborn to break her vow never to ask him for another cent. Instead, she placed a long-distance call to one of her wealthy new friends, Bernard Baruch, who had made millions in Wall Street and would eventually become known as park-bench friend and adviser to presidents. She told him of the girls' plight, and he sent sufficient funds to rescue them. The grateful show girls thanked Grace, and repaid Baruch through Actor's Equity a little at a time.

Following the advice, encouragement, and laudatory recommendations of Charles Dillingham, she was soon singing and dancing in Joseph Gates's *Up in the Clouds*, which played in Detroit, Pittsburgh, Louisville, and other cities before coming, in January 1922, to the Subway Circuit. Robert Benchley of *Life* wrote favorably of her performance, and soon other national publications and metropolitan newspapers began to mention Grace Moore as a rising young star.

Although in future years she would arouse hostility as well as enthusiasm among press representatives, she could always be depended upon for stunning pictures and colorful story material. Not only did she know the value of publicity, she coveted it, prepared for it, and loved it as frankly and passionately as she did the many other facets of the exciting life she was building for herself.

At the studio of Neysa McMein, artist and glamour girl of the famous Algonquin Round Table, Grace first met some of that group of columnists, novelists, playwrights, composers, actresses, and artists. There was constant coming and going in McMein's studio. Her hospitality was casual and warm, and her friends legion. They included such Algonquinites as Dorothy Parker (who had a one-room apartment in the same building), Franklin P. Adams, Alexander Woollcott, Robert Benchley, Marc Connelly, George S. Kaufman, Edna Ferber, Robert E. Sherwood, and Harold Ross. And such diverse celebrities as Feodor Chaliapin, Irving Berlin, Mary Pickford, and Father Duffy. In the McMein studio George Gershwin played his symphonic jazz composition *Rhapsody in Blue*, before it was premiered by Paul Whiteman at Aeolian Hall on 12 February 1924.

A tall, slender young woman with green eyes and molasses-colored hair, with a marvelous sense of wonder and a kindly sense of humor, Neysa had arrived in New York from Quincy, Illinois, by way of Chicago, where she had studied at the Art Institute. Since changing her name from Marjorie Morn McMein to Neysa McMein, she had become successful as a pastel painter of covers for the *Saturday Evening Post, McCall's, Collier's* and the *Woman's Home Companion*. Later she would paint oil portraits of Harding and Hoover at the White House, of Chief Justice Charles Evans Hughes, Jascha Heifetz, Beatrice Lillie, Dorothy Parker, and many other celebrities of the day.

She urged Grace to consult Evangeline Adams, the era's authority on all things astrological, about changing her name. The seer told Grace that she would have her heart's desire if she would change her name to Graziella Morena. Grace refused. She wanted to succeed as Grace Moore, American. She did chop off three years from her age, which made her a year younger than her brother Martin. The Moores understood this stratagem and went along with it. But after 1934, when Grace became a sensational motion picture star in *One Night of Love*, the queries that poured into Jellico regarding her true age caused them much difficulty. They continued the gallant deception and succeeded so well that every road sign, plaque, notation in Tennessee celebrating the famous nightingale's accomplishments lists her birth date as 1901—and her school as Ward-Belmont.

The members of the famous Round Table stimulated each other with witty and sometimes hard-hitting repartee, a mutual passion for the English language and for the New York theater, for word games (especially charades), for cutthroat croquet, and for high-stakes poker. They wielded tremendous influence on the artistic growth of the city. Harold Ross would begin publishing the *New Yorker* in 1925, and many of the others would serve on the editorial board or become contributors. The magazine would become so successful that in ten years it would cause *Vanity Fair* to be discontinued.

The group stimulated the outer fringes, too. Grace enjoyed meeting them and making friends among them, but was wary of Dorothy Parker's acid wit, and, like almost everyone else who came within the orbit of talented, unpredictable, vindictive Alexander Woollcott, she had several spats with him.

One spat occurred at McMein's place at Great Neck, Long Island, where the group would gather during the summers. One day, in a spirit of fun, Woollcott kept ducking Grace's head under the dirty water of Long Island Sound. On her way back to New York City she suffered a high temperature, a touch of delirium and a mastoid infection that required lancing. She never quite forgave Woollcott, and he resented being responsible and never quite forgave her.

Being mentioned in Franklin P. Adams's widely read "The Conning Tower," patterned after Samuel Pepys's diary, and published at that time in the *New York World,* was considered a sure sign that one had arrived. Grace made it first in December 1921: "And so to a merry party at Miss Grace Moore's & Lord! I never saw so many handsome girls in my life, and yet none prettier than Grace."[5] In January 1922: "And so then to Mistress Grace Moore's to dinner, of duck and prune whip, very good too, and a play with her, and I find Grace's mind to be as clearly sweet as her voice."[6]

Franklin P. Adams, or F.P.A., a man of great charm and personality, and the informal leader of the Algonquin group, would occasionally take Grace to lunch at the Algonquin Hotel; and there, at the famous round table in the Rose Room, she came to know still others of the famous group, who eventually called themselves "The Vicious Circle."

Charles Dillingham introduced her to many other famous New Yorkers, some of whom became her lifelong friends, as did Margaret Case of *Vogue,* Frank Crowninshield of *Vanity Fair,* and Condé Nast, publisher of both magazines, who helped launch the careers of many beautiful unknowns. His penthouse at 1040 Park Avenue, decorated by the famous Elsie de Wolfe (who would soon become another Grace Moore friend), was an ideal setting for the parties he gave and the good food he served in great style.

Occasionally on Sunday evenings Condé Nast would take Grace to supper at the Coffee House Club on West Forty-Fifth Street, where Frank Crowninshield presided over an illustrious gathering of such celebrities as Geraldine Farrar, Antonio Scotti, Marie Tempest, Ethel Barrymore, Ina Claire, Lenore Ulrich, and many others.

According to Grace, "These conversations were like the crackling, sparkling discharge of so many electric dynamos. It seemed to me that I was sitting with Olympian gods and goddesses."[7]

One night at a Coffee House supper she had her second encounter with Mary Garden. When they were introduced her idol wanted to know if she was that funny little creature who had been writing her those letters. Grace was still too much in awe of the forceful and exciting woman she admired above all others and was trying to emulate to be able to carry on a conversation with her.

During the previous fall, the *Ladies' Home Journal* had published an article by Mary Garden entitled "Your Career in Opera," in which she had outlined the necessary qualifications, other than talent, of an operatic singer. Her list included good common sense, a healthy and mentally active brain, intellectual acquisitiveness, good health, a love of nature, a vigorous outdoor life, and long hard work. Good looks were desirable but not necessary. Ambition and the will to sing were not enough; you not only had to love to sing, you had to *need* to sing. A dynamic personality and enough money to acquire the necessary training, much of it abroad, were musts. By this time Grace knew that an American singer, and certainly one who insisted on keeping her own name, had little chance of becoming a Met prima donna unless she first studied and performed abroad.

After that second brief encounter, she sailed for Europe on the *Berengaria* with a recommendation from Margaret Chase as to where to live, and another from Geraldine Farrar as to the teacher with whom she should study.

Also sailing for Europe on the *Berengaria* were Condé Nast, Neysa McMein, and several other celebrity friends and acquaintances, including Irene Castle. With her handsome English husband, Vernon, Castle had become internationally famous for ballroom steps—the Maxixe, the One Step, the Tango, the Castle

Walk. Their beautiful dancing and romantic love story had ended in 1918 when the plane in which he was training American aviators at Forth Worth, Texas, plunged in flames to the ground. Her girlish figure, simple dress, and bobbed hair had become the ideal new look; she was largely responsible for the decline from fashion of such lush silhouettes as that of Lillian Russell.

At a dinner party Grace gave aboard the ship, Irene Castle told the story of how she had decided to bob her hair. Before going to the hospital for an appendectomy, she had impuslively picked up a pair of scissors and chopped it off, so that it would be easier to manage while she was in the hospital. After the operation, she had worn a turban while her hair was growing back, but the process was aggravatingly slow. One night she made a little band of black velvet, sewed a string of pearls on it, and tied it around her head. Within a week, hundreds of girls had bobbed their hair and tied a band of ribbon around their heads. Bobbed hair was soon the rage, as well as another symbol of the new woman.

She was also credited with introducing ankle-length skirts because she couldn't dance in long straight ones and eliminating the girdle because she didn't need a girdle.

One of the first moves Grace made in Paris was to bob her hair. The deed was done with several friends on hand to watch the auburn tresses fall—and to celebrate with champagne and laughter.

7 Star Quality

From the moment she arrived at the pension near the Bois de Boulogne until the end of her life, Grace would be a passionate Francophile. She loved all of France, but particularly Paris, the Riviera, and the wine country. Very quickly, she picked up enough of the language to be able to converse with members of the household, and with tradesmen, taxi drivers, waiters, and salesladies. Still a thirsty sponge, she went for long walks with every sense alerted and delighted.

She loved every street scene—the deluxe shops on the Place Vendôme, the kiosks, flower women, the cathedral, the magazine and book stalls on the left bank of the Seine. Of the more than ten thousand Americans then living in Paris, at least three thousand were students. There were also large English, Russian, Italian, and South American colonies. Artists' studios dominated every street in Montmartre; displays of colorful canvasses brightened every sidewalk and café. Literary groups flourished. The sounds of talented musicians practicing scales spilled from many windows. She admired the traditional French family closeness and frugality, and enjoyed the incomparable foods, wines, perfumes, and clothes. She luxuriated in the stimulation of the unfamiliar and rejoiced at finding her second home. But she would remain very much an American girl studying abroad.

On her first night in Paris, Frank Crowninshield and Condé Nast took her to dine at La Pérouse on the Seine, said to be the favorite restaurant of Oscar Wilde and Marcel Proust. Here she first met Elsa Maxwell, who had become famous for her unique talent as a professional social hostess and party catalyst.

Years later in her syndicated column Elsa Maxwell reminisced about how she and Grace Moore met and became such good friends. One Sunday she gave a small dinner party at La Perouse on the Quai des Grandes Augustins for Condé Nast. He tele-

phoned to ask permission to bring a perfectly lovely girl named
Grace Moore and predicted that she would become one of the
finest singers in the world. That is how the long and intimate
friendship began, and it was through that friendship that Grace
met so many celebrities abroad.

Elsa Maxwell invited the threesome to a late supper party given
that evening by Captain Edward H. Molyneux. During the previous year he and Maxwell had opened two nightclubs in Paris—one
called Les Acacias, featuring Clifton Webb and Janice Dolly, one
of the Dolly Sisters, which catered to fashionable Parisians; and
another, for the overflow, called Le Jardin de Ma Soeur, where,
for a time, the American black performer Josephine Baker was a
popular and somewhat controversial attraction.

"Eddie" Molyneux began his fabulous career by doing odd jobs
for the staff of *Smart Set,* and free-lance sketches for stores. One of
his sketches caught the attention of Lady Duff Gordon, then the
ruling power at Lucille's, a London couture house. After World
War I, he opened a couture salon in Paris that quickly became
noted for its afternoon and evening clothes. He and Grace became
friends and later on, neighbors on the Riviera.

Elsie de Wolfe, who later married Sir Charles Mendle of the
British Embassy staff, invited Grace to spend a week at her home,
the Villa Trianon, in Versailles, and arranged a private recital for
her. Before an invited audience, and accompanied by a young
Englishman who would soon become famous as playwright, composer, versifier, and performer—Noel Coward—Grace made her
debut on the European continent—and added still another friend
to her fast-growing and always-cherished list.

"Noel Coward loved Grace," wrote his longtime friend, companion, and definitive biographer, Cole Lesley, in *Remembered
Laughter.*[1] Coward once promised to write a musical comedy for
her, but never got around to it. However, their paths would cross
many times in future years.

Such swift acceptance in international society was heady stuff.
Grace was invited to dine with Cècile Sorel in her sumptuous
apartment overlooking the Seine. The famous French actress was
also noted for her drawing-room wit and lovely bosom. Her service plates were gold, and if that wasn't enough to impress a girl
from Jellico, when Grace retired to powder her nose she sat down
briefly on Madame Du Barry's bed.

Hair bobbed, and costumed in something filmily appropriate to the theme—"Scenes from Pompeii"—she went with Jascha Heifetz, Neysa McMein, and Dudley Field Malone (a New York lawyer with an office in Paris), to the colorful Quatre-Arts Ball, and when Cècile Sorel was hoisted on the shoulders of admiring students and paraded around in the seminude, she saw the famous bosom in all its glory.

Grace also dined and partied with Cole Porter and his Kentucky-born wife, Linda, in their Art Deco home at No. 13 Rue Monsieur, and later in New York in the Waldorf Towers. Cole and Linda Porter had a wide circle of friends abroad, from pretty showgirls to Winston Churchill and George Bernard Shaw. He, too, lived a double life, working hard and playing just as hard.

Despite such an exciting social whirl, Grace managed to live frugally and keep her chief reason for being in Paris firmly in mind. She was welcomed into the studio of the famous vocal teacher, M. Trabadello, as a young friend of three of his former pupils: Garden, Gluck, and Farrar. After she had sung for him, Trabadello, who was thin, old, wore a toupee, high heels and rouge, and spoke in an effeminate voice, asked her to push his baby grand piano across the polished floor while singing "ah." She did so with ease. He had her demonstrate her strength, patience, and fortitude with several such undignified pushings and ah-ings before he smilingly offered to make her a great star, provided she would sign a contract giving him complete control of her artistic career for the next five years.

Five years, she decided, would be much too long to tie herself to a contract that might not produce the results she was after—her name on the roster of lyric sopranos of the Met. Refusing his offer may have cost her the strict discipline and thorough technical training and musicianship that might have made her voice the greatest of an era.

Since she needed to overcome her Southern accent and learn to speak French more correctly and fluently, she chose Roger Thiral, an ex-singer from the Opéra-Comique who specialized in French diction, and reported for lessons once and sometimes twice a day. He introduced her to his friend and colleague, Gabriel Fauré, whom Grace described as "a medium-sized, middle-height, middle weight man with a ruddy, glowing face."[2] Fauré listened to her sing and became another enthusiastic mentor and friend. He taught her much about the history of French music and played his compositions for her. From him she learned that when you are in the presence of genius things right themselves and obtain their proper balance, because genius gives authority. When she sang for him, everything fell into place.

One night, clad in her first Molyneux creation, she went with friends to the Paris Opera to hear Fanny Heldy sing. The admired, adored, and much-talked-about Heldy was not only the top-ranking French prima donna, but also France's top-ranking female jockey, riding her own horses. Grace and her escorts sat in the center box of the golden horseshoe under the blazing chandeliers of 340 burners designed to give one the impression of a crown of pearls. During intermissions, with people watching from every balcony, they joined the slow procession of elegantly attired music lovers in the traditional parade, always to the right and always very slowly, down the grand staircase. The baroque grandeur of the opera house, designed and built under Napoleon III to be the most magnificent in the world, impressed the young American singer even more than did the voice, acting talent, and allure of the famous prima donna.

Paris at that time was the scene of many artistic breakthroughs—in poetry (Ezra Pound), the novel (James Joyce), art (Picasso and the surrealists, abstractionists, dadaists, and pseudo-impressionists), the dance (Diaghilev), and music (Stravinsky). Grace spent many hours visiting museums, browsing among bookstalls, and attending concerts. Living in the midst of so much artistic, intellectual, and emotional ferment provided rich nourishment for her talent and personality. She became steeped in the traditions of French music and adopted the French approach to grand opera as best suited to her voice, taste, and temperament.

Then came another meeting with Mary Garden, at a dinner party given by Dudley Field Malone. No longer overawed, she told her idol of her ambitions and slow progress and asked her advice. Garden advised her to study Gustave Charpentier's *Louise,* and promised to arrange an audition for her at the Opéra-Comique when she had mastered the role.

This was the opera in which Garden, in 1900 at the age of twenty-three, had made her debut at the Opéra-Comique, beginning with the third act, when the French soprano, Mlle Rioton, had collapsed and the doctors had been unable to revive her. Hastily dressed and rushed on stage without warm-up, and without ever before having appeared in a major opera house, Garden was an instant sensation. She sang the title role of *Louise* more than a hundred times there.

Oscar Hammerstein lured her to his Manhattan Opera House in 1907, where she made her American debut in Massenet's *Thaïs* and created another sensation. From there she went to Chicago in 1910, and was still the reigning prima donna at the Chicago Opera House, with thirty-two roles in her repertory. It was said of her that when she put on the wig of a character, she literally became that character. "Mary Garden," wrote James Huneker in *Bedouins*, "in the new opera, is the supreme exemplar."[3] "She paints with her voice."[4] During one of her years in Chicago she would serve as general manager and burden the company with a deficit of a million dollars. She would sing her farewell *Louise* at the Opéra-Comique in 1926. (Her last and greatest opera was *Thaïs*, with the Chicago Opera, in 1929.)

From this third meeting with Garden came a letter of introduction to Edward Herman, a prominent banker, important music critic, and friend of struggling musicians. Although Herman told Grace that she needed a good deal more training, eventually he took her, her coach, and Cècile Satoris (an American music critic), to a rehearsal room at the Opéra-Comique to sing for Albert Wolff. With the maestro at the upright piano, she stood on an empty stage and sang the poignantly beautiful aria "Depuis le jour" from *Louise*.

He advised her to go out and live and then come back and sing for him again, and he would tell her what career she could have. One more year of living and studying was all she would need, Grace thought, to win acceptance at the Opéra-Comique, where Garden had made musical history. It was only a matter of time, her friends agreed, but to Grace it soon became a matter of money. Her savings were almost gone.

Neysa McMein and Jack Baragwanath, a mining engineer, explorer, author, and talented raconteur, were married that summer. Since he had to go to Canada on business, she returned to Paris and shared an apartment with Grace for several weeks. It was the scene of many hilarious parties, and quite a spate of gossip arose about the bride's spending her honeymoon with Grace Moore rather than with her bridegroom.

The popular artist recalled for *This Week* years later her firsthand knowledge of Grace's energy. She would spend hours on her voice, struggle for days with her French accent, and drag McMein off to all sorts of places pretending she was French. If anyone recognized her American accent she would be furious.

One day Grace would find a remote swimming pool and they

would go swimming. On another day she would have a pair of much-too-lively horses delivered to their gate and they would ride for hours, with Grace singing at the top of her lungs. After dancing all night, the indefatigable girl would be up early the following morning exclaiming enthusiastically about a new dressmaker she had discovered.

One day in Paris, Irving Berlin, co-owner with Sam Harris of the Music Box Theater, called to invite Grace to lunch at Ciro's. The 1921 and 1922 editions of his *Music Box Revue* were smash hits; he was now working on the 1923 edition. She had been recommended to him by Robert Benchley, his friend, and Hassard Short, his stage director, for the role of prima donna. He offered her a contract at a generous salary, provided she would return to New York City immediately for rehearsals. Although Grace felt flattered, she was reluctant to interrupt her studies and go back into musical comedy. Money was her greatest need at that moment, however, and she felt compelled to accept. The contract was drawn up and signed on the tablecloth at Ciro's, an amusing bit of business that was used much later in one of her films.

When her teachers and friends tried to convince her that she was making a serious mistake, she told them that she had no choice. She must return to Broadway to replenish her bank account. She promised them, however, that she would be back.

At 8:00 P.M. on Saturday, 22 September 1923, the Music Box Theater on West Forty-fifth Street, known as the "house of hits," was the scene of a crush of happily expectant first-nighters. Backstage almost everyone was tense and short-tempered. Grace prowled her dressing room, warmed up her voice, and strove to control her jittery nerves; the next two or three hours would be crucial to her career. In the short time she had known Irving Berlin, they too had become close friends. She loved the simple and beautiful songs he had written for the show. If she failed in this popular and typically American medium, she could neither expect nor deserve further consideration elsewhere. If she succeeded, big money and Broadway fame would follow, but she might be forever categorized as a musical comedy singer and nothing more. Aware of all the risks, she shrewdly concentrated on making the most of the challenge.

Everything went smoothly. The settings were spectacular. The other members of the cast received generous applause, but Robert Benchley's soon-to-be-famous monologue "The Treasurer's Report" and Grace Moore, fresh from Paris and bursting with

MUSICAL-COMEDY STAR. In the 1920s Grace Moore starred in musical comedies, including two seasons as the prima donna in Irving Berlin's *Music Box Revue. The Frank H. McClung Museum, University of Tennessee, Knoxville. Photo by White Studio.*

beauty, vitality, and talent, singing from the heart a duet with John Steel, a tender ballad, "The Waltz of Long Ago," and an elaborate production number, "Orange Groves in California," were acclaimed by the audience as the surprise hit performers of the show.

As the sparkling notes poured from her throat a kind of magic took place. Grace fell in love with the audience and they with her. She proved that she possessed not only a beautiful voice, but that rare mysterious something called "star quality." When she went out alone to take her first bow and heard a sophisticated New York audience applauding her enthusiastically, she stretched her big moment to its utmost—until voices hissed at her from the wings, demanding that she get off the stage and let them out there too. The angriest voice was that of the tenor. He had a beautiful voice, and it blended well with hers, but the magic that had touched Grace Moore and the audience had not included him.

Until that evening Grace had been able to take the backstage practical jokes (though she hated them), the intrigues, the jealousies, and the cruelties of competition in stride, and had done her full share of scrapping for the spotlight. But the sudden plunge from ecstasy to humiliation was shattering.

Always perceptive and kind, and according to Mrs. Moore caring enough for Grace to spend hours begging her to marry him, Irving Berlin rescued her from the bitter resentments and after-show excitement and took her to his apartment for a quiet celebration. He showed such delight in her performance, and predicted such a brilliant future for her, that she was soon able to regain enough composure to rejoice in the rewards of sudden stardom.

Because of a newspaper strike, she was denied the joy of reading rave reviews about her performance in the morning papers. The combined edition of Monday, 24 September, representing the *New York Herald*, the *Journal of Commerce*, the *Daily News*, the *Morning Telegraph*, the *New York Times*, the *New York Tribune*, the *World*, and two foreign-American language papers carried this paragraph in a short unsigned review:

"So far as the people in the show are concerned, overwhelming triumph was well earned by two newcomers—Miss Grace Moore and Robert Benchley. Miss Moore, whose professional experience so far has been such as to stamp her at best as a high-minded amateur, brought a gracious manner and a voice of genuine operatic timbre to a form of entertainment that has long and sorely needed them."[5]

After the strike was settled, on 28 September, the *New York Times* carried a picture of her on the front page, and, according to Alexander Woollcott, "hats were thrown in the air and cheers resounded from one end of Broadway to the other and a new star was born."[6]

James Craig of the *Evening Mail* wrote, "The one great and joyous contribution, the one thing about its first performance that will stand out sharply when the rest of it sinks into the blur of revue-sated memory, is its introduction of Miss Moore. . . . She has one of those rare soprano voices in which warmth and vitality vie with clearness and sweetness of tone. The sort of voice that grips the emotions and sets them astir. . . . She brought so much serenity and intelligent good humor that we instantly quit looking at anybody else."[7]

With so many influential New Yorkers talking and writing

about her radiant beauty, intelligence, and lovely voice, and with her name up in lights, Grace tasted success for the first time and found it delicious. She loved singing songs so well suited to her voice, inspiring thunderous ovations and reams of publicity, keeping open house for her glamorous and swiftly growing assortment of friends—artists, actors, writers, musicians, financiers, statesmen—and depositing a large slice of her check in the bank every week.

But there were bitter morsels among the sweet. When she was reaching for a high note, John Steel would often step on her toe, or destroy her composure with an ugly remark under his breath. He kept her so upset that she sometimes could not finish a song; the curtain would have to come down. And whenever she would be told that her forte was definitely musical comedy she would suffer twinges of uneasiness. Success in that medium was only a hilltop en route to her dream pinnacle. Biddle and other charming men, some temptingly eligible, some not, persistently sought her favors. Always needing sex and love, and looking forward to marriage and children, Grace would imagine herself in love with this one or that—but never for long. She would avoid, or break off, any commitment that might topple her from the hilltop she had reached, or rob her of the freedom to continue the climb.

Every career woman of that era was vulnerable to feelings of frustration, confusion, and guilt. Women were damned if they did and damned if they didn't. In her search for a measure of inner peace, Grace joined the Park Avenue Baptist Church and attended the Sunday morning services. She would come away from the prayers, music, and sermon feeling calmed and strengthened, only to get caught up again during the week in other stressful situations.

"Emotional powers are your greatest asset," Marafioti would remind her during her daily vocal lessons, "but unless controlled by intelligence, you will never achieve real distinction."[8] He would emphasize the importance of singing with the same ease and fluency as in speaking, and she would practice singing so that a close-held lighted candle would burn without a flicker. In his studio she met Emma Calvé, the prima donna; Roberto Maranzoni, a conductor at the Met and at the Chicago Opera, and one of Garden's close friends; and Italo Montemezzi, composer of the opera *L'Amore dei Tre Re*, which had had a tremendous success at La Scala.

The Moores and other Tennesseans journeyed to New York to see the show, and Mrs. Moore stayed on with Grace for several weeks; this was the first of many lengthy visits in future years.

8 A Heady Hilltop

One evening in the spring of 1924, Grace was seated next to Otto Kahn at a dinner party given by Sir William Wiseman. Kahn was a wealthy and powerful banker, and patron of arts who owned a large share of Met stock and served as its chairman and president. According to his biographer, Mary Jane Matz, "three generations of theatrical performers found him the most genuine, the most unfailingly understandingly helpful man they had ever known."[1]

Grace and Kahn had many traits in common. Each had a shrewd appreciation of public relations; each valued, even loved, publicity; and each was dedicated to the furtherance of art and beauty in America. That evening she set out to interest him in her career, using all the charm, sex appeal, and salesmanship she possessed. Before dinner was over he offered to introduce her to the general manager of the Met, Giulio Gatti-Casazza, and to assistant manager Edward Ziegler.

On the following Wednesday afternoon he escorted her to the rehearsal room, where auditions were in progress, and made the introductions. The rather formidable Gatti-Casazza, bearded, heavyset, and unsmiling, set a date for her audition. The excited soprano rushed to Marafioti's studio to tell him the good news and begin intensive rehearsals.

Montemezzi offered to coach her, so Grace chose an aria from his opera *Giovanni Gallurese* and worked with him almost every day. Between shows and lessons she practiced early and late, sometimes, according to her mother, rising at four or five o'clock in the morning to try again to master a certain difficult phrase.

At last the moment of auditioning came—4:30 P.M., 10 April 1924. With Wilfred Pelletier at the piano, Kahn, Gatti-Casazza, Ziegler, and Artur Bodanzky (foremost conductor of the Germany repertory), listening, she sang better, she later claimed, than at any time or place before.

Although she read approval in every smiling face, Gatti-Casazza informed her that she was not yet ready for the Met. But he quickly took the sting out of his words by adding that she had the potential of becoming another Farrar—if she would work very hard. Perhaps in another year . . .

On her first visit to the opera house she had sat in the peanut gallery, admiring the shabby magnificence of the interior of the old building and listening enthralled to Farrar singing her farewell *Carmen*. At another of Farrar's farewell performances—this time the opera was *Zaza*—she had witnessed the good-bye demonstration staged by hundreds of "Gerryflappers" both inside and outside the theater—a frantic, wonderful tribute. To be mentioned by a top official of the opera company in the same breath with such a sensational prima donna was encouragement of the highest order. But when she compared her qualifications to those of Farrar, who was beautiful, elegant, perfectly trained in English, Italian, and French, and with ample repertory, she knew that she still had a long way to go.

After more than 250 performances business at the box office began to fall off, but the sudden announcement of the engagement of Broadway's newest musical comedy star to a Philadelphia Biddle created such a flurry of publicity and speculation that the sale of tickets picked up. Skeptics called the announcement a publicity stunt, but Grace's friends testified to the seriousness of the romance. Biddle had wired a formal proposal from Paris, and urged her to join him as soon as the show closed. Before sailing for Europe with Jane Thomas, however, she signed a contract at an enormous salary to return for the new revue.

One evening in Paris, Biddle took them to the Opéra-Comique for a performance of *Louise*. Charpentier's beautiful music, the raging conflict between a father and his rebellious daughter, and the familiar Montmartre settings stirred Grace so deeply that she made a passionate vow to herself, and to her companions, to some day sing that role both there and at the Met. From that moment on, the engaged couple's days were spliced with violent quarrels and tender reconciliations. Grace would meet other men and fling herself into a new romance, only to return to the forgiving arms of her fiancé. Not even a tour of Europe that included Venice, the dream city of artists and lovers with its liquid streets, lacy architecture and fascinating history, could put an end to their frequent clashes of temperament.

By the time her vacation was over, marriage no longer tempted her. Despite the worry that she would need more money than she had managed to save, she cabled Sam Harris requesting release from her contract so that she could remain in Europe to study for her next Met audition. The answer was no, Irving Berlin had written some beautiful songs especially for her; she must return immediately. Reluctantly, she sailed for New York, and opened on 1 December 1924 in a new *Music Box Revue,* staged by John Murray Anderson.

She sang the unforgettable "What'll I Do?," "Call of the South," and "Rock-a-bye Baby" and, with Oscar Shaw, "All Alone." The latter, which the two sang to each other from spotlighted dummy telephones from opposite ends of a darkened stage, was one of the show's big hits. Another was the hilariously funny and popular comedienne Fanny Brice, singing "Don't Send Me Back to Petrograd," first as a befuddled Russian immigrant, and then as a confused ballet dancer.

Fanny Brice would often read aloud to Grace the latest letter from her husband, Nicky Arnstein, who was at Leavenworth, Kansas, serving time for receiving securities valued at $1.5 million from criminals who had robbed messengers in the financial district. She had told their two children that he was in Paris.

Grace admired Fanny Brice for her talents, guts, and fierce loyalty to the charming but faithless and dishonest man she loved; and for her remarkable climb from the streets of Brooklyn—by way of amateur contests—to the position of Ziegfeld's top *Follies* star, and a favorite of New York society's Four Hundred. Brice complimented Grace for her naturalness, lovely natural hair, willingness to work hard, and talent.

There was a direct line from the Brice dressing room to Belmont Park. Max Hirsch, an outstanding trainer of horses and friend of Sam Harris, would phone in tips. Sometimes Grace would win more in a day of betting on the races than she made in a week as a highly paid musical comedy prima donna.

Big money, acclaim, and an increasing number of glamorous friends and parties continued to cast a heady spell on her. She became so securely ensconced upon her hilltop that she almost convinced herself that musical comedy *was* her forte, and becoming Mrs. George Biddle her fate. But then her dream of becoming an artist in the truest sense of that word, would recur, and again the spell would be broken.

Eventually, Marafioti recommended a psychoanalyst and suggested one he knew who was a pioneer in the field. She appeared to be quite simple to understand, Freud's disciple told her, but actually she was a highly complicated human being with at least six females, ranging in ages from six to sixty, all living uneasily within one fair body. She was happy only when she was in love and loved; yet she persisted in sublimating her natural interest in men, her instinctive hunger and need for marriage, home, and children, in order to hold fast to her ambitious dreams and make them come true.

During one session he suddenly confessed that he was in love with her and begged her to help him "pull himself together."[2] Since she was supposed to be the patient, Grace walked out. Thereafter, she concentrated on building a comprehensive operatic repertory, and on preparing herself as thoroughly as possible for her second Met audition.

On the crucial day, arranged by Otto Kahn via telephone from Palm Beach, she faced the ordeal sustained by a great deal more training, experience, and self-confidence. This time, after singing two arias, there was silence and no smiling faces. She hastily thanked the Met officials for listening, rushed blindly from the rehearsal room, and collapsed on a bench just outside the Thirty-Ninth Street entrance. When Ziegler and Bodanzky appeared, she implored them to tell her what had gone wrong.

Ziegler, a small man with cool eyes behind rimless glasses and a reputation for gruffness (but with a heart of gold) told her, as gently as possible, that something had happened to her voice; it had lost its color, resonance, and pitch; she would be wise to content herself with her role as top musical comedy star and stop trying for something beyond her ability. Bodanzky added bluntly that she would never sing in opera. For one thing, he doubted if she would ever learn to sing on key.

The stricken girl turned away and spent hours pacing the streets. At last anger and determination replaced the numbness and black despair. Rushing to the telephone, she called Kahn, told him the verdict, and then bet him a hundred dollars that she would make her debut at the Met within two years.

Obviously aware of what her refusal to admit limitations or accept defeat would cost her in self-denial, loss of status, hard work, financial worry, uncertainty—all culminating, most likely, in another negative verdict, Kahn agreed to the bet.

Grace burned bridges right and left after that heartbreaking afternoon, eliminating any temptation to settle for musical comedy and/or marriage and the danger of abusing her voice by singing the

same songs over and over. And now there was another incentive—
to make Bodanzky eat his cruel words.

As soon as the show closed, and after a brief run in Chicago, she
added to her savings by accepting a two-week engagement at the
Palace. To perform as a headliner at the Palace was no small accomplishment. One of the hit songs of her four-a-day appearance
there to packed houses was "Chérie, je t'aime" by Lillian Rosedale
Goodman, who, although she had known Melba, Sembrich,
Eames, Calvé, and Mary Garden, considered Grace Moore by far
her favorite soprano.

After the Palace stint and a session of recording for Brunswick,
Grace bade farewell to musical comedy, Broadway, and financial
security, gave up her apartment, and sailed for Europe. Irving
Berlin protested against such a move, insisting that she would lose
her flair. To make sure that he would not talk her out of going, she
waited until the ship was out to sea, then sent him a radiogram to
forgive her, that she was on her way at last.

That same year, 1925, Berlin met Ellin Mackay, and they fell in
love at first sight. After a courtship that created a sensation, they
were married on 4 June 1926. She was his second wife; the first had
died when they were on their honeymoon. The copyright to the
beautiful ballad "Always," which Grace sang so poignantly, was
deeded by Berlin to his bride as a wedding present.

Part III
To Keep a Dream

My voice, my work, my friends were the big things in my life. . . . I couldn't work without having fun, and I couldn't have fun without working.

9 Now or Never

The opera tenor recommended by Maestro Wolff as a famous and competent teacher was also young, handsome, and flirtatious. Grace went along with his health and posture-training methods, his books-on-chest-and-top-of-the-head routine—a bit of business used later in *One Night of Love*—and enjoyed his ardent Romeo to her Juliet, until the morning the door suddenly burst open and in charged a beautiful female in a jealous rage, screaming accusations, throwing things, and refusing to leave until she had ruined the lesson, the ardent love duet, and the studio.

After several such comic-opera interruptions, Grace wrote a long letter to Mary Garden at the Blackstone Hotel in Chicago, asking for advice. How could she extricate herself from a problem teacher whose judgment of her vocal ability was warped by passion, and whose fiery sweetheart might do her real harm? What would be the best way to prepare for her third audition at the Met in the shortest possible time and at the least expense?

Garden's cabled reply moved Grace to tears. She was to go immediately to Monte Carlo and live for the next six months in the apartment Garden kept there for study, guest overflow, and the use of her family when her new villa at Beaulieu was closed. She was to study with Garden's favorite accompanist and operatic coach, Richard Barthelemy. The cable closed with Barthelemy's Monte Carlo address and a promise to write to him.

Grace entered the salon of Mary Garden's fourteen-room Monte Carlo apartment with the same wide-eyed wonder she had experienced at her first glimpse of Acklen Hall. The draperies, paintings, and furnishings, rich with color and texture, were a charming extension of her idol's dramatic personality. The windows framed exciting vistas of the promenade, the opera house and casino, and a row of colorful shops. The dining room would seat thirty. She promptly fell in love with the bed she chose to sleep in, of green

101

and gold leaf with a gold eagle perched on the crest of the head-board above a cover of green and gold taffeta brocade. As soon as she could afford it, she bought its counterpart in Venice and had Wanamaker's make a chest and a pair of bedside tables to match. They were used in her bedroom at Far Away Meadows. Today they occupy the Grace Moore Room in her brother's house on Lookout Mountain.

Within a short while she felt as much at home on the Côte d'Azur as she had in Paris. Her schedule included daily walks, swims, and letter writing, studying French and a repertory of French songs and Massenet's *Manon* four hours every day with Barthelemy, two hours of piano lessons and practice, attendance at all the performances at the opera house, and, of course, seeing old friends and making new ones.

Living there aided her in concentrating her entire personality on her work and she came to know the rewards success could bring to a singer. But the problem of how and where she could most economically continue to study with Barthelemy for another year soon arose. It was solved by Lady Luck. This legendary angel always kept an eye on Grace Moore, and more than once flew to her rescue. "Grace," says her sister, wonderingly, "was always lucky."

One night she was invited to dine with Louis Kaufman, an American banker, and his wife Daisy, who were touring Europe. The threesome ended up at the Casino, a place she had avoided as beyond her means. The banker did not gamble, but his wife enjoyed roulette. They both encouraged Grace to try her luck, and Kaufman staked her to a thousand francs. After watching the roulette table for a while and receiving a few instructions, she began to play. Number five was her lucky number time after time, and before the evening was over she had won enough to repay her host with interest and pocket forty-three thousand francs!

As soon as they had adequately celebrated her astonishing winnings, she cabled a query to Condé Nast about living quarters on the coast between Cannes and Nice. He advised her to see a Mr. Sella at the Antibes Hotel du Caps. From Sella she rented the Villa de Cedres, a little blue and pink house on the hotel grounds. Ruth Obre Goldbeck, the widow of Grace's first New York beau, joined her there and shared expenses. The two young women were so delighted with their new world that they sent postcards to all of their friends urging them to come to Antibes where life was casual, economical, and free of crowds.

By midsummer 1926, Antibes was the gathering place of many talented Americans and the scene of a series of hilarious parties and pranks that would be told and retold in nostalgic conversations, letters, columns, plays, autobiographies, novels, and motion pictures. Others who had recently discovered the South of France were Gerald and Sara Murphy, the Cole Porters, the F. Scott Fitzgeralds, and Anita Loos and her husband, John Emerson, coauthors of many movie scripts. Her famous female character, Lorelei Lee in *Gentlemen Prefer Blondes,* would soon be introduced to the public and create a sensation. Possibly, Grace Moore inspired whole chunks of Lorelei Lee.

Fitzgerald's novels and short stories of the postwar prohibition era were attracting wide attention; *The Beautiful and the Damned* was published in 1922 and *The Great Gatsby* in 1925. But by this time Zelda had fallen in love with another man and Fitzgerald had fallen in love with the bottle.

Among others who vacationed there were Alexander Woollcott, Harpo Marx, Charles MacArthur, Clifton Webb, and Kenneth MacKenna. The group would swim in the Mediterranean in front of the Eden Rock Restaurant, fish off the rocks, or rent a car for a nickel and drive along the Grande Corniche exploring the seashore towns, the ancient landmarks, and the foothills of the Maritime Alps.

In a hilarious play MacArthur and Fitzgerald wrote for fun, Grace played the Princess Allura, the wickedest woman in all of Europe, and Ruth Goldbeck played the part of the farmer's daughter.

At a farewell-to-a-wonderful-summer party Grace and Ruth gave at the Eden Rock Restaurant, wine flowed freely and many toasts were drunk. Zelda Fitzgerald topped all the others by climbing on the table, removing her black lace panties, and tossing them to the two guests of honor—Alexander Woollcott and Grace's current best beau, Lorenzo "Chato" Elizaga, nephew of President Diaz of Mexico. Woollcott, "that debonair rascally, voluble, bibble-babbler,"[1] was shocked, but Chato, "the gayest and most elegant beau in all of Paris,"[2] grabbed the panties, clasped them to his bosom, and jumped off the rocks into the Mediterranean. The others, fully clothed, soon followed. A little later Woollcott suddenly emerged from the sea and marched off to his hotel room apparently unaware of the fact that he had lost all his clothes and was stark naked. Horrified, the others watched him until he was out of sight; they did not see him again that summer.

Eddie Molyneux, Somerset Maugham, Elsa Maxwell, and Lady Mendle all had, or would acquire, villas on the Riviera. Grace returned summer after summer. She would receive many invitations to luncheons and dinner parties, and usually she would oblige her host or hostess by singing several request numbers. Noel Coward's famous "I Went to a Marvelous Party," which Beatrice Lillie sang in *Set to Music in 1939* contains a phrase about Grace singing from midnight until four. This refers to a beach party given by Elsa Maxwell in 1937 or 1938 at her Riviera villa. She invited Noel Coward, Beatrice Lillie, and Grace Moore, telling them to come as they were—it would be "just marvelous." When they arrived, as they were, they discovered that "just marvelous" meant about one hundred guests, all of the others in evening dress, and that one of the objects of the party was for them to entertain. As they were on holiday, had no accompanist, and were not in any way prepared to perform, they refused. Elsa understood, but her guests were disappointed. Beatrice Lillie was finally persuaded to sing, but Coward and Grace held firm. Noel Coward wrote to Emily Coleman years later that this incident was his original inspiration for "I Went to a Marvelous Party."

When Dr. Marafioti arrived with his family to live at the Hotel du Caps, which remained open all year for the first time, Grace studied her scales and Italian roles with him. She continued her operatic coaching in the French repertory with Barthelemy, who commuted from Monte Carlo.

Grace called on Garden soon after she opened her villa at Beaulieu. She received a gracious welcome and was shown through the villa, which was even more lavish than the apartment in Monte Carlo. At length, Garden led her to the piano and asked her, "with businesslike briskness, to sing."[3]

After hearing arias from *La Bohème, Roméo et Juliette,* and *Louise,* Garden again advised her to concentrate on *Louise* and promised to arrange an audition with Masson and Ricou, directors of the Opéra-Comique, both of whom were her friends. At the audition in Paris a little later, the directors called Grace's voice the kind French music lovers adored, but suggested further training in acting technique. She promptly arranged to take acting lessons from Albert Carré, artistic director of the Opéra-Comique, Garden's onetime lover and still her friend.

One morning after her return to Antibes, as Grace casually opened a business letter, a royalty check for several thousand dollars dropped out. It was for singing and promoting "Chérie, je t'aime"—her good-bye song at the Palace Theater. She knew instantly what she would do with her windfall. She and Ruth went house hunting, and she ended up buying Casa Lauretta, a yellow stucco three-bedroom house on ten acreas of lush hillside in Mougins above Cannes. The furnishings were French provincial; there was a jasmine garden and a view of the sea and the Maritime Alps.

In the early spring of 1927, Kahn arranged another audition for her in the Paris music salon of Edward Herman. Grace looked ravishing, spoke with poise, sparkle, and exquisite diction, and sang "Depuis le jour" with such warmth and beauty of tone that her listeners predicted that she would have a great career. Kahn called her the great hope of the American singers at the Met, adding that her failure at her second audition had been a disappointment to the management. He assured her that Gatti-Casazza would want another audition; she would hear from him soon.

Elated, Grace returned to Casa Lauretta in time to welcome Emily, or "Huff," as she was now called by her classmates at Randolph Macon Woman's College. This was Emily's first trip abroad. While waiting for the call from Gatti-Casazza, the sisters spent happy days partying, taking long walks, lying on the terrace nursing their suntans, and catching up on everything.

A tall, fair young American made history by flying solo across the Atlantic Ocean in a gray-white single-engine plane, on one day of their wait. Lindbergh landed "The Spirit of St. Louis" at Le Bourget Airport, Paris, in the midst of a mob scene and hero's frantic welcome. Grace and Emily were still excited over their fellow countryman's successful flight, after so many others had tried and failed, when the call finally came.

Grace was to go first to Varese, Italy, for a few days of intensive study with Maestro Moranzoni, and report on 12 June to the Teatro Lirico in Milan for her third audition. It took place before Gatti-Casazza, the Italian conductors Serafin and Bamboschek, and Bruno Zirato (former secretary of Caruso, later assistant and then manager of the Philharmonic) with twenty-six other aspirants and Emily and Chato listening backstage. Chato had come from Paris to give moral support, to help Grace celebrate if the audition was successful, and to carry her off to Mexico as his bride if it failed.

With Bruno Walter accompanying her, she sang arias from four operas—*Manon, La Bohème, Louise,* and *Roméo et Juliette.* Although Gatti-Casazza praised her voice, he doubted that she was ready musically, emotionally, and in repertory, and he advised her to remain in Europe another year to gain experience singing in small opera houses before subjecting herself to the critical audiences and especially to the critics of the Met.

It was now or never, insisted Grace. Her money was almost gone; she was ready and eager to take her chances with the Met audiences and critics. The next day a contract was drawn up and signed for the coming season, with her debut to be scheduled for early 1928. Her salary would be seventy-five dollars a week—a small fraction of her musical comedy pay; she agreed to gain fifteen pounds. Only one other American, Everett Marshall, a baritone, won a Met contract at that audition.

Wildly happy, Grace sent cables to her family and friends overseas, and telegrams to all of her friends in Europe. Then the foursome—Grace, Chato, Emily and Zirato—celebrated at an outdoor restaurant with spaghetti and champagne, toasting everyone who had had a part in her triumph, including Maestro Bodanzky, who would now have to eat his words.

"I drank too much champagne," Emily remembers. "I was sick all night."

10 "Mimi"

Early in February 1928, a special train wound its way from Nashville through Chattanooga, Knoxville, Lynchburg, Virginia, and Washington, pausing at each station to pick up members of the Moore family, the press, and more than a hundred other Tennesseans and transport them to New York City for the Metropolitan Opera debut of Miss Grace Moore as Mimi in Puccini's *La Bohème*. The Washington contingent included Tennessee's two senators and two members of the House of Representatives and their wives.

Grace's mother, wearing a stylish new suit, coat, and cloche hat, boarded the train in Knoxville with her husband, sons, and Goldie Garber. She was as worried as she was proud and excited. Knowing almost nothing about opera, she feared she would expose her ignorance before her daughter's many sophisticated friends and embarrass Grace. Her pronunciation of *Faust* was *Fawst;* when Goldie tried to correct her, she exclaimed, "Lord of Mercy! *Faust* or *Fawst,* what does it matter?" Then she added: "I suppose I'll just have to remember to sit still and keep my big mouth shut." Not talking was a real sacrifice for her; both she and her singing daughter rarely ever ran out of conversational steam. Her favorite topic, of course, was Grace. She told her husband that he should keep his big mouth shut, too. He smiled tolerantly and said nothing; he had become adept at hiding his deficiencies under layers of good grooming, shrewdness, and charm.

On the long train ride, Grace's three fun-loving brothers kept things humming. Rich and Jim played their favorite game, betting on anything and everything that occurred to either as a good gamble. Rich always kept a little notebook in his pocket containing lists of names, dates, places, and all kinds of information that would be good for a bet and insure his winning. He would also indulge his penchant for quoting long passages from Shakespeare.

He, as well as Grace, had inherited Richard Moore's remarkable memory; there was a little ham in almost every member of the Moore family.

Emily came aboard at Lynchburg, Virginia; she was the envy of every other girl at Randolph-Macon. She had given her classmates vivid descriptions of the French Riviera, the celebrities she had met, the audition in Milan, and a sight-seeing trip through Italy and parts of Germany and Switzerland she had enjoyed with her wonderful sister acting as tour guide. Whenever Grace replenished her wardrobe, she would send a box of clothes to Emily. The girls would enjoy trying them on, borrowing them, and using them in school plays.

The Tennessee Society of New York City welcomed the visitors with a reception at the McAlpin Hotel, and many distinguished New Yorkers honored the Tennesseans with luncheons, sight-seeing jaunts, and theater dinners. The warmth, good will, and vitality of the Moores more than compensated for whatever they lacked in sophistication.

From its lofty perch on the sidelines, the opera world watched developments with amused tolerance. Many predicted that all the ballyhoo would turn out to be much ado about another flash in the pan. Two years previously, the state of Missouri had made a big to-do over the opera debut, in *Rigoletto,* of its promising nineteen-year-old coloratura soprano, Marion Talley, with a special train and enormous splashes of publicity. She too had been helped by Kahn. Her voice was lovely, but she lacked imagination, flair, and other necessary qualifications for a successful operatic career. Although she was making a fortune concertizing, it was already rumored that she would soon withdraw completely from opera.

The moment Grace walked onto the Met stage for the one full orchestra rehearsal and turned to face the footlights, the conductor, the orchestra, and the vast six-level Golden Horseshoe, awe-inspiring even when empty, she experienced agonizing stage fright. The other members of the cast were gifted and seasoned performers, while she had had no opera experience whatsoever. Edward Johnson, a handsome Canadian tenor who sang Rodolfo, had sung throughout Italy, South America, and Spain; Antonio Scotti, the great baritone, had sung for years in all the opera houses and was internationally famous.

Tickets for the Tuesday matinee, a benefit performance for the Misericordia Hospital, were selling briskly. The distinguished and socially prominent audience would include practically all of the friends Grace had made since her arrival in New York City, plus the trainload of Tennesseans. The peanut gallery would be packed with opera lovers, many of French and Italian descent, and all opera-wise and volatile in their likes and dislikes. The critics would watch her every amateurish move, listen for her slightest flats and scoops. Bodanzky's mercilessly frank remark after her second audition, never far from her mind, began to haunt her.

The debut of another American singer was an occasion looked forward to with great interest and hope by officials, critics, artists, patrons, and the gallery set. To end the monopoly that foreign singers had always enjoyed in American opera houses, Kahn and Gatti-Casazza were eager to find and develop American stars of the caliber of Geraldine Farrar, Rosa Ponselle, and Lawrence Tibbett.

The possibility of disappointing her family, her Southern friends, and everyone else she loved, of becoming another instant has-been, added stabs and twinges to Grace's agony. Knowing she was woefully inexperienced, she feared she could not possibly live up to the expectations of her home state and the Met officials. Somehow she managed to stumble through the dress rehearsal; but the moment she reached her apartment she fell across her bed, wailing hysterically to Jesse Harrison that she was so mad at herself she could spit! She was an impatient fool! She couldn't go through with it! Why hadn't she listened to Mr. Gatti?

Her return to New York in the late fall, after a period of intensive study of the roles of Mimi and Juliet with Bamboschek in Milan and Cannes and the sight-seeing tour with her sister, was heralded in the press with pictures, feature stories, and interviews. In mid-January she was honor guest at a luncheon given at the Bankers' Club by a group of prominent Southerners. Among those who gathered to meet, encourage, and pay homage to Tennessee's emerging opera star were Norman H. Davis, under secretary of state in President Wilson's administration; Frank C. Rand of St. Louis, president of the largest shoe manufacturing company in the world; Dr. George E. Vincent, president of the Rockefeller Institute; Jesse H. Jones, a Tennessean turned Texas statesman; and her own somewhat stunned but very proud father. Grace, the only woman present until the wives joined the party for coffee, charmed everyone with her warmth, beauty, and intelligent conversation. The wives, no doubt, made mental notes thereafter to keep an eye on their entranced spouses.

Colonel Moore, looking as handsome, prosperous, and distin-

COLONEL RICHARD L. MOORE. Mr. Moore was appointed a colonel on Tennessee governor Tom C. Rye's staff in 1916. The original large portrait hangs in the home of Richard L. Moore, Jr., on Lookout Mountain, Chattanooga. *Courtesy of Richard L. Moore, Jr.*

guished as any of the others, had become good copy in his own right. Though his career was not as glamorous as that of his daughter, his success was in the rags-to-riches tradition. He was proud of it, but even more proud of Grace.

That January she also appeared for the first time before a motion picture camera—for Pathé News. Record companies and the fast-growing radio industry, which was changing the habits of millions, had become interested in her debut. Charles L. Wagner had agreed to manage her. Already her dreams had begun to expand to other forms of entertainment, but if she failed at the Met on Tuesday afternoon her chances elsewhere would be greatly diminished, her career forever blighted.

Jessie Harrison brought warm milk to the disturbed Grace and spoke encouragingly to her. Ready or not, Grace went through all kinds of emotional antics to purge herself of all doubts and fears— so that she could throw herself into the coughing and dying of poor tragic Mimi and prove to her father, Jellico, Ward-Belmont, Bodanzky, all the men she had loved briefly and almost married, and herself, that she belonged up there on the stage of her highest dream, the most coveted stage in the world.

She spent Monday in an old robe and comfortable house slippers wandering nervously from piano to window to bed. On Tuesday morning, after only three or four hours of sleep, she read the newspapers, practiced her runs and scales with Marafioti, then, still almost paralyzed with fright, went early to the opera house.

By 1:45 P.M. on 7 February 1928, the Golden Horseshoe glittered with color, lights, and people. At curtain time, 2:00 P.M., the seats in Grand Tier Box 43, reserved for the Moores, were still not fully occupied. The Kahns had given a luncheon honoring Grace's parents and the distinguished visitors from Washington. At the last minute Kahn called to ask that the performance be delayed until his luncheon guests, unavoidably detained, could arrive and be seated. The unusual request, coming from him, was granted.

The longer wait was almost unendurable to Grace. Doggedly she went over the score again, fought to limber up her voice. At last Maestro Bellezza entered the pit and lifted his baton. The lights dimmed. The curtain rose on the cold garret room in Montmartre in which lived, laughed, and worked in Bohemian poverty a poet, a painter, a philosopher, and a musician. The scene always reminded Grace of the walk-up attic apartment she had once shared so gaily with a dancer, a writer, and a sculptress.

Finally, Rodolfo opened the door and Mimi came on stage to a warm wave of applause, clutching an extinguished candle and looking, despite Grace's remarkable vitality, appealingly frail and forlorn. Her voice wavered, trembled, almost went out of control. She was too conscious of being on the stage of her dreams, of the brilliant audience beyond the footlights, of the importance of acquitting herself well, to be able to concentrate on the role she was interpreting.

The history of that stage alone was enough to throw her off pitch and off balance. Here the greatest singers, dancers, and actors in the world had performed—Caruso, Melba, Nijinsky, Pavlova, Bernhardt, Duse, Farrar . . . out there beyond the proscenium arch had sat queens, presidents, the cream of world society.

Suddenly, one of her garters slipped, and she had to continue singing responses to Rodolfo while maneuvering herself behind a chair to pull it up. Her nerves almost gave way completely under this final strain.

After the tenor had sung his first aria in superb voice, Maestro Bellezza gave Grace the musical cue for hers. Determinedly blotting out everything else, she concentrated on singing "Mi chiamano Mimi" with all the beauty, warmth, and tenderness Puccini had written into the famous role. At times her voice rose free and clear; it soared over the orchestra and reached into the hearts of listeners on every level, including the standees in the rear of the top gallery. The applause she received was encouraging.

When the curtain fell on Act I, Mimi once again became an anxious Grace Moore. Numb with strain, and sick over flatting her last high C, she longed to flee, hide, refuse to continue making such a fool of herself. As she stood motionless, in an agony of despair, her head suddenly lifted in disbelief to the sound of thunderous applause. Her colleagues onstage assured her that the applause was for her, and offered their congratulations.

The curtain went up and she executed her first deep bow to a Met audience. Her first, her second, her third . . . her eighth! With her confidence restored, she sang the second, third, and fourth acts with more assurance. At the end of the last act, within seconds after the death of the little embroidery girl and Rodolfo's heartbroken cry "Mimi!" and the orchestra's tender concluding strains, the audience was on its feet, many in tears, crying "Brava! Brava! Brava!" Twelve times she was recalled, making a total of twenty-five curtain calls.

Morris Gest exclaimed loudly that he had known her since she

MIMI in *LA BOHÈME*. **Grace Moore made her debut at the Met in the ever-popular** *La Bohème* **on 7 February 1928. She sang this role many times.** *William A. Fraker. Columbia Studios, film* Love Me Forever.

played in *Suite Sixteen*. That she was a great American girl and a great star.

George M. Cohan leaned over the railing of the pit to impart the information that he had heard her sing ten years ago in Washington and had advised her to study for opera. He kept calling out bravas for the "sweet child."

Edward Johnson predicted that she would have a great future.

After cheering her from the director's box, Otto Kahn told the Moores that only the glorious Southland could produce such a star, one with an exceptional voice, a vivid personality, and the human appeal that would reach into the hearts of her audience. He called her debut the most important since that of Rosa Ponselle.

The gigantic Gatti-Casazza, his face red, puffing from the exertion of continued applause, advised Grace to sing for those who need to hear beauty, who wish to forget the cares and troubles of reality. If she would do this, she would make the world a bit happier.

The first violinist paid Grace a high compliment by lifting his violin and playing an encore for her. Other members of the orchestra put aside their instruments to join in the enthusiastic ovation to the radiant girl, a rare tribute.

The doorkeeper told Zella Armstrong, of the *Chattanooga Times*, that in his forty-seven years on the door of the stage he had never seen such a demonstration of enthusiasm for a singer. To her readers Armstrong wrote that the debut had been a most sublime occasion.

The Tennessee Society had obtained special permission for the visitors to greet the Met's new prima donna on the stage, and catch a glimpse of the world behind the scenes. Family, friends, colleagues, officials, camera and newsmen rushed forward to shower her with love, praise, and extravagant predictions.

Arnold Reuben, Morris Gest, and David Belasco all came backstage to congratulate her. So did Bodanzky, who told her that he never thought she could do it—she was only beginning her career now, and there was nothing she could not accomplish if she wanted to. He not only ate his words, he joined the long list of men who at one time or another fell in love with Grace Moore; and his wife joined the legion of women who suffered pangs of jealousy because of her.

After so much fear, grit, and glory Grace found it difficult to calm down enough to eat a quiet dinner in her apartment with her family. Emily moved in with her, brought warm milk to her bed, rubbed her back. They stayed awake all night eagerly awaiting the morning papers.

Samuel Chotzinoff, of the *World,* wrote:

> Miss Moore's voice is a true lyric soprano, beautiful in every register. It is not just a lovely voice but an organ with a personality—that is, its beauty is not reminiscent. It is exquisitely colored and vibrant, with the deep quality of a good Stradivarius. Musical comedy is a strange apprenticeship for musicianship, but Miss Moore uses her lovely organ with the innate sensibility of a natural musician. Her phrasing throughout the afternoon was a model of refinement. In some unaccountable manner she imbued her muse with the proper colors of the sentiments they described without the smallest sacrifice of tonal balance and musical line. . . . In the first act Miss Moore flatted . . . and her final high C was . . . off key. This was, no doubt, due to nervousness. . . . In the matter of looks Miss Moore was quite the most gratifying Mimi that ever coughed her way through Puccini's tuneful treatment of so-called artists' life.[1]

Leonard Liebling of the *New York American* wrote that Grace Moore "got more than enough applause to stamp her debut a success with her own faithful legion, but she was liked also by the rest of the audience. . . . Miss Moore's voice is a true lyric soprano of ingratiating quality, warm and capable of sympathetic modal modulations. She sings fluently and in proper operatic style. . . . The middle register of the Moore voice is especially mellow. The death scene was sung with veteran assurance and effect. . . . [The debut was] surprisingly good and augurs well for her future activities at our cathedral of lyric song."[2]

W. J. Henderson, dean of critics, wrote an unfavorable review for the *New York Sun,* but he added, "this soprano has a pretty voice of lyric quality, the color tending toward mellowness and capable of more warmth than the singer knew how to evoke from it."[3]

According to Olin Downes's review in the *New York Times,* "Miss Moore . . . has a voice of inherently agreeable but not distinguished quality. Sang with intelligence and best of intentions. Nervousness in first act embarrassed her . . . little resonance and frequently off pitch. . . . In the third act the tone quality improved . . . further experience on this stage may disclose unexpected capacities."[4]

The story of her debut appeared on the front page of the *Times,* and Adolph S. Ochs, the publisher of both the *Chattanooga Times* and the *New York Times* cabled from abroad instructions to his staff to give a luncheon to honor Grace Moore and all his distinguished Tennessee friends in his private dining room, and to make it an unforgettable occasion.

The Downes review, as well as subsequent ones, refutes the gossip that the powerful publisher, himself frequently the center of romantic gossip, had ordered his critics to go easy on Grace Moore because she was a "dear friend." Gay Talese in *The Power and the Kingdom* wrote that Mr. Ochs frowned upon harsh criticism of any artist, but never issued such an order.

With her bed heaped high with letters and cables of congratulations, the telephone ringing constantly, and invitations pouring in, Grace quickly shrugged off the critics who had panned her performance. She had learned from Verdi, Gatti-Casazza, Kahn, Garden, and many others that it was more important to please the people than the critics. When Garden told her she had a "gallery heart," Grace considered the remark a seal of approval.

Not until later when they had become good friends did she learn from "Chotzy" Chotzinoff that after his enthusiastic review of her Mimi gossips and skeptics had spread the false rumor that she had paid him $10,000 to write a favorable review.

Her debut over, Grace thought that she was at last ready to give concerts before packed houses and make new friends, fans, and big money. Her eager optimism would soon receive another severe jolt.

11 A Bitter Dose

O*ne* of her first bookings for a large fee, $3,000, was at the Ryman Auditorium in Nashville, under the auspices of the local Lions Club. The city's newspapers had given generous space to her debut, with full-page spreads of Grace Moore pictures. With so much recent publicity and more to come, including billings as "A Singer from the Southland" and "The girl who has a voice with IT," everyone involved in the concert expected her to sing before a packed house.

The Ryman Auditorium, built as a tabernacle in 1892, had been the scene of many brilliant and memorable concerts by famous musicians including Patti, Heifetz, Kreisler, Schumann-Heink, Paderewski, Rachmaninoff, and, in 1912, Garden. The members of the Lions Club were proud to be bringing Tennessee's lyric soprano to the city and were exerting maximum effort to make the concert an artistic, social, and financial success. The club and Mrs. L. C. Naff, manager of the huge old building with its magnificent acoustics, were as interested as Grace and her manager in the financial returns.

When she arrived at the Union Station, fresh from a much-applauded and favorably received appearance in Atlanta in Gounod's *Roméo et Juliette*, a prestigious committee met her train. The moment she stepped down, stunningly suited, hatted, and bejeweled, flowers were thrust into her arms, cameras clicked, and the mayor handed her the keys to the city, formally designating 1 May as "Grace Moore Day." Governor Henry H. Horton, an honest, religious but naive gentleman, remembered for saying in a difficult situation, "Politics is a sonofabitch," welcomed her and her parents and escorted them to the executive mansion, where they were house guests.

One woman in the large contingent that had arrived from Jellico was heard to say: "Well, now that Grace has made her dee-butt, there'll be no livin' with Tess." She was wrong. Both Grace and her mother were as warm and friendly after as they were before.

One concerned fan, fearing that the ugly experience at Ward-Belmont and her many romances might be exposed in local print, warned Grace to be sure to appear at her very best before the press. "My greatest desire in life," she replied, "is to please my musical public." She wanted no reminders of past mistakes or advice on how to protect her ego, her reputation, or her career. She was under the impression that she had reached that privileged pinnacle where opera prima donnas were free to be themselves upon any and all occasions. If her past, or future happened to shock some people, what the hell! They loved to be shocked as much as she loved to shock them, as much as she longed, adored, and *needed* to sing to them. She craved their approval and love, but on her own terms.

On Monday afternoon, the governor's wife escorted the Moore women to the Centennial Club to a large tea given by the Musical Alumnae of Nashville. Since the organization was comprised chiefly of former students of the music department of Ward-Belmont, Grace was soon surrounded by women who had once rejected her. Their friendliness in 1928 was as different from their hostility in 1916 as she was different from that gawky, overly anxious-to-please hillbilly with a voice who had come to the school to escape small-town tyranny and train for the role of singing missionary to China.

That evening when she strode on stage, clad in a new concert gown of silver cloth, fashionably long behind and short in front, with diaphanous angel sleeves almost touching the floor, she looked both regal and radiant and was given an enthusiastic reception. Her first group of songs, by Haydn, Gluck, and Scarlatti, sung in Italian, won her a standing ovation. Despite the enthusiastic bravas, and her sweet revenge of the afternoon, she was valiantly putting on an act, covering up fresh humiliation. Instead of the packed house she and everyone else had anticipated, there were many rows of empty seats. It was a bitter dose, but Grace managed to swallow it without allowing her suffering to distort her face, her manner, or her voice.

The officials of the Lions Club had expected at least twenty-six hundred paying customers, and had hoped for many more. Counting standing room, the auditorium would accommodate more than four thousand persons. Instead of clearing a substantial sum for their civic work, they lost all the money in their treasury and would end up in debt.

Nashville's music lovers were embarrassed. The city had a popu-
lation of more than one hundred thousand and several colleges
were located within its borders, including the university named for
Commodore Vanderbilt (whose family had also had much to do
with the founding of the Met) and Fisk University (the home of the
internationally famous Jubilee Singers). The city proudly referred
to itself as "The Athens of the South," yet the vast majority of its
citizens had once again betrayed a lack of interest in good music.

The masses had remained at home to listen to country musicians
singing and strumming their "geetars" over Radio Station WSM,
where announcer George Hay's popular *Grand Ole Opry* had
originated and was gathering momentum. They might well have
enjoyed some of the French songs Grace sang in her second
group—by Duparc, Debussy, Hahn, and Charpentier; they would
surely have loved the third group of English classics, and such
popular encore numbers as "Danny Boy" and "By the Bend of the
River."

The enthusiastic and prolonged applause, the many offerings of
flowers, and the brilliant reception after the concert at the new
Andrew Jackson Hotel almost made up to the prima donna for her
disappointment in the size of the audience. But the empty seats,
and the predictions that Grace Moore would be remembered in
Nashville as the girl who broke the Lions Club, continued to
rankle her.

Thus Grace painfully learned that she was not nearly as indiffer-
ent to what was said and printed about her in Tennessee as she had
thought, and that whole ranges of mountains had yet to be climbed
before she could reach the pinnacles occupied by Garden and Farrar. She needed more training, more experience, a more dynamic
approach to her career. She needed more of everything that would
improve her technique, musicianship, and stage presence and
transform the critics and the general public into devoted fans who
would flock to concert halls and opera houses to hear her sing.

On a weekend visit to Jellico she was invited to sing in almost
every local church. Her father urged her to accept the one from
Brother Martin, but that humiliating prayer-meeting experience
was still too vivid in her memory. "I shall never sing there again,"
she informed him. On Sunday morning, dressed in her most stunning Molyneux outfit, she stepped across Fifth Street and sang a
solo in the First Methodist Church.

Always clever at putting to shrewd use her remarkable ability to
transform disappointments into challenges and forge full steam
ahead, Grace soon sailed for Europe to sing in small opera houses

and gain the experience Gatti-Casazza had warned her that she would need.

She made her Deauville debut in *Roméo et Juliette*, and although the opera house was crowded, the applause tremendous, and her appearance there one of the chief artistic events of the year, she was far from pleased with her interpretation of Juliet. Now fully aware of her need for more experience, and of the weeks, even years, of study and daily practicing she still faced, she made a valiant effort to forgo the playgirl side of her life, at least on this stay abroad.

Once she was settled in a small apartment in the Hotel Astoria on the Champs Elysées, she devoted many hours to rehearsing the role of Mimi for her debut at the Opéra-Comique. Since she had learned the *Bohème* role in Italian, she would be singing in that language while the others in the cast would be singing in French. Both French and Paris-American newspapers were generous with their advance publicity. She drew a packed house and sang in glorious voice. At the conclusion of the poignant last act and the many curtain calls, friends, members of the press, and opera personnel jammed into the flower-lined hallway and her dressing room, proclaiming hers to be the most successful American debut since that of Garden.

According to the Paris edition of the *Chicago Tribune*, "the audience put aside its dignity to manifest in no uncertain terms its complete approval of an artist who shows every sign of carrying on the splendid tradition established by Mary Garden and Geraldine Farrar."[1] Louise Schneider of the *New York Herald*, Paris edition, wrote, "No Mimi has ever shown a softer and more melodious voice, above all so well-balanced in both the high and low register."[2]

Grace had kept another dream—become an opera celebrity in the opera house where Garden had become a sensation, and in the city in which she felt so stimulated and free. Her self-confidence blossomed and her dreams began to expand in all directions.

She had, by this time, acquired an exciting new love—the leading tenor of the Paris Opéra, Georges Thill, whom she described as "an extraordinary man, who knew a great deal about music, women and the world."[3] Apparently his wardrobe, like Biddle's, left much to be desired. "He dressed," she wrote, "in the fashion of a small-town dude."[4] Even so, she adored having him follow her from city to city to help her unwind after a performance with wine, food, music, dancing, good conversation, laughter, love.

In Rouen, where she was scheduled to make her debut in Massenet's *Manon,* she staged her first full-blown temper tantrum since becoming an opera star. During the rehearsal, which she had insisted upon, the cast seemed so complacent and disinterested that she suddenly lost her temper. With a blast of choice American and French expletives she stamped off stage, returned to her hotel, took a bath, and crawled, fuming, into bed.

When the manager called her, she told him that she had no intention of singing her first *Manon* under such impossible conditions. Her European tour representative, Alexander Kahn, rushed to Rouen. After listening to her story, he made restitution for her failure to appear. He took her, along with a famous musician and his mistress whom Grace described as "a big, fat, mascaraed dramatic soprano with fat, short, stubby, white hands loaded with demi-semi-precious jewelry,"[5] to lunch at the famous Hotel de la Couronne. They were so friendly and understanding, and the food and wine were so delicious, that her good nature was quickly restored. She was strongly tempted to volunteer to sing without pay. She departed for Paris instead leaving a wake of annoyed and disappointed opera lovers.

This incident was one of many that would contribute to her reputation as extremely difficult and temperamental. When she was under great tension or when things were not shaping up as she thought they should, she would resort to the strong purgative of a good tantrum. If she saw that she could not win her point, she would make a stormy exit rather than compromise. Moments later her sense of humor and good nature would return, but the damage would be done. Thus she made enemies by the dozens, but at the same time her singing won friends and ardent fans by the hundreds, and later on, by the thousands and millions.

With money coming in, she splurged on an entourage befitting a dynamic prima donna—a Hispano-Suiza limousine, a chauffeur, and a French maid. Perhaps because officials, performers, and stagehands were used to the antics of a prima donna, or because they had read her Rouen publicity, she was given a cool reception in Bordeaux. Then suddenly the manager and cast became surprisingly sweet and thoughtful. Grace was puzzled until Georges Thill laughingly explained their change of heart. Her new French maid, Maria, resenting the way they were cold-shouldering her beautiful and famous American employer, had told them that they ought to treat Miss Moore with special consideration since she was the mistress of the richest man in the world, the oil magnate who had many times befriended France. Since John D. Rockefeller had financed the restoration of Versailles, the country was indeed obligated to him.

Instead of feeling mortified or indignant by demanding immediate retraction—or firing Maria—Grace reacted with laughter and calculated shrewdness. The theater was one of many the manager operated throughout France in which she hoped to sing. If a little gossip about her and Rockefeller could arouse his interest in booking Grace Moore elsewhere—what the hell. Her name would later be linked romantically with other Rockefellers. The next day after her debut in *Manon,* which won favorable reaction from both the audience and the critics, the manager indicated that she could sing in any of his houses whenever she was available.

Following several days of studying with Albert Carré, and practicing many hours alone in her Paris hotel apartment, she made her debut in *Manon* at the Opéra-Comique to a full house and critical acclaim.

Before her debut there in *Louise,* the Paris staff of the *New York Times* arranged for her to meet Gustave Charpentier. Pictures were taken of the composer and the new Louise in the Montmartre settings used in the opera. Despite the difference in their ages— Grace was thirty-one and he was in his seventies—these two incurable romantics quickly became friends. She went often to his shabby studio to study the role with him.

Whenever he talked of his famous opera he would explain that he was Julien, that he and Louise had had much happiness, sorrow and visions together. That he had been very fortunate indeed to be able to give back in music some of the priceless beauty and happiness Louise had given him.

Grace Moore's debut in this popular role was a gratifying personal triumph. Albert Carré complimented her during the celebration afterward in her crowded dressing room and asked her to assist in raising money for *Le Maison de Retreat de Point aux Dames,* the organization for indigent retired artists of the ensemble. Grace accepted and did such an outstanding job that she was awarded a marble plaque inscribed with her name, placed, with appropriate ceremony, in the vestibule of the Opéra-Comique among those of world-renowned artists, including Mary Garden.

During those busy and stimulating months in Paris she somehow managed to find the time to take a three-month course, four days a week from 9: 30 A.M. to 5:00 P.M., at the Ecole du Cordon Bleu. In a leased fourteenth-century chateau behind an apartment building on the Rue St. James, connected to it by a narrow bridge

GUSTAVE CHARPENTIER AND GRACE MOORE. The French composer became a good friend of the young star in Paris and personally coached her in the leading role in his opera *Louise*. *The Frank H. McClung Museum, University of Tennessee, Knoxville. Photo by Constance Hope Associates.*

and surrounded by old Paris charm and with several of her friends as neighbors, she enjoyed complete privacy for practicing her scales, puttering in her kitchen, and carrying on her expanding social life. With Emily now in residence as her secretary and Georges Thill still her lover, her days were deeply rewarding; her looks, personality, and voice flourished as never before.

In preparation for the job as secretary to her sister, Emily had studied shorthand and typewriting during her last year at Randolph Macon. She enjoyed the work and the social life, especially meeting so many interesting people, but she soon found the hectic pace too exhausting. She eventually returned home to marry her childhood sweetheart, Thomas Seth Mahan of Chattanooga. Although Grace had vowed never again to sing at the First Baptist Church, she promised to sing at her sister's wedding.

With money to spend she indulged her passion for jewels, clothes, furs, food, champagne, servants, books, paintings, and objets d'art. She gloried in adorning herself with sparkling jewels, most of all emeralds and clusters of bracelets. Some of the choicest emeralds in her growing collection were gifts from men; others she bought herself. She would spend many hours researching the period of the roles she was gradually adding to her repertory, and shop for just the right fabrics, trimmings, and seamstress. Her authentic opera costumes would inevitably draw sharp criticisms because they were new and conspicuous against the background of the threadbare settings and old costumes worn by others in the cast.

When shopping in Paris, she would order several couture creations and concert gowns; in New York she would sometimes buy inexpensive dresses from a bargain rack. Her clothes and accessories were always comfortable, becoming, and appropriate, and she wore the bargains as well as the Paris creations with style and flair.

Upon her return to New York City, after her triumphs at the Opéra-Comique, reporters devoted columns to the Fifth Avenue apartment she rented; her lithographs and drawings by Toulouse-Lautrec; her canvases by Rembrandt, Whistler, Degas, and Gauguin, her autographed photographs of famous friends; and her clothes, jewels, romances. She was publicized in many instances as the most glamorous figure in the world of song. The number of her fans was increasing rapidly both in the states and abroad. Tempestuous prima donnas were not yet a phenomenon of the past; Grace Moore was continuing the tradition with every move she made.

In January 1930 she appeared on the National Broadcasting Company's "General Motors Hour," with Donald Vorhees conducting. The vast radio audience loved her renditions of "Depuis le jour" and "Remember," although some critics frowned upon her daring to sing an opera aria and a popular ballad on the same program. Her potential as a radio star was instantly recognized, and she would soon be termed, among other accolades, "Radio's Darling."

Although her career was zooming in all directions, she managed to keep her promise to Emily. Wearing a deceptively simple red Chanel suit, the skirt three inches below the knees, a small hat the same color, and a gorgeous full-length mink coat, she stepped off the train in Knoxville alone and warmly greeted the welcoming committee—her brothers and two or three reporters. During the sixty-five-mile snowy ride to Jellico she rolled the window down, exultantly sniffed the clean, cold, pine-scented air, waved, and called out exuberant hellos to every mountaineer they passed. "Thar goes Dick Moore's famous gal," several along the road exclaimed, and yelled a welcome to her. At a filling station, where they paused briefly, she spoke to the Italian owner in his own language. He was so surprised that he couldn't speak to her either in his native tongue or in English.

In Jellico word spread rapidly: "Grace has come!" As always, the gossips gossiped, the pace quickened, and she, not the bride, was the center of attention. "What did I tell you?" some sniffed. "She can't help it," retorted others. "She was born to be It." Emily was too excited, happy, and glad that Grace had been able to come to feel overshadowed.

As soon as the prima donna had hugged and kissed every relative, friend, and servant milling about the house, remembering every name, she rushed off to the church to rehearse the songs Emily had asked her to sing. With barely time for a quick bath and change of clothes, she returned to the church for the picture-taking, her solos, and the wedding.

A photographer from Knoxville posed the wedding party for pictures, then placed the exposed films in a leather case on the back seat of his car. A few moments later, when he returned to the car, the leather case was gone. There followed much rushing around, searching, calling in detectives, reporters, and worrying for fear the thief would expose and ruin the film before he was caught.

Grace had looked forward to using one set of the pictures in her scrapbook and another for publicity purposes. She was so upset that she started down the church aisle without removing her galoshes; fortunately, someone noticed in time to give her a nudge. Just before she reached the pulpit, a black cat marched ominously across her path. After helping lure the bad-luck symbol away, she stood on a white cloth not far from where she had once suffered so much humiliation and sang "I Love You Truly" and "At Dawning" so beautifully and lovingly that there was a catch in every throat and a tear in every eye, both inside the church and outside where a crowd had gathered. "Jes' like a bird!" exclaimed one of her black friends and fans. "Jes' like a bird!"

The moment she moved away the drippings from a candle ignited and set fire to the white cloth. A flame shot up in almost the exact spot where she had stood only moments before, but one of the guests quickly extinguished it. At last the wedding march began, and for a few moments Emily became the star as she walked down the aisle on her beaming father's arm, a beautiful bride.

Long after talk of the theft, the cat, the fire, the ceremony, and the cutting of the cloverleaf cake at the reception in the Moore home had died down, the lost and ruined film case was fished from the bottom of Clearfork River, where some never-to-be-caught thief, or prankster, or local rejected suitor, or jealous female, had deliberately thrown it.

12 Dreaming a New Dream

G*race* Moore lost some savings during the stock market crash of October 1929, but fortunately most of her assets were in jewels, clothes, paintings, objets d'art, and real estate. After enjoying seven years of prosperity, the Met was heading into hard times. Many of its patrons had been financially wiped out; a few had plunged to their deaths from high windows. Kahn had lost millions, his health, his dream of building a new opera house, and his dedication to promoting the arts in the United States. Without him, many predicted, the Met would not survive.

The motion picture industry was also heading into trouble. Al Jolson's voice in the first feature "talkie," *The Jazz Singer,* had startled and thrilled vast film audiences all over the world; it was still, in its third year, showing to full houses. Since the top silent stars had been trained to mug and mime, not to speak, act, or sing, their careers were in serious jeopardy. It was obvious that there would soon be a great demand in Hollywood for trained voices and experienced stage performers.

Many opera stars had appeared in early silent films, lured to the new medium because of their experience in exaggerated acting. Farrar made fourteen films, six of them between 1915 and 1918 for Cecil B. De Mille. Caruso starred in *My Cousin* at Paramount in 1918, but the film was a flop, and his second film was never released. In 1917 Samuel Goldwyn made *Thaïs* with Garden, but it lost money and a scheduled second film was canceled. Early Vitaphone shorts were made by Martinelli, Gigli, Schumann-Heink, Lewis, Hackett, de Luca, and Talley. None of these "one-reelers" was considered a box office success. The Irish tenor John McCormack was making a full-length film to be called *Song o' My Heart.* Lawrence Tibbett, a sensation at the Met in 1925 as Ford in Verdi's *Falstaff* and a reigning baritone, had joined the Metro-Goldwyn-Mayer family and was being publicized as the coming singing, sound-screen idol. The potential of sound films had caused a great stir in Hollywood, arousing the fears of silent stars, hopes of many stage personages, and inspiring heated discussion.

Grace was well aware of the changes taking place at the Met, in Wall Street, and in Hollywood, and what they could mean to her if she played her cards shrewdly. With opera in the doldrums and sound movies the coming medium, she dreamed a new dream.

One evening she went to the Met with a party of friends to hear Tibbett in *Pagliacci.* In the corridor her hostess, the first Mrs. Tibbett, introduced her to another of her guests, a Mr. Mayer from Hollywood. Although Grace had little idea of the power Louis B. Mayer enjoyed at that time as vice-president in charge of production at Metro-Goldwyn-Mayer Studios, the word "Hollywood" alerted her. When she found herself seated next to him, she turned on all her charm. During the most moving musical moments he reached for her hand. A dash of flirting, added to her many qualifications, precipitated action. He invited her to the MGM studio to make a screen test.

When she first saw herself on the screen singing an aria from *La Bohème,* she let out an embarrassed shriek and covered her face with her hands. The creature up there wore a bewildered expression and possessed a moon face, two chins, no discernible waistline, and plump hips. But her voice came through with brilliant clarity—a far more important consideration than how she looked.

All but one of the MGM officials who viewed the test agreed unanimously, and with brutal frankness in her presence, that she was pretty hopeless. Two of the top men, J. Robert Rubin and Nicolas M. Schenk, then president of the company, argued against further consideration of her as film star material. Fortunately, they did not convince Mayer, the company's shrewd star-finder and hand-holder. He offered Grace a contract for three years with options, stipulating that she lose the fifteen pounds she had gained as a part of her Met contract and thereafter stay under 135 pounds.

Grace negotiated by herself with a battery of MGM corporation lawyers and other experienced and ruthless businessmen for several days, and won a few stipulations of her own. First she must be provided a private railroad car for the trip to Hollywood. She needed space for a maid, a secretary, and a huge assortment of luggage. More important, since she was aware of the extravagantly sumptuous life the silent movie stars had enjoyed and of the psychology of people in show business, she thought it would be a shrewd move for a prima donna of the Met to make a super-grand entrance upon the Hollywood scene.

Since she wanted her own voice coach nearby to help her prepare for the screen, she introduced Marafioti to Mayer. The throat specialist could do wonders with ailing voices, she pointed out, citing herself as proof; adding that he had worked with Caruso, Chaliapin, Scotti, Galli-Curci, Calvé, Ruffo, and many others. Futhermore, she had heard that another studio was considering hiring him.

The doctor, with his wife, Clara, and their two children, left for Hollywood almost immediately to serve as studio voice coach at a salary of a thousand dollars a week. His first assignment was to work with John Gilbert. MGM had recently signed Gilbert to a four-year, million-dollar contract, but his speaking voice in a color sequence with Norma Shearer in *Hollywood Revue of 1929* sounded so thin and high coming from such a handsome expressive face that audiences snickered. A smash in *The Big Parade* in 1925 and *Flesh and the Devil* with Greta Garbo in 1927, his career was in danger of total collapse. Marafioti's coaching would come too late. Gilbert's death, in 1936, was attributed to a heart attack, but it was more likely the result of a heart that was both broken and whiskey-soaked.

Her picture-making, Grace also stipulated, must be restricted to the summer months so that she could continue building her career in opera, concert, radio, and recording during the rest of the year.

After the contract was drawn up and signed—the ceremony was repeated a half-dozen times in different cities for publicity purposes—she went on a crash diet of little more than thin soup, crackers, tea and lemon, and ordered the works at a beauty salon that specialized in Viennese facial treatments. Eventually her cheeks lost their plumpness and showed lovely hollows and the fine bone structure of her face. One chin disappeared and the other became firm. Her waist became almost as small as her mother's. She emerged from the beauty salon with fashionably thin, high-arched brows and locks of shimmering gold arranged in a coiffure that, with her vivid blue eyes and fair skin, made her more photogenic.

The more than one hundred writers, still photographers, and general promoters in the publicity department of MGM busied themselves putting Miss Grace Moore on front pages all over the land. In the spring of 1930 one could rarely pick up a newspaper or popular magazine without coming across her name and smiling face and a fascinating bit of fact or fancy about the company's glamorous new singing star.

Several other opera stars were battering hopefully at the doors of Hollywood. A few of the youngest, leanest, and most talented would be auditioned and eventually signed. Among them were Gladys Swarthout, Lily Pons, Paul Robeson, Nino Martini, Beniamino Gigli, Risë Stevens, Lauritz Melchior, and Jan Kiepura and his wife, Marta Eggert. Fat prima donnas would begin dieting strenuously. One aging singer made malicious remarks about the young stars deserting like rats from a sinking ship.

Actually, Gatti-Casazza had given the screen-bound Met stars his blessings. In one interview he remarked prophetically that the new sound mechanical devices might well aid rather than spell the doom of opera. The phonographs had promoted music of all kinds. Photography had not lessened interest in painting. He called the switch from silent to sound motion pictures a time of confusion, but not of danger to music. He looked upon the change not as a time of crisis, but as a period of great significance for the future of all music, all art.

Frances Alda, former Met soprano and Gatti-Casazza's first wife, noted for her acid opinions and remarkable bosom, was of the opinion that the talkies were the only medium in which we would ever be able to see perfect opera. Galli-Curci, upon retiring from the Met, declared that live opera was finished; its future lay on the screen. Paul Whiteman, an outstanding popular-music band leader, spoke encouragingly of the role of the phonograph in pioneering musical education, of radio in advancing it, and of the possibility that the sound technique in motion picture would put America in the forefront of nations who were music-minded.

Artur Bodanzky predicted that soon we would be able to achieve the ideal in sound-film grand opera, a flawless performance despite temperamental prima donnas and indisposed tenors. He looked upon this metamorphosis as more important than the great reform Wagner had instituted in opera in his day.

Many perceptive critics remained skeptical. Operatic stage material dissolved into two-dimensional proportions, they feared, would result in flaccid offerings. If opera stars dieted down to the slender proportions of ideal heroes and heroines their voices and health would suffer. If they did not, the public would reject them and fail to show up at the box office.

In all of these discussions, Grace Moore, one of the world's few slender opera stars, was mentioned frequently as the young so-prano most likely to turn movie audiences into opera fans. Holly-wood needed good voices, but it also needed screen personalities. The combination was not easy to find. Musicals as well as opera had fallen into the doldrums, but one good picture would give them new life.

The almost unlimited opportunity Grace now enjoyed was also a tremendous responsibility. After her last appearances at the Met that season, as Mimi in *La Bohème* and as Marguerite in Gounod's *Faust*, she sang Juliette at the Academy of Music in Philadelphia, and Marguerite two weeks later. As usual, an overwhelming num-ber of listeners adored her interpretations and rewarded her with many curtain calls. Only a few reviews, however, could be called raves. Chotzinoff, whose criticism of her debut as Mimi in 1928 had been so favorable, accused her of slurring and of executing one of her deep, dramatic bows before the expected applause had be-gun.

Despite the strain of days of haggling with MGM officials; the trip to Jellico for the wedding; the weeks of concertizing, opera appearances, dieting, and packing; and being publicized, glamorized, criticized, and praised so extravagantly she still, as one observer expressed it, marveling, "radiated good health, good spirits, good thoughts and good sense."

Part IV
Another World

The movies at present are the greatest factor in providing deep love and understanding in the souls of American people. Musical classics in great productions will sooner or later be offered to small towns and rural communities where there has been heretofore no opportunity for the presentation of the highest form of musical art.

13 In and out of Hollywood

The trip to Hollywood in a private railroad car was widely criticized as passé ostentation. As late as 1944, snide remarks were still being made and published about the "Pullman" car. Grace wrote one publisher a sizzling letter, informing him that the Pullman he spoke of was, in reality, a private car, and was rented and paid for by the MGM studios.

During Emily's wedding, Jim Moore and three of his fraternity brothers made plans to hitchhike to California, find jobs, and spend the summer there. Grace invited them to travel with her, rashly promised to get jobs for all of them as extras in her first picture, and somehow managed to keep her promise. They enjoyed observing and participating in the fun that she and Beatrice Lillie, her other guest on the trip, stirred up along the way. The English commedienne had signed with Fox to do a picture called *Are You There?*

One night the car was shunted to a siding in Little Rock, where Grace was scheduled to give a concert the following evening. A delegation including the governor of Arkansas arrived early to take the prima donna to breakfast, lunch, dinner, and on a sight-seeing tour of the city. She aroused Beatrice Lillie and asked her to go in her place, so that she could save her voice and energy for the concert. Lillie reluctantly agreed, and Grace instructed the delegation to tell the governor that Lady Peel of London would represent her.

The Chamber of Commerce day, which included a visit to a new state prison and a sewage disposal plant, put Lady Peel of London in a dangerous eye-for-an-eye mood. That evening, as a thank-you gesture, Grace sang one of her friend's hits—"Come Down to Kew in Lilac Time." In the midst of the first verse, she glanced up at the governor's box and saw Lillie doing a silent takeoff of Grace Moore singing her song. Amid much laughter, she presented Miss

Beatrice Lillie to the audience and invited her to come on stage. There followed what must have been a hilarious bit of impromptu clowning and singing.

A committee of MGM officials and cameramen waited at the end of the line to welcome Grace Moore to Hollywood. When at last her guests, maid, secretary, twelve trunks and twenty-eight pieces of luggage, plus the loot the two femmes fatales had collected from admirers along the way—including a banana tree, a horseshoe of orchids, and a crate of oranges—had been taken care of and pictures snapped, she was whisked off to an old-fashioned Mexican-style ranch house sprawled on a hilltop, just a ten-minute ride from the new Culver City studio.

The Hollywood gossip and speculation about Grace Moore was as widespread as that in Jellico or New York City, but it contained a new ingredient not found elsewhere: fear—fear that she and other opera stars and stage-trained performers would dethrone the reigning galaxy.

Louella Parsons, the powerful gossip columnist who, backed by William Randolph Hearst, enjoyed a monopoly on important announcements from all the studios as well as from the stars, many of whom would bare their souls to her, declared that there was room for both. That we could no more have 100 percent singing pictures than we could have a dinner with nothing but chocolate eclairs. The public wanted and needed meat and potatoes as well as dessert.

The more than one hundred members of the press invited to the ranch house to an all-day patio party to meet MGM's new star made the mistake of comparing her to the reigning beauties of filmdom—Greta Garbo, Marian Davies, Norma Shearer—and were disappointed. But soon her dazzling smile, natural friendliness, and eager articulateness won second looks and thoughts.

Tables had been set up in the courtyard under colorful umbrellas, and members of the Agua Caliente Hotel Orchestra, strolled around in Spanish costumes strumming and singing native melodies while the guests sipped their favorite drinks and nibbled caviar, roast turkey, ham, salads, and chocolate creams. The activities included fortune telling, swimming, racing, and tennis.

Louis B. Mayer and Irving Thalberg arrived at twilight, apparently on their best behavior. Thalberg, "the boy wonder," could be as difficult, as demanding, and as critical as Mayer, but with much more flair and dignity. Grace was destined to clash frequently with both of them.

The press rated the affair a huge success, and Grace Moore a fabulous hostess and potential film star. They proclaimed her to be beautiful, charming, a poised woman of the world, naturally sweet and wholesome, with an endearing sense of humor, delightfully outspoken, deliciously frank, but pervasively intriguingly, unmistakably herself.

After the party, she spent many hours lying on a hard board submitting to the fierce poundings and kneadings administered by Madame Sylvia Ulbeck, the Norwegian masseuse who was famous for transforming any flaws in a star's body into lovely hollows and curves.

Gloria Swanson, the reigning star at Pathé, had first call on Madame Ulbeck's services. Chicago-born and a living symbol to this day of a long-vanished era of incredible pomp, nonsense, and fabulous salaries, Swanson had progressed from notions clerk to one of the highest paid Hollywood stars, and was one of the few to make the transition to sound pictures successfully. A tiny woman with a bright personality and a gift for comedy, she was temperamental and somewhat imperious. Perhaps her best-known pictures are *The Trespasser* (1929) and *Sunset Boulevard* (1950), the latter directed by Edmund Goulding.

Many stars attempted to lure Madame Ulbeck away, without success. She was late for her first five o'clock appointment with Grace, and the prima donna promptly suggested to Mayer that she be hired exclusively. Word spread that MGM wanted Ulbeck at an enormous increase in salary. Gloria Swanson insisted that Sylvia stay with her. Grace retaliated by threatening to deny Gloria the coaching services of Marafioti. Before their tiger claws could do permanent damage, a compromise was agreed upon and the two stars actually became friends.

In Madame Sylvia Ulbeck's book *A Masseuse Looks at the Stars* she recounts the brief feud between Gloria Swanson and Grace Moore, which was settled amicably, and the mistakes Grace made on her first sojourn in Hollywood. According to her, Grace would become peeved at something, or somebody, and just go away for a day or so, thus undoing all the good work she had done for her.

But when she returned to Hollywood for her try at a comeback, she put up such a stiff fight for success she could not fail. The masseuse cheered Grace for being a good fighter.

The story chosen for Grace Moore's first picture was based on the life of Jenny Lind. When some of the studio executives began inventing sexy incidents to spice up the love conflict, letters

HER FIRST MOVIE ROLE. In her first Hollywood motion picture Grace Moore played Jenny Lind, the "Swedish Nightingale," in *A Lady's Morals,* 1931. While not a smash, the MGM picture included the first complete operatic scenes ever filmed. *From the MGM release* A Lady's Morals © *1931 by Metro-Goldwyn-Mayer Inc. Copyright renewed 1958 Loew's Incorporated.*

streamed in from members of the Society for Jenny Lind threatening to burn down the studio if the slightest shadow were cast upon their beloved nightingale. Grace received many warm letters from fans assuring her that she would be wonderful in the Jenny Lind role, adding reminiscences that gave her much needed insight into the famous singer's character. She was prudish and inclined to be a religious fanatic. In Grace's opinion the glory of Lind's career was dimmed by the infinite sadness of her life.

There were fittings and rehearsals of the selections she would sing: "Casta Diva" from Bellini's *Norma,* in Italian; an aria from Donizetti's *The Daughter of the Regiment,* in French; "The Last Rose of Summer"; "I Hear Your Voice" and "It Is Destiny," by Oscar Strauss and Clifford Gray; "Oh Why?" by Herbert Stothart, Henry Woods, and Arthur Freed; "Lonely Hour," by Carrie Jacobs Bond; and "Comin' through the Rye." Sidney Franklin directed; the cast included Wallace Beery playing P. T. Barnum, and Reginald Denny, a fourth-generation member of a famous theatrical family in England, as the composer-lover who disappears from Jenny's life when he learns he is going blind.

When the shooting was finally completed Grace fled to Arrowhead Springs to recuperate, only to be ordered back to do a French version. This necessitated a crash refresher course in French, as well as more weeks of tedious practicing and of trial and error performing before the cameras and the early, imperfect sound equipment.

In the midst of all the strain of performing in film, Rich, Emily, Tom Mahan, and Mrs. Moore arrived for a visit. Grace rented a beach house in Malibu and spent what little time she could spare with her family. One weekend she suggested that they go in her chauffeur-driven car to Agua Caliente. Emily elected to stay with her—and spent the day treating herself to a severe sunburn. While waiting for rooms at the Agua Caliente Club the boys, the chauffeur, and Mrs. Moore drifted from the bar to the gambling tables in the casino. The boys lost all their money except twenty-five dollars, which Rich held in reserve. Mrs. Moore spent the long wait at the chuck-a-luck table. Although she soon lost all her money, she was so sure her number would come up next that she persuaded Rich to part with the twenty-five dollar reserve—and lost again. Instead of checking into the rooms that were now ready, the group, stripped of their last dime, decided to return at once to Malibu. Grace scolded them severely, and they meekly promised to behave more intelligently next time.

NEW MOON. The prima donna was teamed with Lawrence Tibbett in her second motion picture in 1931. *From the MGM release* New Moon © *1931 by Metro-Goldwyn-Mayer Distributing Corporation. Copyright renewed 1958 Loew's Incorporated.*

Long before her first eagerly awaited picture was released, she was rushed into *New Moon,* with Tibbett costarring and Roland Young and Adolph Menjou in supporting roles. The operetta, or musical revue, was produced in 1928 by Sigmund Romberg and Oscar Hammerstein. It included several memorable songs— "Lover, Come Back to Me," "Stout-Hearted Men," "Kiss Me," "Softly as in a Morning Sunrise," and "Wanting You"—and was a hit on the stage. It was prepared for the screen by Sylvia Thalberg and Frank Butler, with Charles MacArthur writing the dialogue.

Although Grace and Tibbett were soon good friends, they were never interested in each other romantically. She was free-lancing at the moment; her most frequent escort was Ivan Petrovitch, a handsome leading man who played in many of Rex Ingram's foreign-made pictures. Tibbett and his wife were on the verge of divorcing; he was in love with the beautiful Jane Marston Bogard, who would become his second wife. He lived in an unpretentious house, had many friends, and entertained frequently. At one party Grace attended his guests included Queen Maria, John Charles Thomas, Roland Young, Charles Farrell, Anita Paige, Janet Gaynor, Hedda Hopper, the Oscar Strausses, the Rupert Hugheses, John Loder, Catherine Dale Owen, Wilfred Pelletiere, Walter Pidgeon, Aileen Pringle, the Erno Rapees, the Basil Rathbones, the P. G. Wodehouses, Eleanor Borden Vidor, and Elsie Janis.

When these two dynamic opera stars were called upon to sing a love duet and make passionate screen love over and over they often exploded into gales of laughter, or else the vibrations of their combined voices would distort the sound recording. The director would order them to stop clowning and hold their voices back—a difficult thing to do. Knowing there would be retakes, they would persist in indulging their bawdy senses of humor. On the day menthol spray was tried for a desired fog effect both stars lost their voices and had to play love scenes with no singing, laughter, or sex attraction, and with menthol tears streaming down their made-up faces.

Grace soon tired of being told she must do this and she must not do that. When Thalberg informed her that she was too plump and must resume her starvation diet, she told him that losing so much weight might damage her voice. She was having too much fun on the set and in her flourishing social life to go on another stringent diet.

Among the women friends she made on her first short stay in Hollywood were Kay Francis and Ruth Chatterton, both of whom entertained in her honor. The beautiful, smartly dressed Kay Francis, with the low-pitched voice and fascinating personality, was starring with William Powell in *The Street of Chance,* her first sympathetic part. It turned out to be one of the best pictures of that year, and she and Powell became a popular team. During World War II she would join the USO and tour with Martha Raye, Carole Landis, and Mitzie Mayfair, and later star in *Four Girls in a Jeep.*

The multitalented Ruth Chatterton, an accomplished actress with a beautiful face, a lovely speaking voice, and a rare quality of elegance that shone on the screen, was at MGM on loan from Paramount to do *Madame X.* She was born in New York City and brought up in an atmosphere of wealth, spacious estates, art, music, and architecture. Unlike Grace's, Chatterton's career blossomed with a minimum of struggle. At the age of fourteen, she went with her classmates at the Pelham School of Girls on the Hudson to Washington, and while there attended a matinee at the National Theater. When she criticized the performance of the leading lady, one of her companions suggested that she get a job and prove that she could do better. Accepting the challenge, Chatterton went the next day to see the manager of the stock company; to her astonishment, she was hired to play the role of a twelve-year-old girl.

After playing in the highly successful *Daddy Long Legs,* Chatterton went to England to do a play, met and married Ralph Forbes, and returned with him to Hollywood, where he starred in *Beau Geste.* Although she made a screen test and was cast in a few silent pictures, it was when talking pictures revolutionized the industry that she became a top star. In the 1940s she would tour in *Pygmalion* and *Private Lives* and star in a revival of *Idiot's Delight* at the City Center. Many of her weekends would be spent as a guest at Far Away Meadows.

There was another young girl in the cast of Chatterton's first play, hired for the part of an eight-year-old—Helen Hayes. She, too, was in Hollywood when Grace was there, starring in one of MGM's biggest 1931 releases, *The Sin of Madelon Claudet.*

The Jenny Lind picture, *A Lady's Morals,* was premiered in September at the Capitol Theater in New York City and at Loew's Columbia Theater in Washington, D.C. It included the first complete operatic scenes ever filmed and promised to be an overwhelming success. The first-night audience arrived in an expectant mood, but went away unimpressed. Most of the reviews were negative; it was a box office flop. The French version, released in Europe under the simple title *Jenny Lind,* fared better. Grace's voice was called glorious, but it suffered from poor recording, or possibly poor reproduction.

Her fate as a super screen personality now depended upon the reception of *New Moon.* Many changes were made before Thalberg would allow it to be released; apparently, he never was satisfied with it. Nevertheless, it was finally premiered and heralded as the picture with two great opera stars that would surely put musicals back in vogue. It did do a little better than *A Lady's Morals* at the box office, but it was by no means a personal triumph for Grace, Tibbett, or MGM. Her acting left much to be desired; her bulges were painfully evident. The sound techniques were still not developed fully enough to do justice to the beauty and warmth of her voice. There was no box office stampede.

At option time Grace Moore was unceremoniously dropped from MGM's roster of stars. Since she knew that she was partly responsible for the two flops, she went to see Thalberg, apologized for all her mistakes and behavior, and pleaded for another chance. She promised to starve herself down to skin and bones, to cut out all clowning and temperament on the set, to learn to act, and to reduce her social life to a minimum. His answer was a curt and final no.

Grace left his office in tears. The enemies she had accumulated cried "I told you so!" and "Serves her right." Louella Parsons, Ida Koveman (Mayer's secretary and former secretary to President Hoover), Miriam Hopkins, Ruth Chatterton, Kay Francis, Dr. Marafioti, Lawrence Tibbett, John Gilbert, and others shared her distress and offered condolence and advice. Tibbett was signed for three other pictures, *Rogue Story, The Prodigal,* and *Cuban Love Song.* None was very popular.

Since no other studio had shown the slightest interest in signing an overweight, temperamental singer who had failed to draw new customers to the box offices, Grace reluctantly packed her belongings and left Hollywood. Bea Lillie had fared no better at 20th Century-Fox. They journeyed back East on the same train, whiling away the hours commiserating with each other.

Grace's most recent love affair was another source of sorrow and regret. As she expressed it: "I had just come through a peculiarly trying situation which involved a musically gifted and sensitive man who threw me in a dither with astrology, psychoanalysis, and a wife who still loved him."[1]

14 Music between Them

Grace had a new manager in the winter of 1930–31 and was available for concerts at half her former price. Since she no longer fitted into any one category, there were few takers. The Great Depression was touching every life and every country. The cities were plagued with breadlines, bankruptcies, and mortgage cancellations. Hundreds of theaters had closed; the Met was in serious financial straits. With the momentum of her various careers lost, Grace was in danger of being dropped and henceforth referred to as another flash in the pan.

The next blow was a serious illness necessitating a hysterectomy; perhaps an abortion was involved. In mentioning this possibility, the writer adds to several strong indications the memory of what F. Scott Fitzgerald is reported by Nancy Milford to have said one day to his wife's doctor. "I scarcely know a beautiful woman of Zelda's generation who has come up to 1938 unscathed."[1] The knowledge that she could never have the large family she had wanted increased her suffering and slowed her recovery. Rumors spread that Grace Moore was finished.

"Those who depend upon public favor," the fallen star commented sadly to friends one day, "cannot afford failure, for the American public is notoriously fickle."

Her almost insurmountable problems included curbing her impatience and restlessness, recovering her health, patching up her badly punctured ego, and doing something quickly to recover the momentum she had lost. More than ever before she was driven by the need to prove herself, to create a demand for her performances, and implant a love of good music in every American breast. Instead of promoting grand opera through films, her two box office flops had convinced Hollywood producers that the public was not ready to accept good music on the screen.

She spent countless hours berating herself and them, going back over and over the mistakes she and they had made. She considered them mercenary, ruthless, and narrow-minded. If only she had not let them misuse her before she had learned the score! If only she had continued dieting! If only she had not overacted, over-clowned, and overindulged in parties and love affairs! If only they had not changed the title of her first picture to that silly, inappropriate *A Lady's Morals*! If only *New Moon* had not been such a flimsy story and undergone so many stupid changes!

Her swift plunge to oblivion, or the next thing to it, rankled to the point of obsession. When she was fulfilling an occasional recital or concert engagement, she would suffer excruciating stage fright. Overly anxious to please, she would come on too strong. Her once dazzling smile and radiant high notes had to be forced, and they no longer intoxicated her audiences. Whenever she betrayed the slightest hardness or shrillness of tone, or sang a note off pitch, the purists among the critics would pounce and jeer.

On the advice of her doctors she spent as much time as possible out of doors—mostly on a golf course. She had played the game for about six years; her average score for eighteen holes was 94 to 96. One day, on the 132-yard hole of the Pinehurst Country Club, she finally broke her bad-luck cycle by making a hole in one. Although Grace always found rest and play savorless unless they were changes of pace between sessions of hard work, the small success gave her a badly needed lift.

Her doctors had also advised her to purge Hollywood from her system and undertake something challenging in another direction—something designed to help her recover her self-confidence and sense of humor. Although she refused to give up her dream of returning to Hollywood some day to redeem herself, she followed the rest of their advice. She engaged the services of a new secretary-companion, Constance Hope, the daughter of the famous concert pianist Eugene Bernstein, and a young woman who could speak several languages, had tact, steel nerves, and enough experience to know how to deal with a temperamental prima donna. The two sailed for Europe on 15 May on the *Ile de France*, with only one appearance scheduled, at the Opéra-Comique.

They spent the first morning on deck playing backgammon. When one of the dice Grace was using bounced off the board, a handsome gentleman picked it up and handed it to her with a charming smile and a courtly bow. As she smilingly thanked him, she noticed his striking resemblance to John Gilbert and Ronald Colman. He moved on, then turned to catch another glimpse of her. Their eyes met again briefly. Without knowing anything about him except his slim, dark, well-groomed good looks and continental manners, she suddenly announced to Hope that he was the man she was going to marry.

Grace spent the next three days laid low with seasickness, wondering who the handsome stranger was. Meantime, he strolled the deck hoping to find her. Both claimed that for days they had the feeling that something wonderful was about to happen. On the last day at sea, as he stood talking to the ship's captain, he saw Grace come on deck, but she pranced on by him without speaking. He told the captain that he would like to meet that young lady. Knowing Grace, and her inquiries about him, the captain only smiled enigmatically.

Since the handsome gentleman, Valentin Parera, had also suffered a touch of seasickness, he had decided to skip both the benefit concert to be given that evening by a prima donna aboard and the captain's dinner in her honor. But on the way to his cabin he ran into Constance Hope. During their brief chat in Spanish, his native tongue, he remarked to her that he would very much like to meet the blonde woman he had seen with her. She informed him that the blonde was Grace Moore, prima donna of the Met, and that he could meet her that evening at the benefit performance.

By the time the captain introduced them, at the dinner, Grace had sized him up as suave, sweet, and intelligent, and he was enchanted with her looks, voice, and personality. Since he spoke little or no English, and she little or no Spanish, conversation was difficult—until they found they could communicate in French. The conversational marathon that followed lasted until almost dawn. With blankets tucked around their feet, and an obliging moon casting glittering paths across the sea, they sat on deck getting acquainted, unburdening their hearts, and making plans.

Parera had been born in Granada, Spain, a few years before Grace's birthdate. His family, "old and respected in all of Spain," he told her, now lived in Madrid. At the moment he was on his way from Hollywood, where he had gone to star in the Spanish versions of Metro's films, to Paris, where he had spent most of his adult life.

Not only had they belonged to the MGM family at the same time, they had left the film capital in bitter disillusionment at about the same time; both had booked passage on the *Paris,* and then at the last minute had changed to the *Ile de France.* Quite clearly destiny had brought them together.

They soon discovered how much they had in common—love of opera, travel, Paris, the French Riviera, mountains, Rolland, Pater, writing, artists, and self-made people, good food, wine, conversation, cooking, gardening, beautiful clothes, gracious living in all its simple as well as its glamorous connotations. The list was endless. They laughed at the same things; they abhorred the same things—bigotry, prejudice, and above all anything that hampered an individual's freedom of mind and spirit. As Grace often said of their romance, "There was music between us."

Parera had become a film actor during the early days of Spanish movie-making and had gone to Hollywood with a six-month contract, but with the tightening of foreign restrictions and the closing of many motion picture houses, he had worked only a few days, in *Paid*, a Joan Crawford picture.

Grace told him how Hollywood had misused her and how she had misused Hollywood, of her dream of going back some day to redeem herself and, by way of sound films, singing to a worldwide audience. They discussed the vast differences in their personalities. He was hot-blooded, but logical, a tranquil, gentle man. She was volatile, audacious, driven by many passions. So what? They were in love! They were ready and eager for marriage. They balanced each other. They *needed* each other. Before parting, they set the wedding date for sometime in July. Grace rushed to her cabin to tell the exciting news to her secretary.

In *Publicity Is Broccoli*, published in 1941, Constance Hope wrote of her three years as secretary, companion, confidante, adviser, and business manager to "that glamorous darling of the opera, radio and screen, Grace Moore," and called the job "thrilling, exasperating and adventurous in turn."[2] She joined other Grace Moore friends aboard—Heifetz and Chotzinoff—and many others, who upon hearing of the engagement, predicted that the marriage of these two impulsive misfits would last about six months.

In Paris, Grace sang in radiant voice the gavotte from *Manon* at a huge party given by Elsa Maxwell, while Val hurried off to Spain to break his engagement to a girl there and tie up loose ends. She admitted later that she felt as anxious and jealous as any young girl in love for the first time. As soon as he returned, she cancelled her one commitment at the Opéra-Comique—and drove off with him to Casa Lauretta.

The wedding took place on 15 July 1931, at the Cannes City Hall, with the mayor officiating. The bride wore a simple white

ROMANCE AND MARRIAGE. Following her initial Hollywood experience, Grace Moore sailed for Europe in May 1931 on the *Ile de France*. After a shipboard romance with Valentin Parera, a Spanish actor, they were married the following July. *From* Opera News, *Morris Gerber Collection.*

gown and plumed hat designed by Molyneux; her bouquet consisted of an arrangement of orange blossoms and flowers from her own garden. Among the guests were Clifton Webb, Samuel Chotzinoff, Edmund Goulding, Gloria Swanson, Michael Farmer, the Michael Arlens, most of the local Riviera society, her gardener, butcher, and baker, and a dozen or so maids who giggled and ogled as if at a king and queen.

Following a reception at the Martinez Hotel, they drove away with "Just Married" signs in three languages splashed on the car and newsreel cameramen giving chase. As a wedding present, Constance and William Gower had loaned them the Palazzo Brandolini, a fourteenth-century Venetian castle on the Grand Canal in Venice, where they had recently spent their honeymoon. Here, during his seven-month exile in 1858–59, Wagner had composed most of the second act of *Tristan und Isolde*.

One night Grace and Val were serenaded by several young Italian singers. Upon rushing to their balcony window, Grace heard, for the first time, the Italian folk song "Ciribiribin," written by Alberto Pestalozza, an otherwise obscure composer. The words and music expressed so thrillingly her own love of life, song, and Val that she promptly added it to her repertory. It would become her radio signature song and her most requested encore number. She would sing it more than three thousand times during the next few years. In 1934, when so many millions all over the world were thrilling to Grace Moore's rendition of his one popular composition on the screen, Pestalozza died.

At Casa Lauretta, the newlyweds plunged into a whirl of domesticity and entertaining. Their house guests included Gladys Swarthout and Frank Chapman, Beatrice Lillie and Noel Coward, and Valentina, the tremendously successful New York couturiere, and her husband, George Schlee.

Grace and Gladys Swarthout had met backstage at the Met when they were cast with Lily Pons, Lucrezia Bori, and Tibbett in *Tales of Hoffmann*. Gladys and Frank Chapman, well-known concert singer, had married in 1930. Chapman and Parera liked each other, and the foursome spent many hours together both abroad and in the States.

Grace Moore and Gladys Swarthout were as different as two prima donnas could be, but each admired the other's talents, beauty, and personality. A sculptured brunette, gentle, gracious, and with great depth, Gladys often compared Grace's personality and voice to champagne. She was inspired by Grace's courage and wild enthusiasms. She admired Val because he was handsome, well-informed, and diplomatic. She considered him to be the balance wheel Grace needed. He proved every day that he adored his wife and was very proud of her.

The Pareras gave a dinner party for another honeymooning bride and groom, Jane and Lawrence Tibbitt. They went often to the villas of Molyneux and Maxine Elliott, where they matched wits with such celebrities as Somerset Maugham, Lloyd George, Winston Churchill, and many other big names of a vanished era.

As a final honeymoon splurge they drove to Spain to attend the fair at Barcelona and visit Val's family in Madrid. In a letter to her parents Grace described her in-laws as numerous, happy, and beautiful in a typically Spanish way. She must have impressed them with her talents and fame, and convinced them that she loved Val. According to his report to her family and friends, they all fell in love with her. She reveled in being called Señora Valentin Parera and gladly relinquished the spotlight to him—at least for a few days. His most recent film, *La Bodega,* was still remembered by his fans. She visited the Prado Museum every day and attended midnight dinner parties given in their honor in Madrid's famous restaurants, collecting more recipes and falling under the enchantment of the company, the food, the guitarists, and the flamenco dancers.

At the American embassy in San Sebastian she gave a concert for the local music lovers and the president of the Republic. In that city she reluctantly went with Val to a bullfight. He had assured her that it was not a brutal sport, but the fairest and most dramatic of all spectacles. She was fully prepared to feel sympathy only for the bull, but, Grace-like, she was soon wildly excited and screaming "Olé!" as loudly as anyone.

One of their first quarrels, she told Frederick C. Schang, her new concert manager, took place that September aboard the *Ile de France* on their return trip to New York. They were playing backgammon, the game that now had for them great sentimental value. Val was winning entirely too easily to suit his volatile bride. One short remark led to another. "You're no gentleman!" she snapped, and watched his black eyes suddenly blaze up in an otherwise calm face.

"You have said I am no gentleman. Very well. I behave as such." He spoke icily, arose, picked up the Morocco-bound board and the ivory pieces, stepped across their cabin to the porthole and dropped the game and the quarrel into the Atlantic Ocean. She admired and loved him more than ever for having so much temper and inward flame.

Using her New York apartment as headquarters, the Pareras were soon caught up in a whirl of parties, adjustments, decisions, and work. "They really love each other!" her many friends agreed, incredulously. "She adores him! He's good *to* her and *for* her!"

Love and marriage softened Grace Moore, restored her health and self-confidence, deepened her emotionally, awakened her, as she expressed it, to even more sensitivity to beauty, and to the joy not only of living and singing but also of sharing. "Now that I truly have something to sing about," she told reporters, "I want to sing my fool head off!"[2]

While she was away, her new concert manager, had booked her in Winnipeg, Oklahoma City, Portland, San Francisco, Sacramento, and Los Angeles. Fortunately for their marriage, and for Grace's career, Val encouraged and applauded her career ambitions. Since her talent, energy and drive far exceeded his, he volunteered to adjust his life-style to hers; to devote all his efforts to helping her achieve her high goals.

Although this arrangement was logical to them, and would be normal procedure today, in the thirties it caused much speculation and many snide remarks about a man living off his wife. Grace considered herself the most fortunate of women to have found such a handsome, loving, congenial, unselfish husband. He was no gigolo. As her business manager, balance wheel, and most ardent booster, he unquestionably earned his keep.

At the first opportunity they stopped off in Jellico. Colonel Moore was as disappointed in her choice of a mate as the Stokelys and Huffs had been with him as Tessie Jane's choice in 1897. He heartily agreed with the town—she could have done much better than marry a dark-complexioned Catholic foreigner who had no job other than waiting on her, who wore spats, couldn't swim, and couldn't even speak the English language.

Grace proudly informed her brothers that in Germany her husband was called "The Ronald Colman of Spain" and in France "the Jack Gilbert of Spain and a true caballero," that he was "the best-loved film actor in all the Spanish-speaking countries." They were not impressed. In fact, they were tempted to rough him up a bit, or at least to ask him point-blank if he planned to live off their sister permanently. For her sake, they settled for teaching him to say *barber* instead of *coiffeur* when he wanted a haircut, and the correct, or Southern, pronunciation of such double-meaning words as *applesauce* and *baloney*.

Mrs. Moore and Emily were charmed by him, and delighted to see the pride and love that shone in Grace's eyes whenever she looked at him or recounted their romantic meeting, wedding, honeymoon, and trip to Spain. With the famous member of the family restored to health, in love, and happy, they found it easy to accept him and, despite the language barrier, make him feel welcome in Jellico.

He was gracious, tactful, and charming to everyone he met. He commented to newsmen that he felt as if he were among his own people. That life in the South had such grace and gentility it reminded him of the Old World.

Val accompanied Grace on concert tours and took care of all the details. He had indeed undertaken a difficult role. Their lives would, of necessity, revolve around her moods, her career, her throat, health, diet, friends, publicity, jewels, clothes, and applause. He played his part unselfishly and diplomatically, thus freeing Grace to concentrate on improving her technique, musicianship, and repertory. Her concerts drew larger and larger audiences, which made it possible for her manager to add new bookings to her schedule almost daily.

As soon as Grace had fulfilled her final Met commitment of the 1931–32 season, she and Val thoughtfully discussed her next move. The Met was still a depression victim. Kahn had resigned in the fall. Many subscribers had failed to renew their subscriptions; many artists were working elsewhere, and others had taken reductions in salaries. The doors of the Met might well close, as some predicted, at any moment. During the following season twenty-eight singers were let go.

It was obvious to the Pareras, and to Schang, that Grace needed to try something new and challenging, something to display her many talents, give her acting experience, and keep her in the limelight. They chose the operetta *The Dubarry*, by Carl Millöcker. The lovely music of the Vienna stage production of 1879, dressed in a smart new book, was a huge success in Berlin and still running in London. Grace plunged into a whirl of conferences, exercises, dieting, costume fittings, practicing her scales, learning her lines and songs, and rehearsing.

The New York premiere at the Cohan Theater on 21 December 1932, was a sellout. Grace sang with joyous abandon such lovely numbers as "I Give My Heart" and "The Dubarry." She loved the part, the songs, the naughtiness, the chuckles, the clothes, the cast, the orchestra, the audience, and especially what the critics had to say about her the following morning:

"Grace Moore sings Dubarry and plays her to the kingly playgoer's exacting taste. As a singer Miss Moore takes full preeminence. Her voice is effortless and brilliant." (Brooks Atkinson, *New York Times*)

"The loveliest light opera that has broken upon this town's ears in a decade or so. Grace Moore is singing divinely." (Burns Mantle, *New York Daily News*)

"Last night's performance can be described as one of the most brilliant solo performances that has yet been given by Grace Moore. The evening took on a joyous importance for which she is to be thanked. Miss Moore conquered her audience more triumphantly than the real Dubarry conquered a king." (John Mason Brown, *New York Evening Post*)

Unfortunately, the theater was too small for the overpowering cast, settings, and songs, the tickets too high, and the mood of the city too depressed. Val kept telling Grace not to fret; something grand would surely result from her triumph even if the show failed to last long enough to be called a hit. He had seen several Hollywood producers in the audience. They could not help but be aware of her many impressive talents.

At that time, the hilarious dialogue between George Burns and Gracie Allen about her brother and the doings of other zany relatives was a smash hit on radio. During one of the last performances of *Dubarry,* Grace came striding on stage in a glittering costume and was given her cue, "Ah, Madame, where have you been?" Her ad-libbed reply, "I have just been out hunting for Gracie Allen's brother," stopped the show for at least two minutes. The audience went into hysterical laughter and so did the staff, the cast, and the orchestra.

Grace accepted a vaudeville engagement after the closing, singing four times a day for two weeks at the Capitol Theater in New York City. She told friends that her vaudeville engagements were "just a lark," but the truth was she needed to replenish her bank account.

One day she signed a contract to give four concerts a week, beginning in the late fall, as the soprano in a foursome with Edward Johnson, tenor, Rose Bampton, contralto, and Richard Bonelli, baritone, to be billed as "The Metropolitan Opera Quartet." A few days later, Schang booked her to sing Marguerite in excerpts from *Faust* in the Hollywood Bowl. The Pareras looked upon her appearance at the Bowl as the break she needed; they began immediately laying the groundwork for her comeback in the movies.

According to Schang, by then a close personal friend, the campaign she waged for a comeback in Hollywood was "planned in every detail, in advance, and executed chiefly alone, without the aid of managers (other than her husband), agents or lawyers." He called it a "masterpiece of business strategy worthy of the chairman of a national political party."

15 Comeback

Grace sang on radio several times in 1933—as guest artist on the "Ford Sunday Evening Hour," the "Goodyear Tire and Rubber Hour," and the "General Electric Hour." The generous fees kept the Pareras in funds, and the warm response of radio listeners kept their spirits high.

To learn to sing for camera close-ups without distorting her mouth, she gave up their annual holiday at Casa Lauretta and spent many hours during the hot months before a mirror practicing scales, arias, and popular songs, especially the high notes. For exercise she played golf, swam, and took long walks. She denied herself the rich foods she craved, with only an occasional greedy-pig splurge of eating, and cooked for Val to economize.

When they arrived in Los Angeles, she was armed with her most beautiful clothes and jewels, a wand-slim figure, golden skin, and clear sparkling eyes. She gained valuable experience in acting *The Dubarry,* and a new collection of favorable reviews and fans from her radio appearances. This time she had a devoted balance wheel who was encouraging her every carefully planned move. Both husband and wife were experienced enough to avoid Hollywood's worst pitfalls. Most important of all, Grace's voice was rich with love, rest, sun, and the self-confidence and intelligent control that comes with practicing and studying conscientiously for many consecutive days.

All she needed to prove that she was not a hopeless dud in films, that the public would pay to see her in a picture containing operatic arias, was a contract with a major studio, preferably the largest and most prestigious—MGM. A large order. An agent, Frank Orsatti, had tried for months to interest a studio in offering her a contract, but without success.

Her appearance in the Hollywood Bowl in the role of Marguerite in a concert performance of *Faust,* with Frederick

Jagel, Myrtle Aber, and Tudor Williams, and Gaetano Merola conducting, was well received. Inspired by the grandeur of the setting—the neo-Greek shell, a spotlight piercing the night sky, the steep hillside seats fanning upward in which sat important stars and moguls among the eighteen thousand applauding listeners, and conscious of the importance of the concert to her future, she gave a thrilling interpretation.

At a party given in her honor that same evening by the Richard Barthelmesses, Thalberg warmly complimented her. She thanked him and waited expectantly. To her disappointment, he had nothing further to add.

The reviews next morning were favorable, and many heads of film companies, as well as friends among the stars and technicians, called to congratulate her. No one mentioned wanting her for a picture. At that time, more than sixteen thousand picture houses were dark. Still, going to the movies was an inexpensive form of entertainment—and starting a new trend, the first "drive-in" theater had opened in June.

Days passed and Grace began to chafe at the lack of action. Val kept assuring her that something would happen soon; she must wait patiently, charmingly, and ever on the alert. Waiting was always difficult for her. Her husband's supreme confidence in her talents, readiness, and avowed purpose bolstered her rapidly dwindling patience and prevented her from exclaiming restlessly, "Oh, to hell with Hollywood! Let's go back to New York!"

One day Goulding called to invite the Pareras to a supper party, adding that he had a very interesting guest coming he wanted her to meet. Soon after she was introduced to Harry Cohn, of Columbia Pictures, he suggested that she come to his office the next morning at eleven o'clock to talk about making a picture. An offer had come at last, but she had never heard of Harry Cohn or of Columbia Pictures. He was president and chief stockholder of the small company, which had offices on Gower Street in the center of Poverty Row. Crude, self-made, and addicted to spicing every sentence with four-letter words, he was avoided by many people in the industry. Some loathed him; but others admired him because he had that extra something—shrewdness, brass, animal magnetism—that so often brings success in show business. A great admirer of talent and aggressiveness, Cohn had two idols—Mayer and Mussolini. Like Grace, he had an enormous appetite for life, challenge, and success. He had attended the first night of *Dubarry*,

had recognized her potential, and hoped to do what Mayer had
failed to do—make her a box office star.

At that time his company badly needed a hit picture. It had one
film—*It Happened One Night,* directed by Frank Capra and starring Claudette Colbert and Clark Gable—about ready for distribution, but it was not considered very promising.

The Pareras stayed late at the party and overslept the next morning. Around noon the telephone rang. Grace answered it and a
rough voice exploded angrily asking her why she wasn't there. She
was supposed to be in his office. She was to "get [her] ass over
there fast."

Cohn's office, designed on the scale of Mussolini's headquarters
in Rome (which he had recently visited), failed to intimidate or
impress her. The contract he offered her, with the understanding
that a suitable story would be forthcoming immediately, sounded
disappointingly vague. Stalling for time, Grace rushed to MGM
and somehow gained immediate entrance to Thalberg's private
office. Most stars would be forced to sit for hours on his "million-
dollar bench" before he would see them.

More than anything she wanted to do the new sound version of
Franz Lehar's *The Merry Widow.* The silent version, directed by
Erich Von Stroheim and starring John Gilbert and Mae Murray,
had been made in 1925. She set out to convince him that she was
perfect for the role, and the music perfect for her voice. The director wanted someone else, he told her. In desperation, she offered
to do it for nothing, and waited while he thought that over and
consulted other executives.

At 4:30 she rushed back to Columbia in defeat and signed the
chancy contract. The great Lubitsch, a director of terrific force and
know-how and a genius at satire, did not want Grace Moore in his
picture, not even as a gift; he preferred Jeanette MacDonald. His
version, using the 1905 operetta merely as a springboard, would
not be as successful as either the earlier silent picture or the first
film Grace would make at Columbia, but today it is considered a
musical classic of that era.

The Pareras moved into a modest apartment and lived quietly;
Grace helped their one maid do the cooking, and concentrated on
the original story under consideration, called *This Love Child,*
written by Dorothy Speare and Charles Behan. Since she thought
it had possibilities but lacked verisimilitude, she went again and
again to the office of the scriptwriter, S. K. Laurens, to suggest

amusing and realistic bits of business drawn from her own experience.

Ten days after the signing of the contract, Samuel Briskin (second in command at Columbia) called her into his office and informed her that Cohn had made a mistake which he regretted, and offered to buy off her contract. The stunned and indignant prima donna, recognizing instantly the damage a sudden dismissal would do to her ego, her reputation, and her career, especially from such a small, unimportant Poverty Row company, used such strong words and wild gesturing that she banged a hand against a window and shattered the pane. "You will buy back this contract," she stormed, "over my dead body!"[1] She came on so strong he quickly gave up.

This savage battle was the first of many she and her tiger would fight to make a picture that would measure up to her artistic standards. She fought to sing "Ciribiribin" and "Un bel dí" from *Madama Butterfly,* but Cohn, who was in the habit of watching every penny, was reluctant to spend a small fortune for them. She fought for Tulio Carminati, the leading man to Eleanora Duse for five years, to play opposite her in the role of the Italian operatic maestro. Cohn preferred Adolph Menjou. She won both battles.

The director, Victor Schertzinger, an accomplished musician, became one of her advisers—the other two were Val and Marafioti—and wrote the music for the title song, "One Night of Love." Gus Kahn wrote the lyrics. Joe Walker (the cameraman who developed a technique for difficult portraiture that flattered stars) and the rest of the crew were wary of Grace's claws, but they applauded her fight for quality. And everyone applauded her nightingale, especially her moments of generosity. Whenever they went on location, she would fill her car with sandwiches, fruit, cakes, and cases of champagne, enough for the whole company, sixty in all, and stage a studio picnic.

During the shooting, the three companies experimenting with sound equipment would scramble fiercely for position and cause many complications and delays. Rumors spread as far as Jellico that Grace Moore was a temperamental terror given to throwing inkwells, slamming doors, and pulling hair to get her way; that Harry Cohn had lost confidence in the picture and was sick of the whole mess. The Jellico version was that when Grace fought with Harry Cohn she would dress him down for thirty minutes and never use the same word twice.

To Grace, being temperamental meant simply that she had an

instinct to protect her art and her belief in it. She was merely keeping her vow to use Hollywood and not let Hollywood use her.

By the time *One Night of Love* was ready for its first preview, everyone except Val was disillusioned and exhausted. He kept saying to Grace and Cohn that it was a hit, that audiences would love it. No one dared believe him.

There was only a small disappointing stir of interest at the first preview, in Glendale; but the many musicians invited to the second one, in Santa Barbara, gave the picture so much enthusiastic approval that Cohn risked a spectacular Hollywood preview with an invited audience of press people, executives, and stars.

At the end of this showing the audience leaped to its feet, clapping, cheering, and screaming approval—an almost unheard-of reaction. The three nervous hopefuls sitting in the back row— Grace, Val, and Cohn—were so relieved and so delirious with joy they wept. Cohn leaned over to kiss Grace and in the excitement kissed Val instead.

Since church leaders, censors, and concerned parents were demanding better pictures than the gangster glorifications being ground out at every studio, the theme—dare to make the most of your talent—was a definite plus. But critics and audiences agreed that the most important of all the picture's assets was Grace Moore, her radiant beauty, personality, and above all her warm and joyful singing.

With *It Happened One Night* also creating a sensation, Cohn was suddenly in the enviable position of having two hits on his hands.

Almost immediately his new singing star was swamped with reporters wanting interviews, photographers wanting her to pose, agents and entrepreneurs wanting her to sign, producers wanting to use her in future pictures. The press called Grace Moore the most glamorous and sophisticated American woman in the world, a free soul, an irresistible singing sorceress. Just before his death in 1932, Florenz Ziegfeld listed her as one of the ten most beautiful women in the world. The others on his last list were Elissa Landi, Greta Garbo, Billie Burke (his wife), Joan Crawford, Jean Harlow, Marion Davies, Sally Eilers, Gladys Glad, and Evelyn Laye. The internationally famous photographer George Heuningen-Huene often spoke of Grace as one of the world's supreme beauties.

With Fox considering signing Val to do Spanish versions of its films, the Pareras agreed that he should not leave Hollywood to accompany her to the premier of her picture at Radio City Music Hall. She was escorted to its first-night gala showing in that fabulous theater, which was opened by the Rockefellers in 1932, by Maurice Chevalier and Condé Nast. While the lights were low, she slipped across the street to the NBC studios to sing "One Night of Love" and "Ciribiribin" on a broadcast with Rudy Vallee, radio's popular crooner. Chevalier waited for her at her hotel while she changed and called Val, then escorted her to the party Condé Nast gave in her honor. The cream of the city's talented, wealthy, and socially prominent were there to drink toasts to her and to the picture, offer advice, and make predictions.

The critics considered it one of the ten best of all time and a four-star hit. Grace would have been completely overwhelmed by all the fuss but for the knowledge that she had earned this triumph with shrewdness, hard work, and Val's help. She always gave him full credit for "his sound advice and limitless effort in my behalf, but even more grateful for his understanding of me as a person."[2]

She often boasted that she and Val had the happiest marriage in Hollywood, that he came first with her and she with him. She claimed that she would cheerfully abandon her career if he should ask her to. Since he was obviously in no position to make such a request she could make that statement and mean it sincerely at the moment—but without fear of ever being put to the test.

Schang's term for their marriage, "a fortunate mating," had so far proved true. Grace had long needed the warmth and security of a deep and permanent love. She not only loved Val, she missed and needed his calming presence whenever they were apart. His contract with Fox did not materialize, or else he gave up trying to complete the deal because he knew how much she needed him. Thereafter, she was his career. He often told friends that he was living only for her.

One Night of Love was so widely shown and so popular everywhere that Grace Moore was rated second that year among box office stars and became known and loved all over the world. After seeing the picture and reading about her long years of daring and hard work, thousands of young women, especially in the South, dedicated their courage, energies, and talents toward achieving the richest and fullest lives possible to them, as she had done. She became *their* Mary Garden.

As always, however, there were complications. Grace pleaded in vain to be allowed to buy off the contract she had signed to tour

ONE NIGHT OF LOVE. Nominated for an Academy Award in 1934, the film was a worldwide success. It established Grace Moore as a top-flight international star. In this scene, as Cio-Cio-San, she sings "Un bel dí" from *Madama Butterfly*. *From the Columbia Pictures release* I'll Take Romance, © *1937, Columbia Studios.*

the country and sing four times a week as the soprano of the Metropolitan Opera Quartet. She was forced to spend months traveling long distances to sing one solo and a few group numbers for a pittance at a time when she alone, as box office dynamite in an era when movie stars in the flesh were treated as American royalty, could have commanded astronomical emotional, artistic, and financial rewards.

Everywhere the quartet gave a concert the audience refused to let her leave the stage until she had sung almost every song in the film. Her enthusiastic fans were packing the concert halls, and she could not bear to disappoint them. She was eager to prove that her voice, without microphones or retakes, could measure up to her extravagant movie billing.

Although Edward Johnson appreciated her position, Bampton and Bonelli accused her of hogging the publicity and the show. One newspaper billed them thus: "Grace Moore Sings and Record Is Set—Bampton, Johnson, and Bonelli Assisting."

By the time the foursome reached Omaha, Grace had had enough. When she announced to the manager that she was too ill to go on, he insisted that he had a sold-out house only because of her. She went on despite a high temperature, and then, to escape from the debilitating combination of frustration, resentment, and exhaustion, had herself rushed on a stretcher in an ambulance, with sirens screaming, to a train bound for New York City. The moment she was free her temperature miraculously returned to normal, her tiredness vanished, and she was soon off on the wings of her nightingale to fill a string of concert engagements at fabulous prices. The others were glad to be rid of her.

But there were other battles brewing. One was a $50,000 lawsuit against Brunswick Recording Company for alleged breach of contract and damages. Grace objected to the songs selected for her and the company objected to the ones she selected. Since the contract did not specify who would make the selections, they had reached a stalemate—and a lawsuit. Always a scrapper, she would wage many fights with record, radio, and film executives for the right, the freedom, to make her own selections. She would choose songs she loved to sing and wanted audiences to love, interspersed with only a few of the sure-fire mass appeal songs the executives insisted upon.

In Chattanooga that November, at the Soldiers and Sailors Memorial Auditorium, her concert drew an audience of more than four thousand, with the boxes and lower floor filled with relatives,

friends, and neighbors. The galleries were jammed with ardent
Grace Moore fans, some of whom had traveled long distances to
hear her sing.

In 1932 Colonel Moore had bought, incorporated, and reno-
vated Loveman's, Chattanooga's favorite department store—
started in 1875 on a small scale by D. B. Loveman. He moved his
headquarters to the thriving city, unique because of the high
mountain and the wide river that guarded and decorated its door-
step. All the Moores loved mountains and gravitated to them.
Their new home on Riverview Road was tastefully furnished with
charming evidence of Mrs. Moore's flair for decorating, her love of
roses, and her pride in her daughter's career. Although she loved
and enjoyed her fine new home, and was proud of her husband's
success, she missed Jellico as much as she had once missed Del Rio
and would never feel at home there. In summers she would return
to her Victorian house on Jellico's Fifth Street for long stays to
tend her roses and see old friends.

Emily and Tom had moved from Knoxville to Chattanooga; Jim
was working in his father's store; Rich was still living in Jellico,
operating the wholesale business; and Martin arrived from Dallas,
where he worked, in time to enjoy a family reunion and his sister's
concert.

The mayor proclaimed a "Grace Moore Week," and Governor
Hill McAlister made her a Tennessee Colonel, the first woman to
be so honored. She teased her father about finally achieving equal
rank with him. When she visited his department store she obliged
the clerks and customers who begged her to sing by jumping upon
a counter and singing "Ciribiribin." She was so impressed with the
family's new store and home that she made arrangements to invest
some of her earnings in Loveman's, Inc., and assign the dividends
to her sister.

That evening, clad in a Lelong gown of white chiffon, her diamond and emerald necklace, a belt of brilliants, silver sandals, and
carrying an emerald green handkerchief, she looked every inch the
glamorous superstar they had come to see and hear.

Everywhere she sang that winter she was interviewed, quoted,
entertained. One Toronto reporter wrote eloquently of her dazzling smile and wondered how she was going to finish a concert
tour that promised to go on and on, start a new picture in January,
and fulfill a radio contract of twenty-six weekly concerts.

In Detroit, where she did a radio broadcast at Orchestra Hall on
the "Ford Sunday Evening Hour," four thousand people had to be

turned away. In Salt Lake City, one writer wrote that she sang and looked like an angel, even if she did not always act like one. The mayor of Seattle embarrassed her when she was taken to City Hall by refusing to pose with her. She told reporters that she could quite understand why the mayor should be camera shy, since he was certainly no Clark Gable. Later she received a letter from W. W. Conners, a prominent citizen of Seattle, imploring her not to judge his city by the stuffy mayor, assuring her that Seattle loved her, and that she was his wife's ideal.

A Chicago critic, Glenn Dillard Gunn, wrote in the *Herald and Examiner*, "Make no mistake about this fine artist, who sings as Mary Garden would have sung if she possessed half the voice that is Miss Moore's. It is one of the lovely voices of this generation."[3]

16 Busiest Girl in the World

Another direct result of the raging success of *One Night of Love* was an immediate outflow of films featuring opera backgrounds. Opera stars were in great demand. Garden was hired by MGM to comb Europe and the United States for talent, but in this project she was not successful.

With opera always her first love, Grace dreamed of singing the leading role in a complete opera on film. By making more and more operas available to everyone, she argued, Hollywood would become the artistic center of the Western world. When she failed to interest producers in such a project, she chided them for taking so long to realize that opera was not the exclusive property of highbrows, that an aria could be not only as popular as a torch song, but an even more thrilling and rewarding experience. She thought film moguls were childish and woefully lacking in musical knowledge, and she accused Hollywood of muffing its greatest opportunity.

That year, many Grace Moore watchers, amazed at how high she had soared, predicted that she had reached her topmost peak and all the rest of her life would be downhill. Proving them wrong was another challenge she met head on. On the day she returned to Hollywood, she resumed lessons with Marafioti, went into a huddle with Cohn and other Columbia executives about her next picture, and into a rehearsal for her first weekly radio show.

The half-hour weekly broadcast, sponsored by Vick Chemical Company, began at 9:00 P.M. on 1 January 1935, over WJZ and the NBC network. The program followed one starring Tibbett and was in competition with Bing Crosby's half-hour over CBS. Billed as "America's darling," she was one of the first performers to talk informally between songs about her selections, her career, and her controversial work-play philosophy. She was also one of the few radio stars who always dressed as glamorously for radio performances as she did for stage appearances. Millions tuned in if for no other reason than to hear her sing "Ciribiribin"—especially her thrilling high note at the end, and then her beautifully enunciated "Goodnight, and may God bless you all."

Hundreds of scores, lyrics, and musical plays from ambitious young people, requests for auditions, and long letters of the type she had once written to Garden showered into her studio. Now it was her turn to advise the talented young.

In addition to the qualifications Garden had once listed Grace told them that everything counted, including natural flair, perspective, objectivity, astute showmanship, and inward flame; that especially they should think of their talent as a service, as a means of reaching out to people and bringing them happiness. Everyone should have a goal, she would emphasize in speeches, letters, and interviews. They should dare to dream, for without dreams, success would be impossible.

Before her second picture, *Love Me Forever,* went into production, the star shrewdly demanded and received the guarantee of a huge fee, plus a percentage of the gross profits. With the large weekly radio fees she was now receiving and the thousands of dollars she was paid for concerts her income was enormous.

To conform to the wishes of her studio and the mores of Hollywood, the Pareras moved into a house in Benedict Canyon, Beverly Hills, and acquired a large staff. Grace described the place as "a mixture of Italian and Spanish Roxy Rococo."[1] Its long flight of spiraling stairs proved to be a decorative nuisance, tiring and time-wasting. Her retinue of teacher, accompanist, secretaries, maid, cook, chauffeur, and valet became increasingly burdensome. Worldwide fame had brought her rich rewards, but she had yet to adjust to her new role.

Since her zest for life and her freedom to be herself were always as vitally important to her as her career, she once again sought a drastic change of pace. One day she said to Val, "The hell with keeping up front!"[2] They went shopping for a Ford and a trailer, and rented a lot near Malibu Beach for seventy-five dollars a year. Weekends were spent in the trailer enjoying a simpler, more healthful, and freer way of life. Val built a terrace at the trailer entrance and surrounded it with artificial grass. He would select the wine and go to a nearby telephone to issue invitations. Grace would satisfy her passion for domesticity by cooking a pot of spaghetti and meatballs and tossing a green salad. Among the many friends who enjoyed their informal trailer hospitality were the

Richard Barthelmesses, the Lewis Milestones, the Samuel Goldwyns and the Irving (Norma Shearer) Thalbergs.

Canadian-born Norma Shearer, one of Hollywood's most beautiful women, climbed from obscurity to Hollywood stardom and marriage to Thalberg. She made her debut in *The Trial of Mary Dugan,* followed by *The Last of Mrs. Cheney.* Her favorite role was that of Jenny in *The Divorcee.*

The Pareras were eventually surrounded by a colony of trailer enthusiasts, including Miriam Hopkins and Anatol Litvak, who set up their trailer right next door. Miriam Hopkins, another star from the South—Savannah, Georgia—was beautiful, versatile, and difficult. Grace claimed that Miriam was the only person she knew who could outtalk her. Hopkins had studied for a career in ballet, but after breaking her ankle became a chorus girl in *The Music Box Revue of 1921.* Later she did several plays. In 1931, she starred in Lubitsch's *The Smiling Lieutenant,* with Chevalier; in 1933, *The Story of Temple Drake,* based on Faulkner's *Sanctuary,* and later, Noel Coward's *Design for Living* with Gary Cooper and Fredric March. She would return to Broadway in *Jezebel,* then go back to Hollywood to do *Becky Sharp.*

Grace used Hopkin's Sutton Place house as her New York headquarters one winter, and her house in Hollywood as her West Coast headquarters. Hopkins lived in Grace's New York apartment one year.

The pictures and stars of two Columbia productions were nominated for the 1934 Academy Awards, *It Happened One Night,* starring Clark Gable and Claudette Colbert, and *One Night of Love,* starring Grace Moore. Bette Davis's remarkable performance in *Of Human Bondage* did not receive a nomination, but there was such an outcry from the public and the industry that the Board of Governors of the Academy allowed a write-in vote for the first time in its history. Claudette Colbert and *It Happened One Night* won the Oscars. Victor Schertzinger received an award as composer of the song *One Night of Love.* With every studio in Hollywood trying to make another *It Happened One Night* or *One Night of Love,* Columbia Pictures had suddenly become an important company and its president, Harry Cohn, a man to be respected and envied.

The Society of Arts and Sciences unanimously awarded Grace Moore its National Service Fellowship Medal for 1934. Only sixteen persons in the fifty-two years of the Society's existence had received the award and only one other woman—London-born Eva

HONORED BY THE SOCIETY OF ARTS AND SCIENCES. At the Ritz Carlton Hotel in New York, on 17 May 1934, Grace Moore received the society's National Service Fellowship and gold medal for "Conspicuous Achievement in Raising the Standard of Motion Pictures." At the head table *(left to right)* are Carl Byoir, then president of the Society; Grace Moore; and William H. Hays, then president of the Motion Picture Producers and Distributors of America. *From* Opera News, *Morris Gerber Collection. Photo by International News Service.*

Le Gallienne, in recognition of her contribution to drama. Grace was the first representative of the film world to be so honored. Other recipients included Thomas A. Edison, Cass Gilbert, Robert A. Milliken, and John Philip Sousa.

More than three hundred distinguished guests attended the banquet given by the Society of Arts and Sciences on 17 May 1935, at New York's Ritz Carlton Hotel. Jellico was represented by the Garbers, Chattanooga and Grace's immediate family by Colonel and Mrs. Moore. The medal carried the following citation: "The Society of Arts and Sciences has taken cognizance of your contribution in the fields of both drama and music, happily combined in an art of great importance through its power vitally to affect our national culture."

The next day the Pareras boarded the *Ile de France* bound for Paris, London, Venice, the Swiss Alps, and the French Riviera. At the urgent invitation of Geoffrey Toye, managing director of London's Covent Garden, Grace was scheduled to sing three command performances of *La Bohème* in June at three hundred pounds each, as a part of the year-long Silver Jubilee Celebration of the reign of King George V and Queen Mary.

After a brief stay in Paris, she stepped off the train at London's Victoria Station into the midst of a mob scene of movie cameras, radio microphones, photographers with flashguns flaring, a welcoming committee from Covent Garden, Maestro Bellezza, who had conducted her first Mimi and with whom she would study the part, and hundreds of excited fans—all trying to greet her at once. She and Val were escorted through the mob to a Rolls-Royce, in which they rode gaily through cheering multitudes along the Jubilee-decorated streets to Claridge's.

At the rehearsal, when she first met the famous conductor Sir Thomas Beecham, he was so coolly polite she knew that something was wrong. Inadvertently, she had created such a splash at the Victoria Station that the arrival on the same train of Arturo Toscanini, the greatest conductor of the age, had gone almost unnoticed. Already skeptical of her ability to sing, many opera lovers were indignant and hostile. Lady Cunard, one of London's social leaders and opera patrons was an American expatriate whom Grace had met in Paris and on the Riviera and who knew very well that Grace had had several years in opera. She went out of her way to register her displeasure over Toye's invitation to "that movie star."

Members of the film press had not been invited to her first press reception—perhaps because they were not music critics, or because Covent Garden officials did not want Grace Moore to be billed as a film star. Grace endeavored to salve their wounded egos by inviting them to a luncheon after her third performance.

Amidst all these emotional disturbances came the important hour of her first appearance. As she rode in a state of high tension from Claridge's to the opera house, located in the heart of London's colorful produce markets, thousands of film fans still waited in line, after many hours, hoping to secure unreserved seats. Just outside the gallery entrance, a solid mass of determined people pushed and shoved for position. Twelve policemen had been rushed to the scene to try to restore order. Twice the doors had to be closed. Screaming women were crushed against the wall as the crowd was forced back. When the doors were reopened, the mass surged forward again.

Humbled, elated, and knowing that she had yet to prove herself an opera singer and not merely a movie star with a voice, Grace stood behind the closed door of Rodolfo's attic studio awaiting her first cue, struggling to purge herself of all emotions, impressions, and fears that might handicap her performance.

Meanwhile, in the lobby, in the audience, and in certain drawing rooms the skeptical remarks continued. With the critics already expressing doubts about her ability, and many of the opera lovers eagerly following Lady Cunard's lead, Cedric Belfrage overheard the man sitting next to him say that he wouldn't be in Grace Moore's shoes for all the money in the world.

It took all the courage Grace could muster to come on stage, and when she heard no welcoming applause she almost collapsed. At the end of her first aria there was only a faint spattering of hand-clapping; what little there was drew many loud shushes. She became increasingly tense and fearful, and was finally convinced that the people of London had made up their minds not to like her or her singing.

"I felt myself sinking," she wrote her mother of that experience. "My heart was like lead and I could hardly stand. I lived a year in that one moment of blank silence." Tears filled her eyes, blurred her vision. The moment the curtain came down on Act I, she fled sobbing to her dressing room and locked the door. Val banged on the door and finally persuaded her to let him in. He and Geoffrey Toye implored her, almost dragged her, protesting all the way, toward the stage to take a bow. She held back until suddenly she heard the audience applauding and many voices calling her name: "Grace! Grace! Grace!"

Tears gone, punctured ego mended, she stepped on stage to wild applause, bravas, and a standing ovation. Bejeweled dowagers and men in evening clothes actually shouted, stomped, and cheered, while the gallery occupants whistled and screamed their adoration. There were thirteen curtain calls before they would let her go.

No one had thought to tell her of the Covent Garden tradition of applauding only at the end of an act, not at the end of an aria! When the curtain went down on the last act the cast, and especially the lyric soprano who had so movingly interpreted Mimi, were given ten enthusiastic curtain calls, while the stage became inundated with floral tributes.

Excitedly, hurriedly, she donned a pale pink evening gown and her favorite diamonds and emeralds, and went with Val to a supper party Geoffrey Toye and Betty Lawson Johnson hosted jointly at Claridge's in her honor. Although she still had two performances ahead of her she lingered until after three o'clock, and no one among the brilliant assemblage was happier or gayer than the honoree. She met many leaders of London society that evening including the Prince of Wales, and Mrs. Ernest Simpson, the attractive American woman who was already causing much whispered concern at Buckingham Palace and much sub rosa gossip and speculation elsewhere.

According to Elsa Maxwell, the Prince of Wales and Mrs. Simpson ran into Lady Cunard on their way out of the opera house. He asked her if she was coming to the party. She told them, somewhat haughtily, that she never went to parties given for cinema stars. The Prince of Wales laughed and declared that she certainly missed out on an awful lot of fun.

The Prince of Wales sat beside the prima donna and complimented her performance enthusiastically. With the greatest love story of the age not yet in full crisis, Grace Moore was the American woman who caused the biggest stir in London that June. By the following June it would be a different story.

Next morning the London music critics hailed her in headlines: "Mimi with Voice of Gold. Never since Melba sang at her farewell performance has there been such a reception accorded a Mimi at Covent Garden as there was last night: *(Daily Sketch)*; "Grace Moore Can Really Act" *(Daily Herald)*; "Last Night Was a Great Occasion" *(Morning Post)*; "Greatest Success at Covent Garden" *(Daily Telegraph)*.

Film fans who had traveled many miles but could not get seats waited in town for her second and third performances, many of them lined up on the sidewalks more than fourteen hours before curtain time. Camp stools, renting for a small fee, were lined up in a row along Floral Street and on around the corner into Mart Street; fans sat on them or used them to mark their places during their long wait.

At her third and last command performance, one act of which was broadcast over BBC, Queen Mary was in the royal box, regal in a pink and silver gown with a long necklace of diamonds and a small pointed tiara. With her were Princess Victoria, the king's sister, Princess Helena of Rumania, and Princess Eugenia of Greece. The latter two were dressed alike in turquoise satin with sunray diamond tiaras.

Although King George had been in ill health for several years, he had planned to accompany his wife to London from Sandringham both to attend the opera and to preside at the Second Court Ball of the Jubilee celebration on the following evening. He had called Grace Moore his favorite actress and *One Night of Love* the best film he'd ever seen. After a sudden attack of bronchial catarrh, his doctors ordered him to remain at Sandringham; he would live only a few more months.

Greatly honored, even awed, by the presence of royalty, Grace tried to express her feeling in her first deep curtsy to Her Royal Highness. The Queen joined in the enthusiastic applause that lasted through twelve curtain calls.

The London papers carried headlines about the most exciting film star in the world, exclaiming that the city had gone mad over her, and calling the scene at Covent Garden astounding. The film critics evened the score with the opera officials by writing that the great days of Covent Garden were gone. Films were more important now than opera, since they were of greater educational value, more influential, and encompassed the whole world. They saluted the American singing actress for taking the beautiful music of Puccini into the lives of millions. For that, the music world was greatly indebted to Grace Moore.

Only a woman of exceptional energy, stamina, and courage could have held up so long under so many consecutive emotional peaks. Performing before audiences comprised of worshipful mobs and highly critical opera lovers, some of whom continuously belittled her ability, called forth the last ounce of courage and strength. Val, the one person who could calm her after a highly emotional performance, found it more and more difficult. Grace needed privacy, quiet, and a long rest.

ROYAL COMMAND PERFORMANCE. When Moore sang Mimi in Puccini's *La Bohème* at Covent Garden, London, the packed house demanded sixteen curtain calls. *Left to right:* Geoffrey Toye, managing director of Covent Garden; Signor Puccini, son of the famous composer; and Vincenzo Bellezza, who had conducted Moore's debut in that role at the Met. *From Opera News, Morris Gerber Collection. Photo International News Service.*

She kept her commitment to sing at a musical party given by Lady Ludlow at her home, Bath House, in Picadilly, but at Val's insistence her manager canceled a scheduled command performance before King Leopold of Belgium. This created another stir; canceling a royal command performance at the last minute was simply not done. King Leopold would never forgive her; who did she think she was? She was a very tired star in danger of nervous exhaustion.

After another short stay in Paris, Val drove them leisurely southward through the French countryside. They talked of building a home in Hollywood. With "Der Führer" in power in Germany, Spain in turmoil, and dark clouds gathering over all of Europe Val advised Grace to sell her villa, give up her lease on the house in Paris, and remove all her valuables to the United States.

Reluctantly, she agreed. But the moment they drove up the winding road from Cannes to Mougins, and she caught a glimpse of her little yellow stucco house, she fell in love with it all over again. She would never sell it, she told him. She would keep it always, and when she retired they would come there and live out the rest of their lives together—she as Señora Valentin Parera, housewife.

17 Her Melodic Grace

The homecoming celebration the city of New York extended to the prima donna in August had the earmarks of a publicity gimmick dreamed up in Hollywood or on Madison Avenue, but Grace loved every moment of it. With much roaring and circling, an airplane escorted the *Rex* into harbor trailing a long scarlet streamer emblazoned with the words WELCOME GRACE MOORE. As the liner entered the Hudson River, tugboat whistles chanted deep-throated greetings, fireboats sprayed liquid silver arches along the way, and high above the ship another plane wrote the star's name in letters of white smoke against the sky.

Among the relatives, friends, press representatives, film, radio, and recording executives, and cheering fans waiting to greet her as she and Val stepped ashore, was her beaming father. Mrs. Moore had wanted to come with him, but her health was failing. She still managed to garden almost every day, and by way of scrapbooks, letters, cables, telegrams, telephone calls, recordings, radio broadcasts, movies, and occasional visits keep in close touch with Grace and live vicariously through her.

The long years of hard work, of shouldering heavy responsibilities as a builder from scratch, and of heading a large business and a high-spirited family through World War I, Prohibition, the Roaring Twenties, and the Great Depression had left Colonel Moore drained of his once-rugged strength. Now sixty years old, he was no longer the rigid hardshell-Baptist father of Grace's rebellious youth. He drank heavily, as did all three of his sons. In Tennessee, both during Prohibition and for years afterward, drinking and politics, and drinking and business, came in pairs, like shoes.

Once the Colonel had been known as "Tess's man;" now he was often referred to as "Grace Moore's father." He was proud of her and always enjoyed talking about her many triumphs. He cher-

175

ished the close father-daughter relationship that now existed between them and the unique status her fame had brought to the
Moores and to Tennessee. But she had catapulted the entire family
into a harsh spotlight, and, as had Garden in her heyday, created
furores of gossip, speculation, and excitement wherever she went.
Adverse publicity always spurred Grace on to greater heights; it
drained her father emotionally and aged him.

Although he often grumbled to his family about the many
Moore relatives who made the trek from the back hills of North
Carolina to his office in Chattanooga with tales of financial woe,
he was thankful to be in a position to help them; rarely did anyone
go away empty-handed. One generous contribution spearheaded
the building of a beautiful new Baptist Church near the place of his
birth; the graves of his parents lie in its shadow.

The welcome-home celebration included a formal ceremony at
City Hall, with Mayor Fiorello La Guardia (another remarkable
dreamer, doer and scrappy fighter, and an ardent opera buff),
presenting an enormous bouquet of American Beauty roses to the
prima donna. He saluted her for having acquired a standing as one
of America's greatest artists.

Although Grace returned refreshed and much better adjusted to
the demands of international fame, she had also indulged her appetite for French food and wine and gained considerable weight. In
preparation for her next screen role, she reluctantly sentenced herself to prison fare and the daily kneading and pounding of a masseuse.

The new series of twenty-six weekly radio broadcasts began on
Monday night, 16 September, over NBC in New York. During
this program she introduced her husband and he fed to her Leo
Carillo's lines; thus Val helped to set the stage for her rendition of
songs from *Love Me Forever*. This was one of the few times he
ever performed with her.

Apparently his European manners and speaking voice impressed
NBC officials. Although his English was still limited, he discussed
with them the possibility of a job in radio. Nothing came of it,
perhaps because of the language difficulty, but more likely because
Grace's career was still zooming in so many directions she still had
constant need of him.

Reporters seemed to enjoy needling Val. Once a reporter overheard him ask Grace about a brooch she had on, and when she told
him that she had received it as a gift from an admirer he jokingly
wanted to know the man's name so he could kill him. The re-

porters spread the word that Señor Parera was violently jealous and would kill anyone who dared admire his wife. In one of the rare interviews he gave, he assured "Gracila's" many fans that he was not jealous of her career, or of the many attractive men who adored her, that his wife's success made him very happy.

Grace was proud of successfully juggling a career and a marriage and still, after four busy and highly rewarding years, not feeling called upon to sacrifice either one. Her many-faceted personality, gorgeous clothes, jewels, regal bearing, sparkling good fellowship, and uproarious sense of humor often dominated Hollywood drawing rooms filled with celebrities. Invitations to the musicals, receptions, and dinners the Pareras gave at the slightest excuse were eagerly sought. With Europe inching toward war the exodus of the titled, the talented, and the wealthy, many of them Jews, had begun. A large number ended up in Hollywood, where Grace's formal dinner parties often won praise from the gourmets among her distinguished European refugee guests.

For more than twelve years she had been collecting, trying out in her kitchen, and serving a variety of recipes of famous chefs. She kept a complicated cross file of favorite menus. Whenever her cook became indisposed, or walked out in a huff—as they sometimes did—Grace would put on an apron and prepare the specialties of the house herself. She was adept at French, Spanish, and Italian cooking and, of course, an authority on fried chicken, corn on the cob, hot biscuits, and other Southern dishes.

Madame Parera always had difficulties with her staff. When a servant fell down on a job she would deliver a stern lecture, and discharge the person for incompetence. She would expect her secretaries to be able to pinch-hit for one of the servants. The secretaries would resent being asked to perform a maid's duties, especially since they considered themselves overworked and underpaid. Despite her enormous fees, she would pay an accompanist no more than seventy-five dollars for a single performance with solo. If he complained, she would remind him that the public came to hear her and not him; the exposure in packed houses would be worth a great deal to his career. He could take it or leave it. He would take it and afterward even the score by calling her a stingy and greedy bitch—or worse. Frequently she would inform her concert manager that 20 percent commission was too much, and insist to her lawyers that their fees were more than they should be. And she would sometimes devote hours to waging a fight over a small bill that she considered an overcharge.

THE VALENTIN PARERAS. This photo appeared on the Parera's 1935
Christmas card sent to their families and hundreds of friends. *Courtesy of
Emily Coleman.*

But just as frequently her nightingale would push ahead again
and she would overwhelm a servant, an accompanist, her concert
manager, or a lawyer, or others with an extravagantly expensive
present. And when she appeared in concerts she would pour out
her personality and voice so unstintingly that the listeners would
receive much more than their money's worth. Every time she
stepped on a stage she redeemed herself.

In November 1935 the trouble all singers dread began to plague
Grace—bad colds, hoarseness, and a sore throat. Dr. Joel Pressman, an eye, ear, nose, and throat specialist and the husband of
Claudette Colbert, prescribed the removal of her tonsils; otherwise, he told his distraught patient, her singing career would be
shortened by half. Despite the risks involved and her busy

schedule, out came the "darling tonsils," as one devoted reporter-fan called them, and off she went to Palm Springs to convalesce. Gladys Swarthout substituted for her on radio.

After only ten days of forced inactivity the highly committed nightingale simply had to be up and about her winging and singing. One morning, when she tried to run her scales, the harsh sounds that came from her throat were such a shock that she began to shake and sob. To lose her voice again just when all those years of hard climbing were beginning to pay off in wealth, fame, and inner fulfillment would be catastrophic. Her retinue of husband, secretaries, maid, and chauffeur came running. Val called Dr. Pressman; he was instructed to tell his wife to calm down, go back to bed, and not attempt to use her voice again for at least two days.

Less than a week later Grace announced to impatient radio officials and anxious fans that she was well enough to return to the air. By the time she arrived at the studio, on a Monday evening in early December, she was in a state of extreme nervousness and self-doubt. Still very weak, she feared her voice might give out and that she might collapse in the middle of the broadcast.

She sang every note with a purity of tone that held the studio staff and her vast unseen audience spellbound; but after it was over, she blacked out. She was awakened by the loud ringing of telephones—from all directions telephone calls, telegrams, and letters poured into the studio praising the added richness and beauty of tone that had come from her throat. With more room for resonance her singing was, to her many fans, more golden than ever before.

Among the many messages and calls the broadcast inspired was a telegram from Mary Garden praising Grace's "glorious" voice. In an interview in Denver the previous March, Garden had said that her greatest wish was to hear Grace Moore in *Thaïs*. According to Garden, Grace was the only star who could fill her shoes. But Grace was too involved with recovering and making up for lost time in all other directions, both musical and social, to take on the difficult task of learning a new operatic role.

18 War with Hollywood

With February, 1936 almost gone, and the shooting of her third picture for Columbia, *The King Steps Out,* still not finished, Grace was caught in a difficult time bind. Her opera and concert commitments were scheduled to begin on 4 March with a *Bohème* at the Met. Schang had lined up a series of dates for the spring in the East and for the early summer in Europe, all at tremendous fees. Contracts had been signed, halls rented, publicity ordered. Should she be detained in Hollywood beyond the last days of February, forcing cancellations, there would be disappointed entrepreneurs, fee losses, and perhaps lawsuits. Frantic communications were exchanged between Freddie Schang in New York and Gracie Moore in California. Determined to maintain her standing as a serious artist and fulfill every commitment, Grace kept assuring her worried concert manager that she would arrive in New York on schedule.

Grace had agreed to make every effort to work harmoniously with Josef Von Sternberg, the director of her new picture (known to be a slave driver on the set, but highly regarded as a pictorial craftsman who concentrated on the photography, lighting, composition, and symbolic values). At first they had called each other "Yo-sef" and "Dah-ling"; now steely glances and sharp exchanges had became daily occurrences. Members of the cast and crew were on the alert for the explosion they saw brewing. It came when the director called upon Grace, as a princess in disguise, to sing while milking a cow. At first she enjoyed showing off the barnyard skill she had acquired on her grandfather's Del Rio farm, but she found it tiring and degrading to be ordered to sing high C's, milk a cow in tempo, smile, and look pretty for the camera all at the same time, over and over until the director was satisfied with the take.

After several hours of smoldering cooperation she suddenly leaped from the milking stool, told Von Sternberg just what she thought of him, his cow, and his directing, and stormed off the set and into Cohn's office. She gave Cohn her sizzling opinion of the director and the picture, reminded him of her long-planned schedule of operas and concerts, and announced that she had reservations on a certain train that would just barely get her to New York in time. She could not and would not delay her departure, not even for one day. For good measure, she tossed in a demand for six months vacation.

His answer was an explosive epithet. Not only was she under contract to him for two more pictures, with the script of one of them almost ready for the cameras, there was a deal being firmed up with Thalberg for her to do a picture at MGM between the next two for Columbia.

One of the stories under consideration at MGM was *Maytime*, with Chevalier. He, too, had pleaded with Thalberg to sign Grace Moore for *The Merry Widow*, pointing out that she had lost weight, looked very attractive, and would accept any price, and, of course, second billing. Thalberg had informed Chevalier that Moore meant nothing at the box office. That was before Grace became a sensation in *One Night of Love*. Now MGM wanted her for *Maytime* and Cohn wanted his take from the deal.

She wanted to do another picture for MGM, if for no other reason than to remove the stigma of her two failures there in 1930, and she looked forward to costarring with Chevalier. Cohn insisted that *his* singing star be given first billing, which was fine with Grace. Chevalier considered second billing unfair to him, refused it, and returned to Paris and the stage.

Another possible role was in *Rose Marie*, but when Grace was available Nelson Eddy was off on a concert tour. Jeanette MacDonald got that part, too. (This may be the reason Grace never liked Nelson Eddy; but when her radio contract was not renewed after two years, she very generously recommended him as her replacement.) She and Jeanette MacDonald somehow managed to remain on friendly terms despite both their rivalry for important singing roles and Hollywood's efforts to stir up trouble between them. Grace was never jealous of MacDonald; she considered herself far superior in voice, training, experience, looks, health, personality, friendships, social standing—everything.

Other business considerations were goading her into tiger, pig, and ass tactics. If she stayed in California for more than six consecutive months, which she would have to do if she did three pictures in a row, she would lose her status as an out-of-state resident and be subject to the state income tax. Since she needed to keep a more careful eye upon her income and outgo—with only an occasional impulsive and extravagant lapse—Grace had this complication very much on her mind.

Although Frank Orsatti, the agent who had failed to interest a studio in signing her to a contract, had been paid $1,500 in full for his services, he was now claiming a $20,000 fee for her two Columbia pictures, and Grace had no intention of paying him, or anyone else, for the work she knew she had done for herself. Her attorneys offered him $2,500. Instead of accepting, he filed suit against her for $98,000. This case was eventually settled out of court.

Her Hollywood world was losing its appeal; the final insults were her clashes with Von Sternberg and Cohn. According to Cohn's biographer, Bob Thomas, someone once asked him why he was so rough on the people who worked for him. His answer was: "I am the king here. Whoever eats my bread sings my song."[1]

Determined to sing her own song, Grace rushed from his office, went home, crawled into bed, and grabbed the telephone. She called Dr. Pressman and asked him to phone Harry Cohn and tell him that a vacation of several months was critical to her health and well-being. Since she did need a rest, he made the call. Grace fretted the night away writing detailed memos to her staff regarding the packing and closing of the rented house.

Cohn followed his flat refusal with a stern, formal hand-delivered letter ordering her to report to the studio the next morning to complete the picture, and to continue to report each succeeding morning up to and including 10 March for added scenes and retakes. He threatened to sue her for breach of contract if she suddenly departed for New York City.

Although she reported to the studio, she stayed only long enough to do a few retakes. Then she departed without any good-byes; she and Val went directly to the train. All the way across the continent she fumed and bristled and told the world, through reporters who climbed aboard for interviews at every stop, just what she thought of Harry Cohn and the film capital.

She resolved to make no more films until Hollywood learned to treat her like a human being. In Hollywood a star had to have the resistance of an ox and the insensibility of a cow. She had a passionate unwillingness to submit to any set formula of living as a person or of singing as an artist. She did not care for the long hours, or for being constantly ordered to do this or that.

In Hollywood, telephones shrilled and tongues wagged. Some

GRACE MOORE IN THE PRIME OF HER BEAUTY AND SUCCESS.
From the Columbia Studios film Interlude © 1936.

top stars, siding with Grace, promptly demanded more consideration and got it. Others rebelled and walked out. Still others
called Grace Moore a traitor to the industry. Critics accused her of
carrying things with too high a hand.

The month of March was a time of much seething and gnashing
of teeth at Columbia Pictures. Grace Moore had dumbfounded
studio officials by departing in a huff before the picture was in the
can, but even more by telling her grievances to the world.

Grace's return to the Met for two performances of *La Bohème*,
after an absence of three years, created quite a backstage stir. Front
stage, too, and all over town. Old friends welcomed her; old
enemies scorned her. Newcomers at the Met, in awe of the pinnacles she had reached, the ardor of her fans, and the David and
Goliath fight she was waging, marveled at her courage, drive, and
the excitement she created wherever she appeared.

The Met had undergone many changes. Flagstad was the reigning soprano, Otto Kahn was dead, and Gatti-Casazza had departed. Edward Johnson, now the general manager, made Grace
feel welcome. She spoke glowingly to the press of his regime and
rejoiced over the many improvements he had made to the interior
of the antiquated opera building, emphasizing how happy she was
to be singing in opera again. The movies were grand, but grand
opera was grander.

The volatile prima donna managed somehow, despite all her
weariness and worries and all predictions to the contrary, to keep
her acting restrained and her voice clear and true. At times, the
golden notes soared over the footlights and the orchestra with such
warmth and poignance that the audience wept. She gave the opera
company a needed spurt of publicity, a kind of shot in the arm,
and surprised the critics. They refrained from pouncing upon her
for singing and acting that was less perfect than that of Farrar or
some prima donna of the Golden Age of Opera, or less perfect
than she herself could have done *if* she had sacrificed a dozen or so
facets of her personality and dreams and devoted her life exclusively to perfecting her technique and musicianship and adding
new opera roles to her repertory.

In writing of his work as a music critic, George Bernard Shaw
once said that he had accused his opponents of failure because they
were not doing what he wanted, when they were often succeeding
very brilliantly in doing what they themselves wanted. Grace

Moore was fighting to do what *she* wanted to do, and her millions of fans defended her right to do just that.

She sang in Washington's Constitution Hall between her two performances at the Met. Always clever at working all the angles, she spent the morning of the day of the concert writing a long letter to Louella Parsons, to make sure the most powerful columnist in Hollywood would have all the facts of her fight with Cohn from *her* point of view.

That evening she was guest of honor at a dinner dance given by the Tennessee State Society in the ballroom of the Mayflower Hotel, with more than a thousand guests including the state's two senators, all the Tennessee congressmen and their wives, and Cordell Hull, then Secretary of State.

In her speech she attributed whatever success she had had to her childhood in Tennessee, saying that she often felt, after she had sung an especially sweet note, one that pleased her, that the note had come straight from the clean air of Tennessee's eastern hills, and she could see herself as a happy schoolgirl skipping along a country road.

Although her speech sounds drippingly sentimental today, she meant every word of it. On stage, on the air, and in the press she would often tuck in between her songs and patter a plug for Tennessee, for Jellico, and sometimes for her father's department store in Chattanooga. She would respond generously to the many requests for help she received from Tennessee and surrounding states, often from someone claiming kinship.

On one occasion, for instance, Phoebe McDonald, a Chattanooga girl working in the stenographic pool at Columbia Pictures, asked her superior what chance there was to watch Miss Moore in one of her scenes and to interview her for the *Chattanooga Sunday Times*. She was scolded and informed that not only was it against regulations; Miss Moore wouldn't like it. She might get mad, and when she got mad she threw things.

One day she saw the star on the set talking and laughing with seven men. Summoning her courage she marched up to the group, introduced herself to Grace, and asked her for an interview. "Now isn't that sweet," exclaimed Grace. Not only did the girl get her story, but the prima donna offered to help her in any way. "I felt suddenly," Phoebe McDonald wrote in her article, "that Miss Moore would be a very good friend indeed."[2]

As to the other part of that sentimental speech in Washington, many experts in the music world, including other prima donnas (notably Garden, Calvé, Ponselle, Swarthout, and Pons) attributed the rare warmth and beauty of Grace Moore's voice to her years of running wild and free in the Southern sun.

Colonel Moore sat at the speaker's table, his dark eyes brimming with tears. Long ago he had given up any ambitions he may have had of keeping ahead of her; he had simply adjusted his affairs so that he could be present whenever she achieved another triumph.

In Atlanta and several other East Coast cities where she sang, Grace continued to wage her fight with Cohn. Her last concert, in Philadelphia, was one of the worst failures of her career. The large, expectant, and highly critical audience was disappointed, the critics brutal. They complained about the program being too short and mediocre, her voice being unextraordinary and already worn, and her intonation being uncertain, her breath support inadequate, and her tone quality uneven.

Grace read the criticisms without anger, except at herself. She knew that she deserved every harsh word, and why. In less than three months she had spent eight consecutive fifty-four-hour weeks under hot lights, rehearsed and given two *Bohèmes* at the Met, given three broadcasts with rehearsals, filled several major concert engagements, made four phonograph records for Brunswick (after settling the court battle amicably), attended to her heavy mail and dictated or scribbled notes to her secretaries, made decisions regarding many legal matters, held dozens of interviews, given out hundreds of autographs, arranged the details of the programs for a foreign tour, attended numerous parties at every stop and the dinner dance at the Mayflower, and all the while continued to wage her public battle with Hollywood!

The weary, conscious-stricken singing actress vowed never again to overload Grace Moore with too many commitments, fights, parties, and split-second train catchings. While in this remorseful mood, she received word from Cohn that she could have her vacation with no need to return for retakes provided that she sign an agreement to report to the studio by 7 August. Grace informed him that it would suit her much better to report on 15 August. Among several other stipulations she included an increase in her advance and a definite time schedule for picture work. Her freedom was still more important to her than any contract.

Although she sometimes infuriated Cohn, he admired her spunk and actually enjoyed scrapping with her. When he began to estimate the value of the free plugs for the new picture she had stirred up, and the prestige her first Columbia picture had brought to him and his company, his anger cooled and his shrewd business sense took over. He was proud of making her a box office star where Mayer had failed.

Although she did not report back to work until the end of August, Cohn was so pleased with the reception of *Love Me Forever* and *The King Steps Out,* and so impressed with her triumphs abroad and the worldwide publicity she was receiving, he not only forgave her for being late but accorded her a queenly welcome. During the filming of her next picture he treated her with much more consideration than previously; he still hoped to make millions starring her.

19 Somewhat of a Goddess

Grace looked forward to a restful crossing on the *Conte di Savois*, but when she found Elsa Maxwell, Colonel and Mrs. Jacques Balsan (the former Consuelo Vanderbilt, author of "The Glitter and the Gold"), and other friends aboard she promptly abandoned any thoughts of resting. She participated in a series of dinner parties in celebration of her victory over Cohn, with Maggie the cow used as the motif and each hostess trying to outdo the others in some hilarious fashion.

The Pareras had planned to go first to Spain to visit Val's mother, who had been ill recently, but with a civil war brewing they were advised to delay their trip. They went directly to her villa at Mougins, where Grace lived for a time in one of her favorite worlds—that of Mrs. Valentin Parera, housewife. She would arise early, don beach pajamas, tie a matching bandeau over her pin curls, stride off to her favorite bakery to stand in line with other local housewives to buy fresh croissants, then queue up again at the greengrocer's.

They would breakfast on the terrace, then spend the rest of the day playing tennis, sunbathing (in the nude whenever possible), swimming off the rocks of Antibes, playing Ping-Pong, or partying with friends. Val, a camera and car buff, spent hours taking picture, working on their car, his expensive camera equipment, or his albums, or playing the records of his favorite Spanish artists. Grace wrote letters, puttered in the kitchen, or ran her scales. They would often drive off to dine at some unusual or exotic restaurant and collect more recipes, which she called "joyous research."

They both enjoyed taking pictures, and would often pose for each other. Grace used an inexpensive Brownie; Val used a new $300 Rolleiflex camera. He would pay close attention to composition, light, shade, and the relation of one object to another; Grace

THE PARERAS AT CASA LAURETTA. Between opera and concert engagements Grace Moore and Valentin Parera enjoyed gardening and relaxing at their villa at Mougins, above Cannes on the French Riviera. *Courtesy of Emily Coleman.*

couldn't be bothered with an expensive camera and such careful technical and artistic preliminaries. She would just walk up to whatever subject she wanted to photograph and go "click." The difference in their methods, was the difference in themselves. Grace regarded the pictures they took and pasted in albums as memories they were storing up for guarantee against inactive old age—memories that would hold them close together.

They spent many hours that spring planting choice American seed they had brought from the states—Country Gentleman corn, watermelon, radishes, carrots, marigolds, sweet peas, pinks, cosmos, petunias, zinnias, Grace Moore asters (guaranteed not to wilt), and Grace Moore dahlia bulbs (a variety created and named for her by a man in California).

Supper would be a simple meal of perhaps a hearty soup, an omelet, at least one green vegetable, and a choice of fruit. The sunbrowned, relaxed, well-fed housewife would retire early, a thoroughly happy and fulfilled woman, and sleep long hours. But after a few weeks of such battery-restoring days, she would become restless and reach toward an exciting new challenge.

In Budapest on 4 May, her summer tour began, with Charles Kullman (at that time tenor with the Vienna State Opera) singing the role of Rodolfo to her Mimi. Admiral Niklos Horthy, Hungarian head of state, and his family sat in the Royal Box. The sophisticated audience was dressed in the latest Paris fashions. A leading musical critic of that city described the audience as sitting in awed immobility drinking in the golden voice.

The night express pulled into Copenhagen, her next stop, at 6:30 A.M. At that early hour she was met by opera officials, reporters, cameramen, critics, and thousands of film fans. When she arrived at the Forum Concert Hall, there was a huge crowd milling around outside still hoping to get tickets. Grace asked the manager to open the windows so the disappointed fans could at least hear her. Since she and Val were raising "Favoralles" hens at Casa Lauretta, and her interest in collecting recipes was well publicized, her dressing room was filled with practical gifts in lieu of flowers. One fan sent her a dozen neatly dressed and packaged chickens decorated with pink ribbons and roses, with a Danish recipe attached to each fowl. U.S. Ambassador Ruth Bryan Owen, the daughter of William Jennings Bryan, solved the problem of what to do with the twelve chickens; she sent them to her chef to be cooked for the dinner she gave in Grace's honor. Others sent fruit, seafood, and poems they had written and dedicated to her. A Danish sportsman named a colt born while she was singing at the Forum "Grace Moore the Second."

King Christian and the entire royal family attended the Command Performance of *La Bohème* in the Royal Opera House, which sold out in forty-five minutes. The response to her Mimi was even greater than to her concert at the Forum. At the end of Act III, she was summoned to the Royal Box and introduced to the king and queen. After a brief chat, during which His Royal Highness asked for her method of feeding her poultry, he presented a gold medal to her, the *Order Ingenio et Arte,* the country's highest artistic decoration.

The American minister to Norway, Anthony Drexel Biddle—a member of the Philadelphia family she had once almost joined by marriage—and a great crowd of fans, all of whom had adored *One*

GRACE MOORE AND SWEDEN'S PRINCE CARL. Honored at a dinner after a concert in Stockholm, Grace Moore's dinner partner was King Gustave's nephew, Prince Carl, Jr. *From* Opera News. *Photo by INS.*

Night of Love, met her train at Oslo, and a huge crowd followed her to her hotel. King Haakon and Queen Maud did not attend the performance at the Coliseum. They were in mourning for the queen's brother, King George V of England, who had died the previous January, but they invited the Pareras to tea in the summer palace where they talked about music, politics, and Kirsten Flagstad's fabulous success in America.

After Grace sang an aria from *Madama Butterfly* and the title song of her hit picture, the two couples strolled through the royal gardens, which the queen informed them she attended herself. The king presented a gold bar encrusted with the royal crown in diamonds to the prima donna.

Her performance at the Concert Hall was regarded as the peak of the whole social season and almost caused a public riot. The audience was enchanted.

At their next stop, Stockholm, a crowd estimated at thirty thousand lined the streets; she rode from the station to her hotel in a grand cavalcade headed by a carriage drawn by four horses. "Val and I, alone in the carriage, stood waving and throwing out our flowers to them as we rode along. We held on to each other, frightened and happy over the tumultuous greeting."[1]

That evening members of the Association of Glee Clubs serenaded her, calling her name from beneath her hotel window, urging her to come out and sing. She stepped out on a sort of ledge, and with Val holding on to her, sang a chorus of "One Night of Love."

One critic proclaimed her to be somewhat of a goddess. He described the warmth and magic of her singing as something divine springing from her heart and going to the hearts of her audience.

For four nights and days the streets of Stockholm continued to be lined with Grace Moore fans. She was guest of honor at many social affairs, including a dinner given by the American Society in the great ballroom of the Grand Hotel. Excerpts from her pictures were shown and stars of the Swedish Royal Opera and a chorus of Swedish music students sang. She was seated next to Prince Carl, whom she described as "a very tall, dashing and romantic blond."[2] Although he was engaged and she was very much married, they enjoyed a brief romantic flurry.

She was invited to dedicate a room at the Jenny Lind Museum which the Jenny Lind Society had named the Grace Moore Room, "as a tribute to the American legend of the Swedish Nightingale."[3] Every night she would linger at the hotel window, watching the flaming streamers of the aurora borealis and reliving her day. She called her welcome in Stockholm "unbelievable, overpowering and cataclysmic."[4]

Next came Amsterdam, where her film fans would not let her go until she had sung "Ciribiribin"—not once, but twice. By the time they reached London Grace was emotionally drained, highly nervous, and extremely tired. Ahead of her loomed ten more busy and exciting days, with an appearance at Royal Albert Hall on 4 June, for which she would receive one of the highest fees ever paid a prima donna—approximately one thousand pounds—and during which the critics would inevitably compare her singing with such great divas who had sung there as Melba, Tetrazzini, Hempel, and Galli-Curci.

Although Lady Cunard scheduled a *Bohème* at Covent Garden on the night of Grace's concert, and made other attempts to embarrass and belittle a fellow American, an audience of more than twelve thousand crowded into Royal Albert Hall and spilled over on the stage and in the lobby. The ovation Grace received was even greater than the one at Covent Garden the previous year. She stood with tears in her eyes during a prolonged siege of frantic applause. The critics praised her in extravagant terms, claiming that never before had an American artist been paid such a tribute by a European audience.

At one of many receptions given in her honor, the Swedish minister presented her, on behalf of King Gustav, the King's Medal of Honor. By this time Grace and Lily Pons were having a friendly medal-collecting competition. Grace would somehow let it be known that she preferred a medal to any other gift, and she always wore her ribbons with great pride.

The Pareras spent a weekend with Noel Coward at Goldenhurst Farms, Aldington, before joining her brother, Jim, and his bride (the former Marian Volkhardt, a Skidmore graduate and member of a wealthy Bridgeport, Connecticut, family) at Casa Lauretta, where Grace had invited them to spend their honeymoon. She was delighted with her new sister-in-law, and they became and remained devoted friends until her death.

There were jaunts to Paris for fittings, to the Palazzo Brandolini to celebrate their fifth wedding anniversary, to Vienna for more sightseeing, to Salzburg for Toscanini, and to the Swiss Alps for a restful stay at their favorite mountain inn.

"I never had such a marvelous summer in my life," Grace told friends upon their return, "and never will again probably."

20 "A Damn Good Buy"

B_{ack} in Hollywood, the Pareras moved into a house at 716 North Palm Drive. Grace gave a large housewarming party to show off her medals; her two new pieces of jewelry—a beautiful brooch and a bracelet of heavy gold bars joined together with diamonds; her new wardrobe; and her vast accumulation of porcelain, linens, Orrefors glass, and other loot.

Their previous landlady soon brought the prima donna down to earth by demanding payment of $1,250 for damages to the walls, floors, furniture, and rugs of the Benedict Canyon house. While Grace had given many parties there, she thought the claim was fantastically high. Her lawyer inspected the alleged damages and offered $500 in settlement. The woman refused and threatened to smear Grace Moore in court unless she was paid the full amount. Upon the advice of the lawyer and Val, she reluctantly paid.

After years of ill health, Irving Thalberg died in mid-September 1936, at the age of thirty-seven. Norma Shearer Thalberg asked Grace to sing at his funeral. From the choir loft, high above the heads of the many notables who filled the Synagogue B'nai B'rith and with ten thousand gathered outside, she sang "The Psalm of David." She had always respected Thalberg's genius and despite their squabbles and his opinion of actors as "charming, vital and beautiful children . . . to be forgiven for their tantrums and other erratic behavior as long as they caused no unreasonable interruption in the making of movies"[1] had valued his friendship.

Grace was enthusiastic about the story, the cast—especially her costar, Cary Grant—the codirectors, Robert Riskin (who wrote the original story) and Harry Lachman, of her new picture *Interlude* later changed to *When You're in Love*. There was only one song she did not care for, Cab Calloway's "Minnie the Moocher"; nevertheless, she took a few lessons in hot-jazz singing and gave a sizzling performance. She found the new technique—recording the

GRACE MOORE AS MASSENET'S MANON. *From* Opera News.

songs in advance and playing them back while the scenes were being filmed—much less arduous than when she was required to sing during every take.

Tempting offers continued to pour in to her and to Schang, whom she called her devoted "live-wire manager," but she was trying to take her husband's advice—be more selective and conserve her energy. As one of the hottest stars in Hollywood, her film income far exceeded that of any other singing star. The big money was still in concert work, and she was receiving offers from all over the world. She loved traveling to new places and singing to new audiences, and was definitely not interested in making films full time.

One day Ziegler notified her manager that her fee for her next appearance at the Met would have to be reduced from $1,000 to $500. Grace sent him word that she would sing for that ridiculous amount in 1937, but not after that. Actually, it was important to her prestige and self-esteem to sing every year at the Met. Except for her pride, she would have sung there gratis rather than not at all. She was paid the full amount.

That fall the Pareras purchased a building site of three choice acres on Saltair Avenue in Brentwood Heights, with a magnificent view of the Pacific and lush plantings of avocados, peaches, lemons, oranges, berry bushes, and cacti. Here they planned to build their permanent dream home, and gather in it all of their most cherished possessions. They spent many happy hours exploring their acreage, studying blueprints, filling folders with clippings of color schemes, patios, and gardens.

Eventually they chose a French manor house, complete with swimming pool, tennis court, playroom, terrace, two guest suites, a bar, a work room, a laundry room, servants' quarters, and garage. An architect was engaged; pink marble was ordered from Knoxville for the breakfast-room floor. Val devoted much of his time to this project and suggested the name "Vista del Rio" while Grace, the breadwinner, dutifully reported to the studio every day.

She celebrated the purchase of the land with a huge supper party to give her friends a "before" look and a preview of things to come. Supper was cooked in the old farm house on the place, which they planned to restore for a guest house. Since there were no chairs, the famous guests sat on pillows on the floor. For dessert, Grace invited them to step into her orchard and pick whatever fruit they preferred right off the trees.

By telegram, Clifton Webb warned her that buying property in Brentwood was silly. She wrote him a long exuberant letter in which she assured him that Hollywood was the only place to have a home, that she had never been happier, that her studio was treating her like a queen.

During the last days of 1936, bad weather and an epidemic of influenza damaged the health and ruined the schedules of many of the film capital's mighty. When Grace was felled by the bug, her doctors insisted that she remain quietly in bed until she had completely recovered. To her, lying quietly in bed and thereby delaying the completion of the picture and perhaps ruining her 1937 schedule was unthinkable.

Despite her resolve to space her commitments more carefully, she found it impossible to turn down offers of as much as $5,000 for one evening's work, especially when her expenses were enormous. She also received as much lift from singing to her fans as they did from listening to her. With the manor house to be paid for and furnished, most of her possessions stored in the East, at her villa on the Riviera, and at the house in Paris to be shipped to California, more taxes to pay, Christmas in New York coming up, and so many requests for help pouring in every day of her life, she needed more and more income.

The infection settled in her throat causing hoarseness, high fever, more delays, and cancellations, yet she bounced back long enough to enjoy one of the merriest Christmases of her life. Cards, telegrams, letters, flowers, and presents were received from all over the world.

After the too-exciting Christmas, the too-busy star again came down with influenza. Her doctors agreed that she must not only rest, she must do so for an indefinite period or suffer total collapse. Val took her to a rest home in Tucson, Arizona, where he wanted her to stay, incognito, the full month of January. But with Cohn fuming, and Schang placating disappointed impresarios, postponing dates, and advising her to pay $1,000 to cover the advance publicity expenses incurred in Milwaukee to avoid being sued by the Chicago Opera Company for breach of contract, one week in a rest home was more than enough.

She returned to work and finished the picture, but within days had to give up again and make more cancellations. The worst blow was having to cancel her Met debut in *Louise*, scheduled for March. Schang managed to have the debut postponed a year, and wrote to Rena Askin, Grace's secretary at the time, that it takes a smart business woman to convince a manager that he is the one in the wrong when she is canceling through no fault of his. Fortunately for him and for her, he had a sense of humor and he was fond of his difficult client, as evidenced by his rhymed description of her:

> Miss Moore is two persons, she's double;
> She's lovable, laughter and trouble.
> Her blood which is Southern and racy
> Accounts for the moods of our Gracie.

Although he was among the business associates and friends whose patience and understanding she often strained to the breaking point, she always managed to redeem herself with him by way of expensive presents, eloquent expressions of gratitude, stimulating friendship, and sensational song.

Val again proved his patience, deep concern and devotion throughout those weeks of illness. Grace began 1937 in a reflective and philosophical mood. To her onetime close friend Blanche LeGarde she wrote of reflecting on the great happiness marriage had brought to her, and wishing deep in her heart that Val would always be there at her side to share all favors, both large and small.

In February 1937, after starting the shooting of her new picture, *I'll Take Romance*, with Melvyn Douglas, she went to San Francisco to fulfill another concert engagement to sing with the San Francisco Symphony Orchestra. The air-conditioning units recently installed on the train kept the temperature so low she contracted another severe cold and was forced to cancel out. Again Val took her to the desert, and again she insisted upon returning to work too soon. The production schedule had to be extended several times. She finished the last takes with a temperature of 103 degrees.

During March and April she was well enough to sing in a few radio shows, and to sail for London to sing in a concert with the London Philharmonic Orchestra at Royal Albert Hall as a part of the Coronation celebration. By the time the ship docked, however, she was suffering from a severe cold and was forced to bow out and arrange for a last-minute substitute. Although hoarse and running a temperature, she appeared long enough to greet her

GRACE MOORE—SINGING STAR OF RADIO. *From* Opera News, *Morris Gerber Collection.*

disappointed British fans and introduce Marjorie Lawrence, the Australian soprano. Then she and Val departed, she in tears, for Cannes and a long rest at Casa Lauretta.

Word spread that Grace Moore was desperately worried about her health, that she had been advised to make no commitments whatever for at least a year, and that she had foolishly, while still in her thirties, burnt herself out. No one, man or woman, critics and colleagues agreed, could carry on such a whirlwind social and career pace without ruining both voice and health.

Inquiries swamped her studio, the radio stations, her secretary, and her concert manager. Her family and close friends were worried too; but knowing her superb vitality and resilience, they hoped that she would soon recover and henceforth take better care of her health.

After many days dedicated to relaxing in the Riviera sunshine, taking long walks and vigorous swims, eating properly, going to bed early and sleeping late, catching up on her reading, writing, and thinking, her throat healed and her strength returned. Again she was raring to be off to meet a new challenge—this time it was to prove to everyone, especially to herself, that Grace Moore was far from finished. Grace Moore had hardly begun.

On the last day of her vacation, she sang in concert at the Opera House in Cannes before a distinguished audience which, she was informed, included the former King Edward VIII of England, now the duke of Windsor, and his bride, Wallis Warfield Simpson—to be known henceforth as the duchess of Windsor. Their marriage had taken place on 3 June 1937 (he had abdicated the throne on 11 December 1936) and the publicity about their romance, her divorces, and his abdication in favor of "the woman I love" had finally died down. Grace honored the ex-king—or so she thought—with one of her most dramatic curtsies. The next day she sailed for New York without the slightest idea that she had created another furore.

When she reached quarantine, she found a message awaiting her from Emily Coleman, of *Newsweek*, warning her to prepare for an avalanche of newspapermen "as per Windsor story." Baffled but alerted, Grace met the scores of reporters with a smile and a quick inquiry about her friend Emily Coleman. They had met briefly when Grace appeared in concert in San Antonio. Emily, a breezy Texan, explained that her curtsy to the duchess had incensed the public, that the press wanted the complete lowdown as to why she

GRACE MOORE PROUDLY DISPLAYS MEDALS. The prima donna on many occasions wore some of the fourteen medals awarded her by heads of state, especially the Legion of Honor from the French Republic. *From the Frank H. McClung Museum, University of Tennessee, Knoxville. Photo by Toppo, New York.*

had curtsied to the American woman who had divorced her second husband and caused a king to abdicate.

Thus forewarned, instead of explaining that she had thought she was honoring her friend, the ex-king who, unknown to her, had been unable to attend the concert, Grace informed the reporters that the duchess was due the same courtesy any other woman in her position would get, and would have got if she hadn't been an American. When she refused the photographers' request that she pose curtsying, and Val informed them sharply that they were being rude, many reporters walked out in a huff. Although they returned later to take pictures, and she and Val posed smiling radiantly, she was still annoyed with them and not a bit sorry she had aroused their ire. They had aroused hers—and not for the first time.

This wacky incident was the beginning of the warm friendship that developed between Grace Moore and Emily Coleman. Emily says of her: "Grace was not a musician—an instinctive one perhaps—but not in today's accepted meaning of the term. She was instead a soaring, gutsy, vibrant and magnetic personality who became a singer because she happened to like to sing better than anything else."

Upon her return to Hollywood, to film a script called *At the Sound of Her Voice*, Grace rebelled at doing another warmed-over version of *One Night of Love*. As long as she was doing pictures she could be proud of, pictures that would turn her millions of fans into opera lovers, she felt challenged. She had hoped to do *Of Lena Geyer*, by Marcia Davenport, and then a prestige musical for MGM. But with so many musicals being made the market was glutted. The returns from her previous pictures were dwindling; her box office appeal had passed its crest. Since producers were interested only in turning out films that would make millions— such as MGM was making with Jeanette MacDonald and Nelson Eddy—her disillusionment was almost complete.

She now agreed with Clifton Webb. The new manor house, almost ready for occupancy, was a silly show-off place, totally unsuited to their needs. Furthermore, making pictures all day and watching them all evening was a silly, shallow, ingrown way to live. She began lecturing her Hollywood friends. They should travel more, expose themselves to the cultures of other countries, use their riches to bring more cultural advantages to California. She had reached the point of feeling as stifled in Hollywood as she had once felt in Jellico.

The Pareras counted the days until the picture would be finished and made plans to take off in their car and trailer for a leisurely tour of Canada, with stops here and there for concerts, and then return to Europe for further study. Henceforth, Grace Moore was to be taken seriously as a lyric soprano of the Metropolitan Opera and not as a glamorous Hollywood movie star.

One morning in September she awoke with another sore throat. Her doctor advised her to cancel her travel plans and undergo an operation immediately. She would require at least three weeks of intensive care, without visitors, talk, singing, or excitement of any kind. And after that a long convalescence.

Stunned and contrite, she put herself into the hands of a skilled surgeon. The nature of the operation and the name of the hospital were kept secret, but Louella Parsons, Walter Winchell, and other gossip columnists dug up enough details to inform their millions of avid readers that Grace Moore was not only through in Hollywood, she was a very sick and shattered woman. Her career was at an end.

Weeks later, when at last she was allowed to test her vocal chords, she found them healed and functioning normally. She was concentrating on rebuilding her once-vast reserves of strength and finishing the long-delayed, warmed-over version of her first hit picture when her final Hollywood tantrum took place. One afternoon, on the set, with her strength, patience, and artistic integrity already stretched to thin threads, the producer tried to tell Grace Moore, prima donna of the Met, how to sing. Since he had no musical training whatsoever, she considered his instructions impertinent and working with him another moment impossible. With flashing eyes and sizzling sentences she blasted him and all his forebears and descendants. Then she walked out, vowing to Val as they drove away that she would buy off her contract no matter what it might cost her and leave Hollywood forever.

Since her contract called for three more pictures, she lost half a million dollars at the least, plus the $55,000 in cash she had to pay. She called the freedom to return to New York and concentrate on climbing to new pinnacles in grand opera—the medium she found most challenging and fulfilling—"a damn good buy."

Part V
War Clouds

Singing is not a question of two chords that you manipulate at will, but something that flows from an inward source. Everyone is endowed with special gifts as well as human weaknesses. My special gift, my voice, has saved me many times from giving in completely to my human weaknesses—from kicking over the traces, from marrying the wrong man, from destroying my health. . . .

All freedom and no duties make a life that's not worth living. You've got to be going somewhere; you can't just drift. My voice has kept me on the track when I might have been derailed. Do you wonder that my thanks come pouring out in every song?

21 Louise

The Pareras drove across the continent and reached Chattanooga in time to spend Thanksgiving with the Moores. Although they narrowly escaped a serious accident on the way, both the long drive, and the family reunion were wonderful therapy. So was the successful concert she gave at the University of Tennessee, planned to inaugurate the University Concert Series and lay groundwork for the Grace Moore Musical Scholarships.

They went next to Connecticut to visit Jim's in-laws, the Volkhardts; and there, one day, the final healing took place. On a drive along narrow country roads to see historic landmarks they drove through Newtown, with its charming Old Inn, built in 1787, and the many gracious old homes set far back amidst tall trees, and paused finally in a tiny village, Sandy Hook, to admire a weather-beaten saltbox house called Far Away Meadows Farm. Set on a hillside not far from the road, it was shaded by two giant maple trees and surrounded by softly rolling hills that fell away in every direction. The farm, known originally as the Old Plum Gray Place, was the home for several generations of the family of Raphael Gray, an uncle of a prominent neighborhood writer, Leland Stowe. At one time the house was used as a general store.

After one swift, all-encompassing look, the second miracle of falling in love at first sight happened to Grace Moore—this time not with a man, but with a house. The unpretentious saltbox appealed to her much more than had the big new show-off manor house still standing empty and unloved in Hollywood. Its charm and potential awakened in her a deep longing for roots planted firmly in good rich American earth amid growing things, enfolding hills, and kindred spirits.

Upon their return to the Volkhardts' home they found a young reporter, Humphrey Doulens, waiting there to interview the famous Miss Moore. He was young, bright, eager, with a delightful

GRACE MOORE AS FIORA. When Miss Moore made her debut in *L'Amore dei Tre Re* on 7 February 1941, the composer, Italo Montemezzi, conducted. *From* Opera News. *Photo by Toppo, New York.*

THE TWO-HUNDRED-YEAR-OLD SALTBOX. Far Away Meadows, Sandy Hook, Connecticut, before the Pareras began extensive improvements. *Courtesy of Emily Coleman.*

sense of humor and zest for life. When he offered to help her persuade the George Waldos, publishers of the *Bridgeport Post*, to part with Far Away Meadows, she knew she had found a new friend. With Doulens serving as go-between, and many others waving their wands, the Waldos reluctantly agreed to sell. Grace bought the saltbox and almost three hundred surrounding acres at a reasonable price, and called the buy her birthday present to herself. The house in Hollywood was put up for sale; it was eventually bought by Tyrone Power.

The excited new owners rushed from room to room exclaiming over the exposed beams; the huge three-way cooking fireplace beautifully restored to add grace and give warmth to the main hall; the dining room and the little front parlor; the wide plank floors; the quaint corner cupboards; the nine-over-eight window panes; and the cunning turns and twists of the all-but-hidden stairs.

Donning hiking clothes, they explored their farthest hills.

They chose tentative sites for a guest house, a swimming pool, a barn, a tennis court, and an outdoor grill. An architect was engaged to submit plans for the guest house and for the addition of a studio, a playroom, a terrace, a wine cellar, additional baths, a garage with servants quarters above, and the installation of steam heating.

All too soon the proud new owner had to tear herself away to prepare for a *Bohème* in Chicago before an audience of opera lovers whose friendship and critical opinions she valued highly, particularly since Chicago was Garden's home town. The Chicago critics were enthusiastic, using such words as *glorious* and *superlative*.

The trouble-prone year, 1937, ending on such a happy note gave Grace Moore reason to reflect upon her past triumphs and recent mistakes and reach a new maturity. She attributed the added richness, beauty, and warmth in her voice to a love of singing, of her husband, family, friends, home, and country, and her simple faith in God.

Miriam Hopkins's townhouse on Beekman Place was her New York City headquarters that season, but frequently Grace would catch a late train to Connecticut and eat a boxed supper en route. At the slightest break in her schedule, she would hurry home to Val and Far Away Meadows. When that was not feasible, she would spend every spare moment prowling through antique shops and attending auctions, happily searching for the perfect furnishings for her home.

Before her first Mimi at the Met that season she was informed that the Polish tenor Jan Kiepura would be making his American debut as Rodolfo. Although word came to her that he was vain, ungallant, and ruthlessly ambitious, rehearsals went smoothly. The tenor's voice blended so beautifully with hers, and he was so charming and friendly, that she began to think someone had libeled him.

During her long wait for the opening bars of Mimi's music, as she peered through the little peephole, she saw him pushing upstage the chair in which she was supposed to faint. After her entrance, frantic signals to him to put the chair back where it belonged were ignored. She had to faint into the misplaced chair and sing her aria with the tenor standing between her and the conductor. When the curtain finally fell, she stormily informed Johnson and Ziegler that she would never sing with Kiepura again. They agreed that his conduct was ill-mannered and inexcusable, assured her that together they had given a great performance, and refrained from reminding her until later, when her fury had subsided, that her contract called for another Mimi to his Rodolfo. Once more she good-naturedly gave in, saying philosophically that what must be must be. For the second time she saw him stoop to remove her chair from center stage, but her swiftly rising anger gave way to gleeful chortles. Her friends the stagehands had nailed the chair to the floor.

Despite tenor trouble, the performance was a critical as well as a popular triumph. "*La Bohème* delighted an immense audience yesterday afternoon at the Met," wrote Olin Downes. "The special attraction in the cast was Grace Moore, whose movie fame has greatly increased public interest. . . . It was a pleasure to discover how conspicuously she had advanced as singer and dramatic interpreter. Her voice is larger, warmer, and much more capable of emotional expression. . . . [She] has more to give . . . afforded pleasure and moved her audience. Tone fuller, freer and much better controlled. . . . Her vocalism was completely at service of dramatic revelation. Presumably experience and persistent work have wrought these changes."[1]

To celebrate their seventh wedding anniversary, the Pareras returned to Casa Lauretta and to the Palazzo Brandolini. One evening they dined with the duke and duchess of Windsor at their French Riviera villa. During the dinner, the duchess thanked Grace for acknowledging her new status so graciously before the world. Grace wisely refrained from explaining that her curtsy toward the royal box during her Cannes concert had been intended for the duke, and ever since had been termed a publicity stunt.

The duchess and the prima donna had much in common. Both were Americans who had known lean as well as rich years. Both had become sophisticated, controversial, world-famous. Both had flair and enthusiasm for gracious living; both took pride in their clothes, decorating, cooking, entertaining. Both attracted men, publicity, gossip. Both loved their husbands, their native land, and France. Both had husbands who adored them, and both were working against tremendous odds to make their marriages last.

Obviously the ex-king, who had given up an empire for love of Wallis Warfield Simpson, had the ex-actor, who had given up a country and a career for love of Grace Moore, topped in many ways, but Grace coveted neither the charming man, nor the impressive titles, riches, and fame he had bestowed upon his American bride. She preferred to win her own laurels. She coveted the fulfillment that comes only to those who have expressed their artistic selves individually and on a large canvas. The success a woman enjoys by way of marrying an important man, or helping a man become important, would never have fulfilled Grace Moore. She gloried in being a wife and a homemaker, and she would have gloried in being a mother and in helping her husband achieve his full potential, but it was not in her nature to be content with these roles however happy, grand, or challenging. The world was full of challenges; she yearned to meet and conquer every one. Fortunately, Val did not want her to narrow her scope, only to space her endeavors so that she would not exhaust her energy—or his.

In August 1938, Casa Lauretta was the scene of several exciting story conferences between Grace, two French motion picture producers and the elderly French composer-librettist, Gustave Charpentier. The seventy-eight-year-old Charpentier had agreed to sell the screen rights to his popular opera *Louise* because he wanted to share its musical salute to Paris and to young love with the world of nonopera goers, and preserve it on film for posterity. He also wanted to buy a Riviera villa so that he could spend his last years in the sun.

Apparently as thrilled about the project as she was, he offered to supervise every aspect of the filming and made all the necessary cuts himself. After the plans were firmed up the rested, suntanned prima donna and her husband settled in Paris for another siege of concentrated work. Her schedule included losing several excess pounds, taking a refresher course in French diction, and mastering the title role of *Louise*.

The shooting began in September in the Paramount Studios at Joinville, fifteen miles from Paris. One of her former lovers, Georges Thill, was signed to play the role of the poet lover, Julien. Others in the cast were equally well known. Between shots the artists would gather around a table in the garden of a nearby restaurant to drink aperitifs or tea and discuss their exciting venture. Sometimes they would argue heatedly. Grace was impressed by their gallant regard for each other's ideas and feelings.

The project got off to a splendid start, but there was trouble brewing. Big trouble. Hitler had taken over Austria in March; now he was demanding a large slice of Czechoslovakia. Partial mobilization in France was under way; almost every day the little company lost another valued man to the military.

During the anxious days when Chamberlain and Daladier were

trying to placate the German dictator and avoid a major war, the company feared it would have to disband. Despite the American ambassador's suggestion that all Americans return home immediately, Grace assured her worried colleagues that if they were willing, she would stick it out in Paris until the picture was completed, come what may.

Although their safety and the outcome of the ambitious project remained far from certain, the company fell to work with a sense of urgency to capture on sound film before it was too late all the poetry and passion of old Montmartre. In such an atmosphere of danger and creative challenge, Grace was in her element. If all went well the film would be released the following February, premiered in Paris, and shown in New York City at the same time she would be making her debut in *Louise* at the Met. She expected the picture to do even more for serious screen music, for opera, than had *One Night of Love*.

After the signing of the Munich Pact on 30 September, and Hitler's subsequent takeover of the Sudetenland the war scare subsided. In November, Grace made a quick trip to London to give a concert in Royal Albert Hall for the benefit of Queen Mary's favorite hospital for children. In top form physically, psychologically, and vocally, she redeemed herself with all the fans she had disappointed the year before; later in the month she sang in Brussels before the king of Belgium. Here, too, she redeemed herself for that previous cancellation, and she hurried back to work on the picture proudly wearing another royal decoration—the Belgian Order of Leopold.

The recording for the film was done at Salle Pleyel, the French equivalent of Carnegie Hall, under the supervision of the French representative of Victor Records. The crew ran into many technical difficulties which caused delays and anxious experimentation. When the artists first heard the playbacks they sounded so clear and natural that everyone was elated. Grace considered her recordings of *Louise* the most exciting achievement of her career.

The last day of shooting was devoted to the big scene in Act III when Louise, surrounded by three thousand extras representing every type of Parisian, is crowned the muse, or queen, of Montmartre. Champagne for everyone was provided by the American prima donna and the French producers. The last few feet of film were used to capture the dramatic scene of all members of the company standing on a balcony with glasses raised to drink a toast to Paris—to the Paris of Old Montmartre, to the tense but still beautiful city of 1938, and to whatever the place they loved so dearly would become in the future. Since both producers and many others involved in the making of the picture were Jews, the toasts were solemn and eloquent expressions of concern, a fond farewell to each other and to the end of an era.

Soon the Pareras boarded an express train for a concert tour of Warsaw, Bucharest, Constantinople, and Sofia. When the train rolled into the Berlin station a German, probably of the Gestapo, rudely confiscated the *New York Times* Grace was perusing. The sudden loss of her favorite newspaper—and more pointedly her freedom to read whatever she pleased—shocked and infuriated the volatile freedom-loving American. If Val had not cautioned her against making a scene she might have found herself in serious trouble. The incident heightened their awareness of the dangers involved in the tour and their fears that war was not only inevitable, it could start at any moment.

Everywhere in Warsaw there were evidences of war preparation. The city was tense with foreboding. The concert was well attended, but her entrance elicited only a slight spattering of applause. The lower floor was filled with uniformed men and glitteringly attired women; above were the peasants, all staring at her with unsmiling faces. But when she had finished the last of her first numbers, an aria from Mozart, there was wild applause. Startled and bewildered, she bowed and made her exit. The manager, wiping his brow, explained their strange behavior. The audience was relieved because they had not spent their money for nothing. They had thought she could not sing a note without a "horn." Their idea of a microphone had come from pictures of the horn in Victor's "His Master's Voice" advertisements.

Grace had to wage a fight for her accompanist, a Jew, to be allowed to cross the German border. They also had trouble with Val's Spanish passport, and lost $300 to a bodyguard assigned to protect them from being swindled. In Bucharest, some members of the audience stood on their seats to peer at her through binoculars, and others uttered loud, insistent cries for certain numbers. Grace scrapped her program, assumed the "what-the-hell" facet of her own personality, and sang all the hit songs from her pictures. She called the American-Rumanian love feast "the damndest thing."[2]

Relieved when the concerts scheduled for Constantinople and Sofia were abruptly cancelled, she hurried back to Paris to study the title role of *Louise* with Mary Garden for her appearance at the Opéra-Comique on her birthday. "She had a mellow approach to

MARY GARDEN AND PROTÉGÉE. In the Green Room of the Opéra-Comique, Grace Moore and her idol-mentor discuss the prima donna's outstanding performance in the title role of the opera *Louise. From the Frank H. McClung Museum, University of Tennessee, Knoxville. Photo by Raymond Voinquel, Paris.*

teaching," Grace wrote of her mentor's coaching. "She imbued you with such enthusiasm and friendliness and was so uncanny in pointing up strengths as well as weaknesses that her reactions were immediately absorbed in your own interpretation, naturally and spontaneously."[3]

During the big scene in Act III, as Garden had suggested, Grace moved closer to Julien to sing directly to him and through him in patriotic fervor to Paris. The audience, led by Garden, responded with such prolonged applause that she repeated the aria "Depuis le jour"—and was sharply scolded by some critics for doing so. The prolonged applause was a tribute to Garden as well as to Moore. The elder prima donna stood up, took a bow, unpinned the flowers from her chinchilla wrap, and tossed them on the stage at her protégée's feet. Grace always cherished that moment, and the pictures taken afterwards, as another high point of her career.

On Saturday afternoon, 28 January, 1939, she sang the title role of *Louise* at the Met for the first time, with René Maison as Julien, Ezio Pinza as the Father, and Doris Doe as the Mother, and scored one of her greatest personal triumphs with the audience, the millions of radio listeners, and the critics. Her knowledge and love of Paris, and her sympathetic understanding of the yearnings of the little French girl who defied her father for love, gave her interpretation, according to some critics, more warmth and depth than that of Garden, Farrar, or Bori. Olin Downes called her Louise "a thoughtful, sincere and dramatically effective accomplishment."[4] Others were even more eloquent in their praise. The opera had not been heard at the Met since Bori sang it in 1930.

During one intermission, the French ambassador to the United States, Count René de Saint Quinta, read a formal announcement over the air of the award to Miss Grace Moore of the Chevalier of the French Legion of Honor "for services to French music and culture generally." This great honor had come to her, Grace believed, at least partially in gratitude for the role she had played in the twenties in helping open up the French Riviera to year-round visitors.

Emily Coleman was with Grace when she read the reviews. When she found that every criticism was favorable her eyes filled with tears. She celebrated the keeping of another dream by adding a codicil to her will requesting that excerpts from the music of the third act of *Louise,* her favorite opera, be played at her funeral.

Less than two months later, Hitler swallowed the rest of Czechoslovakia; for his next feast he was whetting his appetite for

LOUISE—HER FAVORITE OPERA. With war clouds hanging over Europe, Grace Moore starred in *Louise,* for the French movie production of the opera, with Charpentier doing the arranging and serving as consultant. *From the Frank H. McClung Museum, University of Tennessee, Knoxville. Photo by Raymond Voinquel, Paris.*

the Free City of Danzig. Alerted and fearful, Grace and Val decided to risk spending one last summer at Casa Lauretta.

It shocked them to find the Riviera hotels overflowing with merrymakers, the harbor flecked with yachts, and parties as frequent and lavish as ever. When a guest dared mention war, the others would cry "spoil sport." She gave concerts in several French cities, and sang at the Musical Festival in Geneva before the International Woman's Peace Party headed by Perle Mesta (the wealthy and popular American widow who later became ambassadress to the Grand Duchy of Luxembourg, and was spoofed on Broadway and in Hollywood in *Call Me Madam,* as the "Hostess with the Mostest.")

"All things had taken on a perhaps-never-again nostalgia," Grace wrote of that last summer at Casa Lauretta before the war. "We sailed the blue Mediterranean waters in the yacht of our friends Jessie and Jimmy Donahue, picnicked and sang together under the spreading cedar trees on the Ile St. Marguerite. Serge Lifar danced in the moonlight on our terrace to the music of *Tristan und Isolde.* But everywhere gay abandon seemed shrouded with impending disaster. Even the birthday dinner I gave for Val on August 15th in our villa at Cannes had this same feeling of sad finality. I remember particularly that when Douglas Fairbanks, Senior, rose to toast Val and me, he said: 'It is wonderful to drink to two people still so happy in their original marriage. It gives us all hope. But I also want to say goodby to a world we have known and loved here and which I think I shall never be part of again.' "⁵

Douglas Fairbanks must have had a premonition of impending death as well as impending war. His divorce from Mary Pickford in 1935, after fifteen years of marriage, had shocked their millions of devoted fans, and saddened him. He died in his sleep in December 1939, at the age of fifty-six.

The Spanish Civil War ended in July. Val heard from his family; they were all safe. But 183 towns had been devastated, more than six hundred thousand of his fellow countrymen had died, two million more had been wounded or mutilated, one hundred thousand would be shot, and two million jailed or removed to concentration camps. Apparently he suffered and worried in silence about the future of his family and his country. He rarely mentioned the Spanish holocaust.

One afternoon in late August, when Grace, Val, Elsa Maxwell, and several others were relaxing on the terrace of the Grand Hotel, a man suddenly rushed up to their table with grim news. He had just heard over radio that Germany was signing a ten-year treaty with Russia. White-faced and unbelieving, they rushed to the nearest radio. Before the first shock had worn off, and the full meaning had sunk in—that now Hitler was free to wage war in the West—there was another ominous announcement: the sailing of the *Conte di Savois* had been canceled!

Within minutes the people of Cannes were in a panic of indecision. The women questioned each other, wailed, wrung jewel-laden hands. What to do? What to believe? Dare we stay? If not, where to go? Hundreds rushed to telephones or to the railroad station to clamor wildly and fruitlessly for train reservations. Yachtsmen hurried to their beautiful craft, which had suddenly become white elephants, to lift anchor and churn away. Frenchmen rushed off to don uniforms and report to their units. Cab drivers and farmers in ancient vehicles crowded the streets offering to drive people to Paris.

One of the few women to keep cool and use her head was Grace Moore. She grabbed a telephone and held on until she had reached a friend in Paris, Countess de Montgomery, head of the *Magazine Marie-Claire*, who would surely be able to give her some definite answers. The countess advised her to close her villa and leave at once, otherwise she might not get out at all. Grace called Elsa Maxwell and other unbelieving and immobilized friends and urged them to pass the word. Then she got in touch with another influential friend who secured a place for her in a third-class railroad compartment with eight other women. Meanwhile, Val loaded the back seat of their car with cans of gasoline, determined to drive to Paris.

The couple paused in their hurried packing long enough for a farewell ceremony at Casa Lauretta. Julien, their faithful gardener, showed up in uniform, having walked from his barracks in Nice to say goodby. Val opened a bottle of his best brandy, and the little group—Grace, Val, Julien, his wife Blanche, and their son—drank toasts to France, to their safety, and to their early return. With one last spontaneous hug all around, they hurried off in their separate directions.

After a slow uneventful trip to Paris, Grace reached her hotel and devoted nine hours to telephoning. With the help of still other friends, she finally succeeded in securing tentative reservations for herself, Val, Elsa Maxwell, and several others on the S.S. *Manhattan*, which was scheduled to sail from Le Havre in a few days. Finally, with her husband long overdue, she began to pace the floor in frantic worry about him. Hours later, he stumbled in pale and spent. He had been held up by traffic jams and convoys, stranded in a fierce lightning storm, and almost asphyxiated by leaking gas fumes.

Following the advice relayed by Grace, Elsa Maxwell reluctantly closed her villa and drove all night, passing what seemed to her and her companions to be millions of soldiers on the road. During a stop for lunch the following day, she saw a touching sight—a group of crippled soldiers from World War I, holding a meeting and solemnly passing a resolution dedicating what was left of their broken bodies to France. Putting up at the home of friends near Paris, she soon found that she was one of more than sixty thousand Americans scrambling for reservations on the S.S. *Manhattan*. In a feature story published in the *New York Journal-American*, she recounted her flight and gave Grace Moore full credit for prodding her and many others away from their villas in time, and for securing passage for many of them on the ship.

On their last night in Paris, while Grace was dressing for a dinner engagement with Molyneux, Valentina, and Schlee, all the lights suddenly went out. Paris was experiencing its first blackout. The Pareras groped their way by flashlight along the Champs-Elysées to the terrace of Fouquet's to meet their friends. Later the group went to Maxims where the lights were still bright—the banter still gay and the entertainment still flamboyant. Many of the thousands who had rushed to Paris tried to hide their fears behind bravado, while others rejoiced over being safe from Hitler's armored columns behind France's "impregnable" Maginot Line.

Before returning to their hotel, Grace and Val went to the Boulevard des Italiens to see the film *Louise* for the first time. It had premiered two weeks previously. Ignoring the blackout and the lateness of the hour, more than three hundred people were waiting in line. Grace felt amply rewarded for the risks she had taken. Her appearance at the Opéra-Comique the previous December would be the last opera performance of *Louise* in Paris for many years, and her film version would, she hoped, provide badly needed musical entertainment during the dark years ahead.

Upon reaching Le Havre, and learning that their ship would not sail for at least another day, the Pareras checked into a hotel and then went out for a last dinner. Before the meal had progressed to the second course, Grace suddenly discovered that her jewel case, which she had elected to carry herself at all times, was missing. With a frantic wail, she left Val at the table, rushed into the street, which ran through the heart of the red-light district, and created a commotion trying unsuccessfully to summon a cab. Windows flew open all around and bordello girls leaned out to make appropriate inquiries, and eventually to offer assistance. One girl obligingly put a coat on over her kimono and drove Grace in her little car to the hotel.

When she tore into the lobby an American professor, who had just found the case, was standing with it at the concierge's desk. He must have been startled almost witless when he was suddenly showered with cries of joy, thanks, hugs, and kisses by a gorgeous creature, who then clasped her jewel case to her bosom and rushed away. Upon her return to the restaurant, Grace ordered magnums of champagne for the obliging girl and her bordello friends.

By the following morning, many of the Americans who had rushed to Le Havre began to have second thoughts and proceeded thereafter to believe only what they wanted to believe. Why should they behave like frightened sheep? There were so many last-minute cancellations all the tentative reservations Grace had managed to secure were honored, including space in the hold for their cars! Cots were lined up in all available places for the more than fifteen hundred passengers. Elsa Maxwell slept on the bridge, which was laughingly called the "hotel for women." The captain slept on a couch. Grace and Val bunked separately, each sharing a room with many others.

At Southampton, the ship crept through a mine field. Some of the mines were visible to the passengers as well as to the cautious crew. No one breathed easily until this danger zone was behind them. Two days later, at sea, the dreaded word reached them: Germany had invaded Poland. In grave silence they listened to the British prime minister, Neville Chamberlain, announce by radio a declaration of war. Soon Grace was at the microphone leading a song-fest of national anthems—"God Save the King," the "Marseillaise," and "The Star-Spangled Banner." She would sing these moving expressions of love of country many times and in many places during the next few years.

22 Far Away Meadows

The unusual apartment the Pareras rented at 280 Park Avenue amused and stimulated Grace, and gave her friends and foes something new besides the war in Europe to gasp about. "The champagne of my life, I think, lies in contrast," she said once. "If I am grateful for my triumphs, I am also grateful for my defeats."[1] Her three places of residence—Casa Lauretta, Far Away Meadows, and the new Park Avenue apartment, were indeed a study in contrasts.

There was a high-ceilinged living room with a balcony at one end, a low platform at the other, and a huge fireplace and stone mantle on one side. There were banners and shields and other antiquities reminiscent of a throne room. When she added her collection of autographed photographs of kings, queens, and other heads of state and personages of importance, the setting was perfect for interviews, picture-taking, and entertaining in the grand manner. Here Grace played the role of Queen of Song for all it was worth.

In greater demand that fall than ever before, she sang to sold-out houses for fabulous fees. Everything in her life was running so smoothly, only occasionally did one of her demons outdistance her nightingale. It happened in Chicago one day during a rehearsal of *Louise* when the maestro told her how he wanted her to sing so that the backstage conductor would have time to direct the chorus. Grace said haughtily, "I studied this with Charpentier, and I shall sing it the way he taught me."

"It will be sung my way," the maestro retorted, "even if we have to use another prima donna."

She sulked for a while and refused to use her voice during the rest of the rehearsal; but the next day she sang the role his way and received magnificent applause and reviews.

The filmed version of *Louise* was premiered in America at the

Little Carnegie Playhouse on 2 February 1940, the day after her second *Louise* of the Met season. Another of her dreams was now a reality, though a year late. With English titles and a foreword by Deems Taylor, it was heralded by tremendous publicity.

Most of the critics gave the picture favorable reviews and credited Grace Moore with being the chief reason they had liked it. A Chicago critic informed his readers that he liked it for many reasons, but mainly because he always enjoyed Grace Moore; she seemed to love to sing so much she swept her audiences up in the embrace of her enthusiasm and made them love it. He called her one of the most vital personalities of public life.

Although the sound proved to be far from perfect when heard in inadequately equipped motion picture houses, the film was saluted as a pioneering effort of great interest and worth, a remarkable achievement.

Grace's sister and brothers and their families spent Easter at Far Away Meadows. The weekend was a combination Easter celebration, family reunion, and housewarming. This was the first of many house parties held there.

The lines of the original saltbox had been retained in the new wing, but with a huge bay window added to overlook the swimming pool, the tennis court, and the rolling hills beyond. The main house, guest house, garage, servant quarters, studio, and stretches of rail fence were painted white, the shutters a shade of blue lighter than Royal Copenhagen, darker than Mediterranean—nearer the rich deep blue of Grace Moore's eyes. Her friends called her favorite color, which she used often in her clothes, jewels, decorating, stationery, the ribbon of her typewriter and the ink in her pens, "Grace Moore blue."

The music room, large enough for informal recitals, was built with wide plank floors and a high-arched ceiling supported by hand-hewn and darkened oak trusses to match those of the original house. Her Bechstein piano, upon which stood autographed photographs of Mary Garden, President Roosevelt, and other famous and valued friends . . . her collection of opera scores, sheet music, and song books occupied the most important corner of the room. The walls were hung with her excellent collection of etchings, lithographs, and drawings by Toulouse-Lautrec, and paintings by Whistler, Degas, and Gauguin.

Grace had found yellow-cabbage-rose wallpaper and a yellow-

FAR AWAY MEADOWS FARM. Some of the exterior improvements and additions are shown on the Pareras' 1940 Christmas card. *Courtesy of Emily Coleman.*

rose rug for the little front parlor, and had chosen mint green striped fuchsia cushions for the chairs. There was a needlepoint footstool, a little harmonium, and lots of Victorian bibelots.

The old kitchen had been converted into a passageway, lined with shelves and cupboards and painted several shades lighter than Grace Moore blue. On display here was her collection of fine china and porcelain. Beyond this was a modern kitchen with stained and rubbed knotty-pine cabinets. On the wall behind the recessed and indirectly lighted electric range was a mosaic of Spanish tile in colorful fruit, vegetables, and game. Herb and spice jars and French copper pots and pans were handy to her touch, and a garden of herbs grew just outside the kitchen door.

The walls of the stairwell leading down to the playroom, and the well-stocked wine cellar on the lower level, were covered with autographed photographs of many of her friends; still others hung on the warm pine walls of the playroom. The floor was red tile; there was a small bar and an informal arrangement of comfortable sofas and chairs. Near the door leading to the terrace and the swimming pool were dressing rooms, a shower, and other conveniences for outdoor sunbathing and swimming.

Another staircase, to the left of the front entrance, led to the second floor's two spacious bedrooms and baths, ample storage closets, and dressing rooms. Grace's bedroom was a charming garden of tiny bouquets of flowers, no two alike, hand painted by an Italian artist on canvassed walls in pastel colors. In the center of the ceiling the artist painted a delicate floral rosette with sprays of blossoms drifting out in all directions. Draperies were hand painted on the wall behind the Venetian bed. The wide plank floor was painted white, the rug and fabrics were a soft blue.

After a heavy snow or rain, the country road leading to the entrance gate was impassable. Sometimes the Pareras and their guests would have to park their limousines on the main road and walk almost a quarter of a mile. In one letter she received from the governor of Connecticut, he welcomed her formally as a new resident of the Nutmeg State. In another he invited her to sing at some local function. Grace replied that she would be delighted to sing for him, provided he would see that the road leading to her property was improved. He agreed. Weeks passed without the governor living up to his part of the bargain. Tired of waiting and of spending her own money on a public road, she sent him a terse message that produced results: "I took the high road, now you take the low road."

Grace had always loved to entertain, and now more than ever. Invitations to Far Away Meadows were eagerly accepted. Busy celebrities would cancel engagements and travel long distances to attend her parties. "When she'd had a glass or two of champagne," one friend recalled recently, "she was more fun than anyone else I've ever known."

Grace always cherished her friends and rewarded them with steadfast devotion. At the same time, far back behind those dazzling blue eyes her revved-up computer would be reckoning how best a certain friend could be used to further her own interests. When asked about using her friends she would say, "Isn't that what friends are for?" Her many friends would leap at the chance to be of use to her; she was their inspiration, their catalyst, their hilltop. The poet-novelist Robert Penn Warren once said; "Your passion is your identity. If you have no passion for something, you might as well be dead." She had no time for people who lacked passion, or inward flame.

Coleman and Chatterton spent several Christmases and many weekends at Far Away Meadows. They would arrive in Chatterton's Rolls-Royce, complete with chauffeur and maid, and stay in

HOMEGROWN AND HOME-COOKED. Grace Moore collected hundreds of recipes from famous foreign chefs, studied at the Cordon Bleu in Paris, and became a gourmet cook. She always took pride in her homegrown vegetables and fruits. *From* Opera News, *the Granger Collection.*

the guest house, where the maid served their breakfast. No guests were welcomed at the main house until after noon. There would be a dinner on Saturday evening and another at 2:30 on Sunday afternoon. Their hostess would prepare a late Sunday night supper of perhaps baked eggs in individual casseroles, a delicious salad, hot homemade bread, and cheese. Val would keep firm control of the keys to the wine cellar to make sure no one would overindulge.

"Everything we serve, except the wine," Grace would proudly remind her guests, "is homegrown." Her love for cooking was rooted in her childhood. At a county fair she once won a red ribbon for being third-best soloist, and a blue ribbon for a cake she had baked. She collected eighty-eight famous recipes for chicken, but salads and desserts were her specialties. She loved to experiment with new mixtures for salads. A combination of figs, oranges, and grapefruit was a favorite. She always questioned the need for cooking when nature provided such delicious natural foods.

She appeared on many lists as one of the ten best dressed women in America. She loved striking accessories, perky hats, scarves, sweaters, costume jewelry, and furs, and she always emphasized appropriateness of dress for an occasion. She wanted American women to learn simplicity of dress, which was the basis of French women's chic. She urged American designers to learn the meaning of simplicity. She was convinced that she sang better after she gave up high heels. She believed that uncomfortable feet cause more crow's-feet and furrowed brows for women than wayward husbands. She loved wedges and sandals and helped make low-heeled casual footwear popular.

In the world of dieting she was, from long years of experience, an acknowledged authority. She claimed she could smell a candy store a mile away. She loved desserts, and had she let herself go would have become enormously fat; her slender figure was the result of eternal vigilance. Her ideal weight was 125 pounds. Whenever she went over it, she would sentence herself to walking, swimming, golfing, gardening, and horseback riding, and to another round of thin soups, vegetables, toast, and tea.

Grace searched for a way to help ambitious and talented young people. She found that although more than $35 million a year was spent in America on musical education, no more than two percent of the students achieved even a slight musical success. The wholesale influx of experienced European singers to America and the traditional policy of always giving foreign artists preferential treatment had enriched American opera—but the policy made the competition so fierce that young Americans scarcely had a fair chance.

To help remedy this unfortunate situation, she founded the Grace Moore School of Singing, designed to equip young singers artistically, and also to promote and actively launch their careers. Lessons were to be given at Far Away Meadows in summers and at New York's Steinway Hall Building in winter months. Val agreed to serve as business manager. Two famous teachers were engaged: Ostalgo Pescia, of Rome, considered one of the finest masters of the old bel canto style, to head the vocal department; and Isaac Van Grove, of Chicago and Hollywood, to coach and head the operatic department.

Grace elected to hold the auditions herself, select the pupils, inspire and guide them, teach them the importance of proper balance between work and play, and when they were ready, launch them on their careers. Talent and inward flame—the driving force that insists that music is the only goal—were all that interested her in applicants.

The press gave editorial approval to the ambitious undertaking, acknowledging both the need and the artist's unique qualifications to carry it out. She herself would reap a harvest of good will and favorable publicity, and an interesting job for her husband. Her supercharged energies would also be so harnessed between concert tours that she would have little time to worry over the fate of France.

That May the Nazis invaded the Netherlands, Belgium, and Luxembourg. Chamberlain resigned and Winston Churchill became prime minister of Great Britain. Germany crossed the French frontier, and entered Paris on 14 June 1940. When France surrendered on 22 June, Grace suffered the country's humiliation almost as keenly as if she were a native. She had offered her villa as a refugee home for French orphans, but no word of its fate reached her. At Far Away Meadows she kept busy every minute—planting a garden, putting up fruits and vegetables, testing recipes, experimenting with salads and desserts, planning her school. When friends urged her to slow down, she would say, "If I didn't keep busy, my heart would be so sad."

Among the twenty-two young people who enrolled in the first session of her school was her star protégée, Dorothy Kirsten. The previous year the columnist Dinty Doyle had introduced the young singer to her. Kirsten had all the qualities Grace looked for in a protégée—voice, blonde beauty, and inward flame. She worked as a troubleshooter for the New Jersey Bell Telephone Company during her high school years, and after graduating took a year's leave of absence to try singing in radio and operetta.

One day Grace said to her agent, "Freddie, I've discovered my successor." After his skeptical "Who?" she told him about her find, adding that she had arranged an audition at Steinway Hall so that he could hear the girl sing. When it was over, she asked eagerly, "Well, what do you think of her? Will you take her?"

"No," he replied. "She's not ready. In three or four years . . ."

"Oh, she won't need you then!" retorted Grace.

"That," he countered, "remains to be seen."[2]

Kirsten accepted Grace's offer to underwrite a year's study with Maestro Pescia in Rome. She credits Grace Moore with opening magnificent vistas to her and changing the course of her life. In 1971 she celebrated her twenty-fifth anniversary at the Met.

Another promising pupil was blue-eyed, ash-blond Helen Huff. Grace very much admired her father, the pastor of the First Baptist Church in Chattanooga where the Moore family worshipped. Until he was seventeen years old he could neither read nor write. He tried school for a time, but left it one day with no money, no prospects, and with what little he possessed in a wheelbarrow. On his way to nowhere, he met a man who cared enough to question him, and then hand him a hundred-dollar bill, with these words: "See how far you can make it go."

Helen's father went back to school, got an education, and spent the next fifty-two years as a Baptist preacher, changing pastorates only three times. Although his daughter eventually chose marriage rather than a career, she looks back on her training under the supervision of Grace Moore, highlighted by her summer at Far Away Meadows, as the most exciting and rewarding year of her life.

"We worked hard and played hard," she remembers fondly, and described the delicious meals they ate out-of-doors, mentioning Southern baked ham, fried chicken, and huge platters of home-grown corn on the cob dripping with fresh country butter. The pupils had the use of the swimming pool, the tennis court, the coke bar, and the music library. Helen met many of the greats of the music world, listened to stimulating conversations, and attended operas and plays. She adored Grace Moore and her voice, and is today proud of having been her pupil, friend, and number-one fan.

Four times that busy summer Grace made the long trip by train to the West Coast—to perform at both the opening and the closing of the Golden Gate State Exhibition, to study the role of Fiora with Montemezzi, and to sing at the Hollywood Bowl with Richard Hageman, formerly of the Met, conducting. In September she sang in the bandshell in Grant Park, Chicago, to an audience that stretched south across the spacious grounds between the drives from the bandshell almost to the Field Museum, estimated variously to be between two hundred thousand and three hundred fifty thousand, reported to be the largest crowd ever assembled in one place up to that time to hear an artist sing.

There was a marvelous rapport between the performer and the listeners, and Grace was in magnificent form. Deeply stirred, Grace paused at one point in the program to exclaim that seldom in her career had she known such a great experience. The roar of applause assured her that seldom had they known such exaltation as she had provided them.

She returned to Nashville that fall to open the concert season at the packed War Memorial Auditorium. A conquering heroine of international renown, she was in full prime mentally, physically, socially, and artistically. As a bow to the Grand Ole Opry, she sang an Appalachian folksong "Red Rosy Bush," and as a tribute to a local composer, Julia Robards Herbert, "In My Garden." As a salute to the school that now was so proud to be known as her alma mater, she sang as an encore "The Bells of Ward-Belmont."

An invitation to visit the school, where in 1916–17 she had been so sternly rejected, was graciously accepted. She stood in a receiving line in the spacious and elegant reception room of the Acklen mansion acknowledging with warmth and friendliness the greetings of the faculty, the alumnae, and the students, awing them with her radiant beauty, exquisite diction, high-fashion clothes, jewels, sophistication, poise, fame, and generosity in establishing a Grace Moore scholarship fund at Ward-Belmont.

23 Without Her Balance Wheel

A blow of staggering impact struck the Valentin Pareras in January. Val had been plagued with bad colds all winter; a thorough examination and consultation revealed a serious lung infection. Doctors prescribed immediate hospitalization for an indefinite period at the tuberculosis sanatorium at Saranac Lake, and perhaps an operation later.

Grace insisted on dropping everything to remain by his side until he was completely well. Her first concern, she told him and the doctors, was his welfare. Without him her career would be nothing at all.

Val knew that her first reaction would not, could not, be the right one for her—or for him. She would be breaking contracts right and left, disappointing many colleagues and millions of fans. The momentum she had so spectacularly built up since buying off her contract with Columbia Pictures would be lost. Some day she would want to resume her career, and she would have to start near the bottom again. Meantime, the inward flame that fueled her amazing energy and ambition would be burning just as briskly as ever. Inevitably she would become restless, frustrated, and overburdened with unspent energy and talent, a condition that could very well lead *her* into a serious illness. She could no more relinquish all her exciting worlds and settle down to nursing a sick husband than he could allow her to attempt such a sacrifice.

Grace persisted. He had devoted himself to her when she was ill; now it was her turn. He demanded to know what she would do with her eager self. Finish the cookbook she'd dreamed of writing, she told him. She'd always had the urge to write, and she had enough material to keep her busy for years.

231

It was a gallant argument, but at this point the doctors informed her that her sick husband needed days and nights of fresh air, complete rest, and utter quiet. What he did *not* need was the everyday presence of a superwoman fairly bursting with success, vitality, and sacrificial love. No matter how much she loved him and wanted to be with him, or believed that it was her wifely duty to be with him, and no matter how much he might love her and want her nearby, it was definitely not in his best interest. He would recover much more quickly without her daily presence at Saranac. Reluctantly, Grace left him there and hurried to Philadelphia to sing *Louise* on 7 January at the Academy of Music.

In addition to worrying about him and loving him with a fierce protective tenderness, she missed his steadying hand, quiet devotion, and passionate love. Once again she became prey to extreme tension; it mounted relentlessly before every appearance. The electric entrances and dazzling smiles with which she would greet and excite audiences had to be forced, and when the performances were over there was no one with Val's understanding to help her unwind. Without her silent partner, her balance wheel, Grace began to falter, to lose her hard-gained self-confidence and poise. Her nightingale fell behind her demons. The temper tantrums became more frequent; sometimes she would become almost hysterical.

Humphrey Doulens had joined the staff of the Columbia Concert Bureau and was acting as her tour manager; Jean Dalrymple had become her publicist. Unwinding after that first difficult appearance without Val proved to be an ordeal requiring the help of these two and several others among her closest friends.

With great reluctance Grace gave up some of her most challenging projects, including the Grace Moore Singing School, so that she could concentrate on the ones most vital to her operatic career. Without Val, she would need to work harder than ever before just to keep the place she had won in the world of opera, and even harder to keep her dream of singing the role of Tosca before the year ended.

Following her last performance of *Louise* on 28 January, she was the honor guest at a party given by Mrs. Joseph B. Thomas (a charming and talented painter of fine murals and the wife of a descendant of the Wells Fargo Express Company) in her delightfully unique townhouse on East Ninetieth Street. At this very posh affair, Grace read an unfavorable review by an important music critic whose good opinion she greatly desired—Virgil Thomson. He had returned from Paris in 1940 as music critic for the *Herald*

AS TOSCA. Grace Moore fulfilled another dream when she won unanimous rave reviews for her interpretation of *Tosca. From* Opera News.

Tribune, a post he would hold until 1954. Thomson damned her performance with faint praise, adding tersely "She leaves me cold, just the same."[1]

At this difficult time in her life, it was devastating to have the man whose compositions were played more frequently than those of any other new composer, whose opera *Four Saints in Three Acts,* with libretto by Gertrude Stein, had created a sensation in Hartford and in New York City in 1934, so bluntly reject her efforts. It took all the resilience, courage, and determination she could summon to keep her smile intact, but, as always, she managed to shrug, fling her head high, and exclaim that her career had been built on such bad notices.

After her successful Met debut as Fiora, with Ezio Pinza as Archibaldo, the management rewarded her with the role of Tosca for the fall season. With her husband's health improving, Grace could now relax on her visits to Saranac Lake. She brought vivacity, charm, and a beautiful voice into the lives of patients, nurses, doctors, and the citizens of the area.

Her spring tour called for many long train trips. At every stop admirers would surround her and shower her with flowers, compliments, and invitations; some would follow her from city to city. Between Fargo, North Dakota, and Winnipeg, Canada, the train on which she was trying to snatch some badly needed sleep was halted for more than six hours in a fierce blizzard. Since there was no dining car, it appeared that the passengers would have to endure a long wait without coffee or food. Grace marched into the club car and checked the larder. Then she routed the porters and helped them prepare eggs, toast, and hot coffee for everyone on the train.

On Easter Sunday, a few minutes after soloing with the Minneapolis Symphony Orchestra, she was rushed by special car to the airport to fly to Mexico City on her first good-will tour for her country. Before boarding the waiting plane she changed from concert gown to travel suit in the ladies room. She was accompanied by Ernesto de Quesada, tour manager; Isaac Van Grove, accompanist-conductor; and Jean Dalrymple, publicist, personal representative, and friend. The plane touched down hours late, but still waiting at the airport to welcome her was a tremendous crowd of cheering fans and four prominent fellow countrymen—Bernard Gimbel, Stanton Griffis, Reed Kilpatrick, and Robert O'Donnell.

Grace enjoyed the excitement and challenge of appearing in Mexico, even though she had to fly and go so far away from Val. Although he would worry every minute she was in the air, he had agreed that the role of U.S. Good-Will Singing Ambassadress was too important to her country, and to her career, to be rejected.

Before her trunk arrived, she learned that she was due almost immediately at a Pan American Reception given in her honor at the palace of Exequiel Padilla, Mexico's minister of foreign affairs. As often happened when she was tired and needed sleep and release from tension, she chose this inauspicious moment in which to balk. "To hell with receptions!" she exploded wearily. "Let's have a quiet dinner somewhere and then I'm going to bed early." To the consternation of her three fellow travelers, she strode into her room, shut and locked her door. They had expected temperament but not so soon, and certainly not in the form of an obstinate refusal to make her very first appearance. Beginning on the wrong foot meant the good-will aspects of the tour were doomed. They sank into chairs and stared at each other, pale and speechless.

Meanwhile, Grace stretched out luxuriously on her bed and closed her eyes. But instead of relaxing, she kept wondering why the hell Jean, Quesada, and Vanny weren't banging on her door, loudly protesting her rebellious behavior. The reception was being given in her honor and she had proudly accepted the assignment from her good friends Nelson Rockefeller and Cordell Hull of the State Department. Since Padilla was a champion of full cooperation with the United States and its foreign policy at this critical time, what did it matter that she was too tired to smile and chat with strangers? Or that her beautiful Hattie Carnegie and Valentina clothes had not yet arrived? Her conscience as well as her curiosity were needling her.

Getting up quietly she tiptoed across the room, opened the door a tiny crack, and peeked out. Her three colleagues were still just sitting there in such a slump of silent despair she threw the door open wide and burst out laughing. "Oh, all right! To hell with how I feel and look! If you think it's so important, let's go!"

After much sighing with relief and rushing around, the top of one evening dress and the skirt of another got pressed. Grace hurriedly fixed her hair and powdered her nose. She soon made a dramatic entrance at the reception, and the American ambassador, Josephus Daniels, and his wife, old friends of hers from the South, introduced her to Padilla, who was a tall, olive-skinned handsome Mexican of great distinction. Within a few moments she had met and charmed many of Mexico's top political, diplomatic, social, and artistic leaders, including Chato Elizaga, one of the men she had almost married.

The next morning, as she and Dalrymple were dressing for a luncheon with Padilla and the four North Americans, the hotel began to shake. They rushed to the street in time to witness buildings toppling, Mexicans crossing themselves and falling on their knees. The city had suffered its worst earthquake in a quarter of a century. Although they experienced only a few moments of fright, a report spread that Grace Moore had been killed. Dalrymple and the local photographer she had employed quickly informed the world that the North American Good-Will Ambassadress was very much alive and singing in glorious voice to the largest and most enthusiastic audiences ever assembled in Mexico City to hear an American artist. The Grace Moore pictures were used all over the world, and she was awarded both the Medal of Honor of Mexico City and the National Decoration of the Mexican Order of Aztec Eagle, the country's highest honorary award.

Her mission brilliantly accomplished, she flew to Saranac Lake. The doctors informed her that Val would be able to return home in July. She immediately reactivated a long-held dream to celebrate their tenth wedding anniversary with a large gathering of all their friends at Far Away Meadows. Guests arrived from near and far. Luncheon tables were set up under the trees near the swimming pool. There was tennis, swimming, and other games during the afternoon, supper at dusk, and breakfast the following morning for those who had stayed overnight. Champagne flowed freely and many toasts were drunk to the continued happy marriage of the Pareras.

Fresh air was prescribed for tubercular patients, and Val slept on a tiny glassed-in porch off his bedroom. Although he held up remarkably well during the prolonged celebration, after only a few days it was obvious that he was too weak to resume his difficult roles as business manager, farm superintendent, and husband to a highly sexed and busy prima donna. All too soon he suffered a relapse and had to return to the sanatorium, with an operation indicated.

Grace was frantic with worry and remorse. Celebrating birthdays, anniversaries, moves, and get-wells was as natural to her as taking sunbaths. Instead of providing the peace and quiet he needed, she had allowed her happiness over his recovery, her love of sharing exciting hilltops with her many friends, and her natural optimism and need of sex override her common sense and concern for his health. Furthermore, she had made many important and exciting commitments for the rest of the year.

Since her daily presence at his side was still inadvisable she went to see him between engagements, worried about him constantly, and continued to miss his steadying presence. The Met's dazzling mezzo-soprano, Marilyn Horne, said recently that an opera singer carries her instrument in her body, so if her big toe hurts she feels it in her voice. Grace's heart hurt, and so did her conscience. The strain began to affect her singing.

24 Tosca

The Mexican trip was such a success that a tour to all the South American countries was scheduled by the State Department, with Grace Moore singing as North American Good-Will Ambassadress. With France occupied, England under heavy air attack, and the United States on a gigantic lend-lease program and on the verge of mobilization, the friendship of all the Latin American countries was vital.

Although she was reluctant to leave Val for almost six weeks, and add to his worries and her own by flying over inaccessible jungles and the high Andes Mountains, the doctors convinced her that her husband still needed to be very quiet for long stretches of time. She considered it her patriotic duty, as well as an exciting privilege, adventure, and honor, to be winning friends for her country at such a critical time in history.

Repressing his almost obsessive fear when she traveled by air, Val assured her that he wanted her to go. Although he promised to concentrate on getting well while she was gone, he began to have second thoughts during the last days of frenzied preparation and after the Pan American plane had taken off. Premonitions about her flying, resentment of the illness that had prevented him from accompanying her, and jealousy of the hordes of attractive and virile men she would meet plagued him. The contrast between the busy and exciting life she had created for herself with his help, and was still enjoying, and his sterile routine, uselessness, and complete dependence upon her caused him many hours of agony.

The Pareras could no longer fill each other's needs. Val needed peace, quiet, and rest; Grace needed challenge, excitement, a sense of accomplishment, romance, and applause. Their worlds were now light years apart. And yet, still loving each other, each continued to cling to the other and to the remnants of a once-happy marriage.

With the same retinue that accompanied her to Mexico City she flew down the East Coast, crossed the Andes to Santiago, Chile, and up the West Coast, with seventeen pieces of luggage, including her jewel case containing perhaps a half-million dollars' worth of "accessories." Everywhere she went she was a sensation.

In *September Child*, Jean Dalrymple gives a vivid description of Grace on the plane flights. She would travel with her hair done up in pin curls, covered by a gay bandana fastened under her chin with a sunburst of diamonds. Just before the plane touched down she would retire to the ladies' lounge with her makeup kit, emerging a few moments later looking as beautiful and chic as if she had spent hours in the hands of beauty experts.

Although she was enchanted with Rio, she staged what her publicist called "one of her stuffy spells" on her first day there. She refused to attend a luncheon given by Dr. Oswaldo Aranha, foreign minister of Brazil, and his longtime friend, Rolanda Norris, because she thought the affair should have been given by the foreign minister and his *wife*. When Dalrymple returned with a glowing account of the party and listed the brilliant guests, including Madame Vargas, the president's wife, and one of her sons; the ministers of commerce, agriculture, and propaganda and their wives; and many of the music lovers, art patrons, and millionaires of the city, Grace became furious at herself. "I'm so mad I could spit!" she stormed. "You had no right to let me be such a damn fool! Make sure to invite all those people you met to *Tosca*."[1]

With Frederick Jagel and Alexander Sved, both Met stars, she sang *Tosca* and *Manon* before brilliant cheering audiences. She received the greatest ovation accorded any artist in years for her beauty, luscious singing, and the perfection of her dramatization of the role. President Vargas awarded her Brazil's highest medal of honor, the "Sign of the Southern Cross." She was the first foreign woman to be so honored.

She stood alone on the stage of great Teatro Colon in Buenos Aires, facing a tremendous but skeptical audience and fighting against the fear of disappointing her listeners; of letting herself and her country down. She missed the costumes, the orchestra, the cast, and all the operatic decor of *Tosca* and *Manon*. She missed her husband too. Why should Grace Moore be frightened? she kept asking herself, and pitched in with such an outpouring of songs, that the critic of the country's leading newspaper, *La Prenza*, was lavish with accolades. She gave two concerts there and made many new friends for herself and her country.

She was still in Buenos Aires when she received word that Val was worse. She immediately announced that she was canceling the remainder of the tour and hurrying home to his bedside. Ambassador Norman Armour and his wife urged her to stay at least long enough to sing at the charity concert they were sponsoring, to be given at the American embassy. Grace agreed, and despite her worry about Val, the affair was a brilliant success. To the consternation of American embassy officials, she insisted upon canceling all other scheduled appearances. The members of her staff and many others tried to impress upon her the importance of keeping her commitments, pointing out the loss in money and especially in good will that such action could cause. Considering her reason for canceling, understandable to anyone with half a heart, Grace remained adamant. Val needed her—nothing else mattered.

When she found that there would be no reservations from Buenos Aires to New York available for more than a week her anger, anxiety, and frustration built up to another tantrum; boosted, one suspects, by pangs of guilt for being so far away, meeting so many interesting people, and enjoying so many triumphs when her husband might be dying. When the emotional fireworks sputtered out Stanton Griffis, yachtsman, chairman of the board of Paramount Pictures, and later U.S. ambassador to Spain and other countries, managed to talk her into continuing the tour, at least for the days she would be waiting for a reservation.

Her flight reservation finally came through, but in Quito, Ecuador, Grace and her publicist were unceremoniously bumped off the plane to make way for a junket of U.S. congressmen. When told that there would be no other plane for three days, she lost her temper again and became a raging tigress. She so cowed the few people at the tiny airport that a seat was quickly found for her on the plane; whereupon the temperamental prima donna burst into tears, vowing that she would *not* leave Jean stranded for three days with all their luggage at the end of nowhere.

Word had reached the American ambassador that a tiger was on the loose in Quito. He rushed to the airport and promised the all but hysterical Good-Will Ambassadress that he would take good care of Jean. Within seconds Grace's tears vanished; with gay farewells she boarded the plane and flew away. Dalrymple breathed a sigh of relief; at last she could relax and enjoy her forced stay in Quito.

"I came back," Grace reported to Secretary Hull, before hurrying to Saranac Lake, "with a sensation of how vast, yet how integrated, the Western Hemisphere is, and what a future there is in it for all of us."[2] Her tour was applauded by the State Department and by officials of all the countries she visited. Her tantrums received no official notice; they were overlooked, forgotten, or forgiven. Grace Moore was the first American artist to make a good-will singing tour and was one of the pioneers of the Cultural Exchange Program of the United States Department of State.

Val's operation was successful and his recovery rapid. "He looks well," Grace wrote her mother and father, "and is so sweet & wonderful & courageous there is nobody in the world like him & he must get well for I could never be happy with anyone else."

While in Lima, she bought a vicuña rug, or bed cover. When she showed it to the others in her party, Dalrymple said it looked to her like an "old dog." Vice President Herrera (with whom Dalrymple had become good friends when she was in Peru previously with Jose Iturbi) gave Grace presents of antique silver and Inca carvings, and Dalrymple a beautiful vicuña rug which she described as "all white and biege squares and as light as eider down." The rugs were rolled up together and shipped to New York.

Soon after Dalrymple reached her New York apartment, she found, to her surprise, that the "old dog" had been delivered to her. She called Marion Graham, Grace's secretary at the time. Graham informed her that she had cleared the rugs through customs herself and that Grace had taken possession of the most beautiful one and carried it to Far Away Meadows.

Immediately, the indignant Dalrymple called Grace, who admitted candidly that she had it. "You were right. When I saw them together I realized the one I bought did look like an old dog." "But the pretty one's mine!" protested Dalrymple. "The Vice President gave it to me." "Yes, I know," retorted Grace, coolly. "But what are you going to do about it?"[3] She burst out laughing and, eventually, so did her friend and personal representative. After all, what *could* she do about it? Without Grace Moore there would have been no South American tour. Besides, during their stay in Rio Grace had bought her a lovely jeweled pin, as a token of her appreciation for her part in making the tour a success.

Val's operation was so successful that the Pareras were able to enjoy a little time together at Far Away Meadows before Grace opened her fall concert tour. She traveled by air and kept in communication with her husband by transcontinental telephone rather than by letter. But by mid-October he was back at Saranac Lake gravely ill. Several times the distraught wife cancelled appearances to hurry to his bedside. As soon as he was pronounced on the mend she would resume her tour. She was in Chicago doing another *Bohème,* celebrating her birthday and Val's recovery, when Japan attacked Pearl Harbor. Grace immediately dedicated her talents, energies, and fortune to helping her country gear up for a war that must be won no matter the cost.

Puccini's *Tosca,* composed from Sardou's dramatic vehicle for Sarah Bernhardt, was first sung at the Met in 1901 with Milka Ternina in the title role and Antonio Scotti as Scarpia. The interpretations of Ternina, Fremstad, Eames, Farrar, and Jeritza followed. On Thursday evening, 18 December 1941, it was Moore's turn. With Charles Kullman singing Cavaradossi and Lawrence Tibbett Scarpia, she threw herself into the role of the temperamental and impulsive Roman opera singer, Floria Tosca, with every bit of talent, training, experience, and inner flame she possessed. Val had returned home in time to attend the debut. With proper care he need never go back to the sanatorium. Everything was, as Doris Doe expressed it, "copacetic."

According to many opera lovers who heard her that evening, Grace performed with fire and authority. Yet, while the audience gave enthusiastic approval, the important critics were not impressed. In her column, Elsa Maxwell wrote that she had heard many Toscas but that of Grace Moore was the most moving. She was indignant over what she considered the undeservedly harsh criticisms Grace received, calling their unfavorable reviews a blitzkrieg.

To the surprise and admiration of everyone, including the critics, Grace refused to accept any evaluation of her Tosca as final. She kept studying and growing in that role as well as in all others she sang at the Met and elsewhere. Her repertory of only ten roles was a source of aggravation to critics. Another source was Hollywood. According to a comment Andre Previn made on television, "Critics are always prejudiced against artists who have Hollywood in their background."

Nevertheless, when she sang two Toscas at the Met in January and two in February, one of which was broadcast, the critics at last began to sit up and take grudging notice. In the *Herald Tribune,* Virgil Thomson wrote a long article entitled "The Grace Moore Case," which created a flurry of indignation among Grace's colleagues, friends, and fans. Parts of the article were bluntly unfavorable, but in one paragraph he wrote, "After seeing her in *La Tosca* the other evening I am inclined to think that the expenditures were not wasted after all, and that she has 'arrived' as people used to say. . . . Miss Moore gives a thoroughly worked out rendition of whatever she does . . . a sincere attempt to observe a great tradition. And somehow, by sheer good will, hard work and intellectual modesty, Miss Moore manages to produce the best performance available in that tradition."[4]

After reading the article and all the cables and letters of protest she received, Grace assured her many concerned friends that she felt complimented, and anyway she could take it. At least she no longer left him cold.

In his autobiography, Virgil Thomson wrote, "I had not meant to hit so hard. But in the 1930's no one pulled his punches. Indeed the whole decade was to be marked by such intensities, by violent loyalties and passionate betrayals, by idyllic loves and out-of-joint ones, by friendship indivisible and by threats relentless, by panoramas of poverty and shocking displays of wealth."[5]

On her forty-fourth birthday, after triumphant Toscas in Canada, she sang the role the second time in Chicago. The puller of no punches, Claudia Cassidy, was lyrical in her praise, "Grace Moore celebrated her birthday with the best *Tosca* this town has heard in almost a decade. It had distinction and it projected both the warm lyricism of Puccini and the shrewd melodrama of Sardou. Out of her disappointing *Tosca* of a year ago, Miss Moore salvaged the material of success. Even her costumes have changed for the better, flaring to a picturesque peak in the second act gleam of emerald on white shot with silver. For that matter, her entire performance was curved to the crescendo of the second act, when she hurled all her resources into a performance of *Vissi d'arte* that had poignancy, passion and a kind of prescient beauty."[6]

When she gave the season's last two interpretations of the Roman opera singer at the Met on 19 and 30 December 1942, she was at the zenith of her powers. From the moment she made her first electrifying entrance in the Church of Sant' Andrea della Valle, to the last melodramatic scene when the tortured woman leaped to her death, Grace Moore literally *was* Tosca. The audiences were ecstatic. At last the purist critics had only praise in their reviews, calling her performance magnificent, her acting remarkably free and dramatic, and her voice beautiful, compelling, and effective. Her rendition of "Vissi d'arte" was acclaimed as truly magnificent and deserving of the long applause she received. They agreed that she sang with lovely tone and deep feeling, that her acting showed a remarkable gain in freedom and dramatic power, and that her singing betrayed not the slightest hint of strain.

Part VI   War Years

We must see to it that politics doesn't enter in the world of art. Already the concert halls are beginning to show signs of boycotts, already there is some under-the-breath talk of not performing this and that opera. Art is above politics. That is one of its great privileges.

25 Ravishing Prima Donna

The war gave Grace fresh incentive and challenge, motivating her to play less and work more. She was in great demand in concert halls, opera houses, military camps and canteens, at war benefit rallies, and on radio hookups from coast to coast. She became a USO volunteer long before a schedule was set up, hired her own accompanist, and paid her own way, often sacrificing concerts to travel from one camp to another. Gone were any thoughts she may have had of retiring.

Although her dread of air travel was very real, and Val continued to have ghastly premonitions whenever she flew, it was the only way to go from city to city and camp to camp and return home quickly. Since he still was not well enough to accompany her on her many strenuous jaunts across the land, he would remain at their New York apartment or at Far Away Meadows, watching his diet and resting.

Grace did much traveling, performing, and partying without him, and there was gossip and speculation about the status of their marriage. Perhaps before the Latin American tour, and certainly afterward, she began to need, and to lean on, other men—for escorts, guidance, stimulation, sex. Many of the most charming, talented, and successful men in the world were her lovers as well as her loyal friends. To salve the lingering remnants of the Baptist conscience that still, at times, surfaced to plague her and to cause her occasional stuffy spells, she devised her own moral code with a fine line drawn between sex, love, and fidelity, and lived by it with candor, gaiety, and daring.

"Now art and sex are correlated," wrote James Huneker. "Sex is the salt of life. Art without sex is flavorless, hardly art at all, a frozen simulacrum. All great artists are virile. And their greatness consists in the victory over their temperaments . . . the harmonious

247

comminglement of intellect and artistic material. . . . The noblest art is the triumph of imagination over temperament."[1]

Inevitably, there were many who were as appalled and shocked at Grace Moore's trailblazing life-style as the purist critics were at her refusal to sacrifice all else to her art. More and more insecure wives and sweethearts began to fear the ravishing prima donna. Since she had no permanent designs on their men, Grace thought they were behaving rather stupidly. One of her pet peeves was women who jumped to the conclusion that every other woman was dangerous because this prevented naturalness among them. She disliked women who tried to worm details of her personal life from her by telling her some of theirs.

Wherever she sang in concert she would invite, as her guests, some of the troops stationed nearby, and ask the local management to seat them on stage. Crowded on the stage would be rows of young Americans or Canadians resplendently uniformed, with barely enough space left over for the piano, the accompanist, and the star. Wearing an exquisite concert gown, her golden hair arranged in the new and very becoming upswept fashion and crowned with a dashing bow, a silken American flag in one hand and her word book, covered to match her gown, in the other, she would stride on stage and electrify the audience with her vitality, radiance, and good will. Then she would turn her back to the audience, hold the flag erect over one shoulder and sing "The Star-Spangled Banner" straight at the rows of standing and saluting men in uniform.

The troops loved it. The audiences loved it. And Grace Moore loved it. She brought comfort, excitement, and inspiration into the lives of millions of homesick soldiers and hard-working civilians during the war years. She fired their patriotism and sold millions of dollars' worth of war bonds.

Both her "live-wire" manager for twelve years and her tour manager for four years joined the U.S. Army Air Corps, and were sent to the Officers Candidate School at Miami Beach for training. Many times on tours Grace had peppered Schang with messages blaming him for a draft in a hotel room, a bad train ride, or an uncomfortable bed. Fun-loving Private Doulens, with Captain Schang in on the joke, sent a wire to his old office: "My tent is drafty, and my bed is hard as nails. What are you going to do about it?"

Grace heaped coals of fire on their heads by flying to Miami Beach at her own expense and giving an all-request program in the

SOLDIERS' FAVORITE. Grace Moore shown in Camp Show uniform, entertained World War II Allied troops at home and abroad, even before the formation of the USO. *From the Frank H. McClung Museum, University of Tennessee, Knoxville.*

Flamingo Park Bandshell before more than ten thousand officers
and enlisted men, officer candidates, and supporting civilian personnel.

During that winter and spring she gave eighty-three concerts,
with as many as three hundred soldiers on stage each time, admitted free; and she was one of the first to join the group of
musicians organized to provide the armed forces with a permanent
supply of music for the duration. Once she was asked how much
of an honorarium she would expect for singing the national anthem
at a war plant "E" awarding ceremony. She told the man that she
would be glad to sing for him, but no one could pay Grace Moore
to sing "The Star-Spangled Banner."

She made several appearances on the "Chesterfield Hour," on
the "Famous Artists Series" of the "Telephone Hour," and did
many broadcasts for the U.S. Treasury Department's war bond
drive. No matter what she sang, her voice was one of radio's most
thrilling.

With the Victor Symphony Orchestra, Wilfred Pelletier conducting, she recorded a miniature concert of the French chansons
and opera arias that had won her international acclaim. This album, Victor M918, captured her vivacious personality and vocal
beauty more compellingly than any of her previous ones. It was
the only one of her many records that she liked; it is now a collector's item.

By the beginning of 1943, reporters began to use the word
buxom in describing the forty-five-year-old prima donna. Her
reaction was to sentence herself to another strenuous siege of dieting, massages, and exercise. Some of her Columbia pictures were
being rerun in movie houses across the country, and as she dashed
about giving concerts and singing to troops she amazed everyone
by looking ten years younger and far more ravishing than the
Grace Moore of the 1930s.

She would always stipulate in a concert contract that a white
cloth be stretched on stage from the wings to the piano where she
would stand. If the cloth was missing, no matter what excuse the
manager would give or how loudly the audience would whistle and
stomp, she would refuse to go on until the contract was fulfilled.
She was not merely throwing a temper tantrum—she was determinedly protecting the hems of her expensive concert gowns and
freeing herself from a petty worry, so that she could concentrate
on singing at her best and on giving her listeners more than their
money's worth.

When she learned that her favorite opera, *Louise*, never as popular in America as in Europe, was to be dropped from the Met repertory, she charged into Edward Johnson's office bristling with indignation. After arguing and pleading with him, and with Frank St. Leger, assistant manager, she threatened to resign. They knew that she could not afford to lose the prestige and the drawing power her name on the roster of Met sopranos gave her, and so did she. When finally she realized that she was not to have her way, she stalked out. After sulking for a few days, she shocked the Met management and all the music lovers who leaned toward keeping grand opera grand by signing a contract to sing four times a day at the Roxy Theater, for the largest salary in the house's history— $10,000 a week. A dressing room was redecorated in her favorite shade of blue, a piano was installed in it for between-act vocalizing, and fresh flowers were provided daily to keep the glamorous Miss Moore happy.

Here, with Val now well enough to be with her every day, she would entertain a constant stream of friends between performances, then sing to packed houses all kinds of songs, from "Minnie the Moocher," which she would refuse to sing at her concerts, to "Vissi d'arte."

Her retort to those who persisted in scolding her for doing something as trifling and undignified as singing in a four-a-day movie house was that she never stuck to tradition. Her greatest ambition was to reach as many people as possible, and the movie houses offered the audience of largest possible size. People seemed to be turning to music during wartime for emotional release. Her audiences that summer were the biggest ever, and the most appreciative. She became a frantic hit.

One day at a port of embarkation, when she was introduced by a USO official, the thousands of scared and homesick young men in uniform rudely proclaimed with loud hoots and groans their desire to see Betty Grable's legs or hear Bob Hope's jokes—not listen to a middle-aged opera singer warble high-toned tra-la-la's. Looking radiantly beautiful and supercharged with that electric something that rarely failed to bring an audience to instant attention, eyes blazing and hands expressively raised, she proceeded to smack several thousand clean-shaven young cheeks. She told them that being there was no more fun for her than it was for them. But if they would remember their manners, they might all have some fun.

With her audience in sudden shock, she proceeded to enrapture them. After her first few songs they applauded wildly and shouted for More! More! More! They loved her and hated to let her go. She loved them and hated to say goodbye. Among their many requests were shouts that she come sing for them "over there." With smiles, bows, and thrown kisses she promised to come as soon as possible.

Before keeping that promise, she signed a book contract with Doubleday, Doran & Company and committed herself to a deadline. She had already spent many hours on planes, in dressing rooms, and in hotel suites making notes, dictating, and selecting from the hundreds of recipes she had lured from reluctant European chefs during her many trips abroad and tested in her own kitchen. Whenever she found that a chef had left out one or two important ingredients, she would march into his kitchen on her next visit to his restaurant, confront him with his cunning, and try to charm or shame him into revealing the secret ingredients. Often she would return to the table, where her husband and friends would be waiting, grinning triumphantly. But when she was not successful she would vow, in strong language, never to patronize or recommend that restaurant again, and make a stormy exit.

That summer she and Val spent a month at the Broadmoor Hotel in Colorado Springs, ostensibly to rest and enjoy her first vacation in years. The real reason was to provide the long hours necessary to meet that swiftly approaching deadline. Nelson Doubleday, one of her ardent admirers, suggested that the manuscript be divided into two books. She put her collection of recipes away, intending to write the cookbook later, and concentrated on the story of her life.

Grace had a penchant for starting interesting projects, and then, for lack of time or for some other reason, dropping them. She managed, somehow, to complete her book. As soon as the galley proofs were sent to her for corrections, she fell prey to prepublication jitters. Having written the manuscript off the top of her head, she knew it was far from accurate. She sent out a frantic SOS to two of her closest and most competent friends in the writing business—Jean Dalrymple and Emily Coleman.

The three women spread the galleys on the living room floor of her new apartment on the seventeenth floor of the Savoy Plaza and fell to work. That is, her friends fell to work; Grace paced back and forth, defiantly sluffing off their many questions, watching with mother-hen nervousness the brutal slashing and switching around they contemplated doing to her brainchild. "Oh, to hell with it!" she exclaimed suddenly, swooping up the galleys from the floor and bundling them off to her publisher.

You're Only Human Once, tagged a "frank and informal autobiography," was published in March 1944. For the next few months, wherever the singer-turned-author gave a performance, she was wined, dined, and interviewed by book as well as music editors. She attended many autographing parties, attracted large crowds, and made cash registers ring.

The critics who mattered to Grace wrote very complimentary reviews. By April, her book was number two on the nonfiction best-seller list, topped only by Gene Fowler's *Goodnight, Sweet Prince*. In fiction *A Bell for Adano*, by John Hersey, and *A Tree Grows in Brooklyn*, by Betty Smith, were the top sellers.

Although *You're Only Human Once* was filled with unedited inaccuracies, merely skimmed the cream off her life, and did not mention the long serious illness of her husband, it did sparkle with the champagne and grit of her personality, vivid splashes of name dropping, and generous servings of her work-play philosophy. Her brief sojourn in the literary world gave her a tremendous feeling of accomplishment, and her frankness about her love life amused some readers and shocked others.

Colonel Moore died in late November 1944. The prima donna flew immediately to Chattanooga. The funeral was held at the First Baptist Church with the Reverend Mr. Huff officiating; the burial was at Forest Hills Cemetery, at the foot of Lookout Mountain. Before rushing back to New York to sing two *Bohèmes* at the Met, Grace said to her mother, as they stood together at her father's flower-blanketed grave, "I want to be buried in this beautiful spot right here beside him."

26 "Talons, Great Wings, and a Strong Heart"

As soon as plans could be worked out with the military and with the USO, she flew to Paris by way of Newfoundland and the Azores to keep her promise to the American soldiers. She served as manager, master of ceremonies, and star performer of the small company which included Nino Martini, tenor; Joseph Haber, violinist; and Warner Bass, pianist. She found her favorite city, Paris, only slightly damaged physically by the war, but deeply scarred emotionally. She was profoundly shocked at what she saw in all the cities in the Allied-occupied zones: thousands of buildings and homes reduced to rubble or hollow shells, men and women in rags picking up cigarette butts from gutters, and half-naked children running around in packs like hungry dogs.

Every afternoon for a week she stood on the stage of the huge Sportsplatz in Nuremberg, where Hitler had held so many spectacular party conventions and hate rallies, singing operatic arias and hit songs from her movies. The thousands of eager young American faces and waves of applause inspired her as nothing ever had before. For six weeks the company toured the European Theater of Operations, giving performances in allied troop centers. When their plane landed at an air base near Rheims the company was rushed to the local opera house, where an audience of American troops, disappointed by the sudden cancellation of a scheduled show, had waited for hours hoping Grace Moore would come.

Tired, her uniform wrinkled, her face without makeup, she rushed on stage and greeted them with a smile and a few words of explanation. If they could stand entertainers in their traveling clothes, and didn't mind that their apparel and music hadn't arrived, because no performance had been scheduled for that day, they would be glad to perform. Their loud and prolonged cheers

254

CELEBRATING THE LIBERATION OF PARIS. Following a concert at the Paris Opéra on 24 July 1945, Grace Moore stepped onto the balcony and sang to a tremendous overflow of jubilant Allied troops and citizens. *From the Frank H. McClung Museum, University of Tennessee, Knoxville.*

told her of their homesickness, need for entertainment, and gratitude.

Following two concerts at the Théâtre Trocadera in Paris, Grace was at last free to go to her villa in the hills above Cannes. During the war years she had received disturbing as well as reassuring news about its fate and the fate of her many friends along the French Riviera. Her little yellow stucco house looked as sweet and colorful and well-kept as she had remembered it, and Julien and Blanche welcomed her with tears and hugs. The villa had at first been used as a home for orphans; then, during the German occupation, as Nazi quarters; and finally, as a hiding place for members of the French Underground. Julien had managed somehow to remove her furniture and other treasures to a safe hiding place and had just recently brought them back. During her brief stay, Grace gave concerts in the hospitals and churches of Cannes and Nice for

the benefit of the French hospitals desperately in need of instruments and other medical equipment, and for the orphans of French
prisoners of war.

Although her contract with USO Company Shows had expired
on 30 June, she received an invitation from Special Services in
Paris, and special permission from General Eisenhower, to return
to the liberated city to give a concert at the Paris Opéra. Every seat
for her 24 July appearance was sold quickly, and thousands of
civilians and Allied forces, hungry for music, had to be turned
away. She agreed to sing a few songs after the concert from the
balcony overlooking the Place de l'Opéra. Notices, or throwa-
ways, were dropped over the city; four hours before the time set
for her appearance on the balcony the square was crowded with
troops of all Allied nations, and with recently liberated citizens of
France. Military bands played intermittently, and there was much
jockeying for closer position.

It was a beautiful night, made even more radiant by floodlights.
The moment she appeared on the balcony, clad in a white concert
gown trimmed with touches of red and blue, her arms opened
wide, the eager throng greeted her with shouts of "Our Grace!"
and "Vive l'Amerique!" As far as she could see in every direction,
the floodlighted square was a mass of smiling upturned faces. In a
voice rich with emotion, she sang the "Marseillaise," "God Save
the King," and "The Star-Spangled Banner."

The cheers of the vast audience were loud and prolonged. They
were saluting her as an artist, as a Francophile whose name was
emblazoned on a plaque in the Opéra-Comique, as a woman entitled to wear the ribbons of the French Legion of Honor, and as a
brave and tireless trouper. They were also saluting General
Eisenhower and all America for their part in the successful fight for
liberty.

Within little more than thirty hours, a tired Grace Moore was
back in her Savoy Plaza apartment trying to convey to her relieved
and proud husband, and to a gathering of friends and reporters,
just what the tour had meant to the troops and to her. She told
them that she was afraid she could not go back and sing to stuffed
shirts anymore, that singing twice a day under all sorts of conditions was an overwhelming experience.

A Far East booking agent, A. Strok, had arranged for several
American artists, including Grace Moore, to tour the Orient in
1937. He had a contract with her to do a series of concerts in China
and Japan, but the war had interfered. After four years of intern-

ment, Strok sent her a cable notifying her that he had been liberated, was regaining his health, and was grateful to be alive; he wanted to know how soon she could come to the Orient, pursuant to the contract. Grace looked forward to going to the Far Pacific to entertain all the troops and seamen stationed in that area, and to keep her contract with Strok.

On the night after the second atomic bomb was dropped on a Japanese city, 9 August 1945, she appeared at Lewisohn Stadium as soloist with a symphony orchestra. The enemy had finally made overtures of surrender, and during her program she announced "Un bel dí" from *Madama Butterfly*, and added, "Thank God, we can sing this again now!"[1] The audience remained completely still, while she sang that poignantly beautiful Puccini aria, and stayed that way for several moments afterward, as if transfixed. When at last the applause and cheers broke out, she stood in regal splendor, spotlighted in the soft night air, her face all smiles, her arm outstretched, eagerly drinking in and giving out countless sparks of love and joy. She adored the aria from *Butterfly* and always sang it with moving warmth and beauty of tone; unfortunately, she never got around to adding the complete role of Cio-Cio-San to her repertory.

This performance at Lewisohn followed a highly successful *Bohème* and preceded a benefit concert entitled "Songs Our Soldiers Love." On the day of her third appearance there, 14 August 1945, the long-awaited announcement of the Japanese unconditional surrender was broadcast. When Mayor La Guardia presented her with a Certificate of Merit of the City of New York for her many contributions to the war effort, the audience expressed its approval in wild applause.

With the end of the war many new voices began to be heard at the Met. Among the new names listed on the roster of sopranos for the 1945–56 season was that of Dorothy Kirsten. Grace had recommended her to the Chicago Lyric Opera and she made her debut there in November 1940 as Musetta in *La Bohème*. In 1942, in Chicago, she sang Musetta to Grace's Mimi and both received critical acclaim. In 1943, she made her debut at the New York City Opera, and in December 1945, a highly successful debut at the Met as Mimi. Grace sat in Box 1, threw sweetheart roses on stage, exclaiming proudly, "She's all inner flame, that girl."

Although both on stage and off Grace continued to draw tremendous audiences with the excitement of her personality, the drama of her life, and the beauty of her voice she would now frequently forget the words of a song, or start off on the wrong key. With a disarming grin she would say, as she stole a glance at her word book, "There I go making another boo-boo. Let's start over." Frequently too, now, she would drink a split of champagne between acts, remarking with a grin, "It relaxes my throat, you know."[2]

In October, she stopped between concerts in Chattanooga for a brief visit with her family. Mrs. Moore was far from well, but she was excited and happy to have her famous daughter sharing her large and lonely home. Grace played the piano, sang all the songs her mother loved, browsed through the many carefully tended scrapbooks and albums, strolled around the rose garden. She graciously submitted to interviews and posed for the local press. She went for long walks in the rain, visited Emily and her family, drove to the top of Lookout Mountain to visit Jim and Marian, and Rich and Nancy, then paused at the cemetery to say a prayer at her father's grave.

Her brothers, Rich and Jim, had become busy and prosperous executives, carrying on their father's work and making Loveman's, Inc., one of the South's finest department stores. One evening she stood on the terrace of Rich's new castlelike home, viewing the colorfully carpeted Georgia valley far below, and exclaimed ecstatically, "Oh, Rich. I've never seen a more magnificent view anywhere." The doting brother and sister-in-law beamed; this was praise they would cherish all the rest of their lives.

Minutes before her last appearance in Washington—a *Tosca* at Constitution Hall, she waged a fierce backstage battle with a Deputy U.S. Marshall who suddenly appeared at her dressing-room door. He had come to serve a summons upon her to appear in District Court in response to a lawsuit for $10,000 filed that morning by a concert booker for her alleged nonappearance for an engagement in Richmond, Virginia. She had been unable to appear there because of a taxicab accident and had thought the matter had been settled by her manager. Grace was in a state of extreme tension, struggling to calm her taut nerves, relax her throat muscles, and get into the proper mood to interpret the highly dramatic and demanding role.

The distinguished audience beyond the footlights, eagerly awaiting her entrance, included Margaret Truman in the president's box, and topmost members of Washington society, government, and diplomatic corps. As always, she was geared up to give her listeners, many of them old and valued friends, her very best performance. She was also looking forward to the reception to be given by Evelyn Walsh McLean, society leader and owner of the fabulous Hope Diamond, at her famous estate, Friendship.

The instant she realized what the man wanted, her tiger took over. She told him off in unprintable language, kicked him on the shin, or foot, and savagely shoved him out the door. Seconds later, she strode on stage and enthralled the audience with her fiery interpretation of the beautiful and ill-fated Tosca. The Washington press gave the incident almost as much headline attention as if another world war had begun. Grace informed the world that she was a good strong Tennessee hillbilly and hoped that she had hurt all five of his toes.

The critics called her onstage performance great operatic art, her tones full and rich, her voice in best form.

At the reception, according to one society reporter, she was as slim, vital, and blond as the Grace Moore of ten years ago and tremendously dramatic in her trailing evening gown.

Her final commitment of that season, a *Tosca* on 9 February 1946, was also her last appearance on the stage of the Met. After that, she was free to fly the Atlantic again to sing to the occupation troops and the liberated peoples of Europe.

In Paris she broadcast to America an appeal for food for France. "If every one of you, my dear fellow Americans, could see France and other parts of Europe as they are you would sense why there is such anxiety, and why France so badly needs the helping hand of every American. . . . The French farmlands have been bombed, their plows have rusted, their soil has had little fertilizer for six years. . . . The French are proud. That is why I, as an American who knows France, speak for them and make this appeal to you. Send France food. And quickly. . . . Please . . ."

Of that second tour, she sent the following information to members of her fan clubs and to Emily Coleman:

Salzburg was a great high spot and I'm the only American to ever sing there and the first concert ever given in the Festspielhaus and the first time French music was done. The critics are superb and my visit to all that part of the country was a memory for all life. We visited Berchtesgaden, Eagle's Nest, and the Heidelberg concert with the Philharmonic was only for soldiers. Salzburg used to be dark & gloomy but Hitler had Italian (2,000) laborers work 2 years to change it & it's all gold and white and beautiful for concerts. They want me to come next season and sing Marschallin in *Rosenkavalier*.

In Vienna—I was flown from Paris in Gen. Clark's private plane with Drew Pearson and Col. Ladue and on our arrival at airport I was motored into Vienna in Himmler's car, the glass 6 in. thick—all bullet proof and 16 American M.P.'s as an escort. What a scene for my Vienna debut. I return there end of Nov. to sing *Tosca* at opera.

Deauville, where I wore my new musical career dress by Schiaparelli— white & gold with first bar of music & the words from all my favorite operas & one or 2 songs—was in the same theatre where I made my debut in 1929 as Juliet. We had a very distinguished audience, mostly British, and Lady Cunard (who as you know from the book was unkind in London) thanked me with tears running from her eyes that she had never been so moved. So you see—life takes care of itself!

She flew back to the States in time to spend the Fourth of July with Val at Far Away Meadows. Just ahead were two performances at the Lewisohn Stadium and a *Bohème* in Montreal. On her first night at the stadium, where the year before she had been a sensation not once but three times, she gave her worst performance since that failure in Philadelphia years before. She had a bad cold; but more than that, her voice had begun to slip badly and her technique, never perfected, had become so insecure that many listeners became embarrassed for her. Furthermore, she was desperately tired and she could no longer feel as inspired as when she sang for the troops. The harder she tried to rise above her cold, her tiredness, and lack of inspiration, the worse she sang. The applause was heartbreakingly meager.

Next morning the critics slashed at her mercilessly. Grace Moore was definitely through. She read their cruel words with fire in her eyes and heart, admitted that she had been in wretched voice, and vowed to redeem herself and prove to them that Grace Moore was far from through. Someone substituted for her the following night, and she would never again appear at Lewisohn Stadium. She went on such a rigid health-restoring program that by the time she sang Mimi in Montreal she did a creditable job. Immediately after this performance, her last on this side of the Atlantic, she and Val departed for a long vacation at Casa Lauretta.

After a long rest there, she could no more resist accepting the flood of offers that came in from her European concert manager than she could resist giving and attending frequent parties. Her ambitious plans and bookings for the rest of 1946 and on through 1948, and her optimistic belief that Val would soon be a well man, served to convince her, or almost convince her, that her life was still on an upward spiral.

ONE OF HER LAST PHOTOS IN THE UNITED STATES. Grace Moore
flew from La Guardia Field, New York, on 24 July 1946, for Europe to meet a
heavy schedule of concert and opera engagements. *From* Opera News. *Associated Press Photo.*

She returned to Casa Lauretta from a tour of the British Isles to find Val again seriously ill. Nothing he ate agreed with him. Doctors recommended a stricter diet, no smoking, and bed rest. Torn between wanting to cancel all the contracts she had so optimistically signed and remain quietly at home with him, and not wanting to disappoint her European fans, Grace compromised. She canceled all American commitments at the Met and elsewhere that would take her across the sea, and kept only some of those nearby. She would stay with him until the very last possible plane departure, and despite bad weather, his premonitions, and her own fears and forebodings fly to some European city, give a performance— or a series of performances—then fly back to him as quickly as possible.

One day several officials came to the villa to notify her that she was to be made an honorary citizen of Cannes, the first foreigner to receive such recognition. A special medal was to be designed and awarded to her at a dinner and reception to be given in her honor. Pleased and excited over this tribute from her French neighbors and friends, she and Val flew to Paris where she sang *Louise* on 4 December for the last time at the Opéra-Comique. The performance, publicized as a huge postwar gala and the return of the American prima donna who had sung the last *Louise* there before the war, brought more ovations and critical acclaim.

A doctor in Paris diagnosed Val's recent illness as a stomach ulcer, and prescribed a special diet and an operation as soon as he had built up sufficient strength.

27 Final Curtain

On 6 January 1947, Grace dashed off the following note to Helen Ruth Matthews, her last secretary to be relayed to the members of her fan club:

> There will be a gala concert on February 7 after I become a citizen. We had all the Mayors in last night & I cooked Beef Strogonoff [sic]. It was gay & interesting, & they are such charming people that being a citizen is not only a great honor but it brings me closer to all the people.
> . . . Today there is snow like Conn., & although the garden is full of green vegetables the trees & grass are glistening with snowflakes that do not bother to kill anything—they just give the countryside a beautiful look. With this 6-inch snow which never happened before we are all laughing so hard about St. Moritz 'moving' down here. Our weather has been heaven, & the sea & mountain air are wonderful.
> I will go to Paris & Denmark on the 19th for 10 days, before back to Lyons for *Louise* on Feb. 1, citizenship dinner on 5th, concert gala on 7th, then Monte Carlo for opera, a trip to the mountains for a rest & South Africa in April, returning to the Riviera about May 20.

Her schedule included returning to New York City in the late summer, Val's health permitting, for appearances during the Met season and elsewhere; recording a complete album of the opera *Louise;* and a tour of Australia and other appearances in the far Pacific in the spring of 1948.

Val had looked forward to accompanying her to Denmark and Sweden, where they had been received so royally in 1936. As the date of departure drew nearer they agreed that he was not yet strong enough to undergo the operation he needed, much less accompany her on a strenuous concert tour in harsh winter weather. Reluctant to go without him, and still prey to forebodings about the flights through snow, sleet, and high winds, Grace decided to cancel all commitments and remain at home with him.

ARRIVAL FOR LAST CONCERT. Grace Moore deplanes in Copenhagen for what was to be her last performance. The prima donna flew in all kinds of weather to fulfill concert engagements and then hurry back to their villa to be with her ill husband. On Sunday 26 January 1947, the takeoff from Kastrup Airport, Copenhagen, ended in disaster with all twenty-two persons aboard killed instantly. *From the Frank H. McClung Museum, University of Tennessee, Knoxville. Photo by Press Association, Inc.*

But when her European concert manager insisted that she *must* keep her concert engagements in Denmark and Sweden, otherwise she would disappoint thousands of her most devoted fans and cause great financial loss to local impresarios, she reluctantly agreed to go. Moments later, she called Dalrymple in New York and urged her to fly over right away to accompany her. Because of an important commitment to Bert Lahr, the ever-busy publicist and friend could not get away. Disappointed, Grace said chidingly, "All that I don't believe. You've just lost your sense of adventure."[1] Dalrymple laughingly denied it and promised to come for a visit in May.

Her next call was to Ivor Newton, in London, the pianist who had accompanied her on the singing tour for the American Occupation Forces in Germany and Austria the previous summer, and on her tour of Britain in the fall. He could not serve as her accompanist because of such short notice and previous plans, but he assured her that he would do so on the South African trip. A substitute was quickly found, a young French pianist, Jean Loup Peltier, who must have regarded the unexpected assignment as a wonderful break.

Despite the strong winds and zero weather, the plane from Paris touched down on a Kastrup Airport runway, Copenhagen, with ease. The city lay silent beneath a stiff coating of snow. Grace gaily answered questions and told the welcoming committee and reporters that more than anything she wanted a new opera, one in which the soprano did not die; she was tired of that. That was one of the reasons she loved Charpentier's *Louise* so much: Louise is still alive when the curtain falls.

On Saturday evening an audience of more than four thousand excited Grace Moore fans gathered at the largest hall in the city, which had been converted for her concert. When she swept on stage and broke into her first wide, eager smile, she was greeted with a joyous roar of welcome. Before she sang a note the Moore magic had connected her heart and theirs in an electrical fusion of nostalgia, anticipation, and love. No matter that her body was a bit thicker now, and her voice, when she began her first number, a little darker; she could still charm away their burdens and anxieties and give their hearts an exciting lift.

She began with settings from Shakespearean works, then pieces from Sullivan, Buzzi-Peccia, and Debussy; "Un bel dí" of course, and all her big film hits. Four of her favorite composers were next—Bizet, Duparc, Hahn, and Tchaikovsky. According to the critics, her voice was at its best in Hahn's poignant "Si mes vers avaient des ailes" and Tchaikovsky's "Toi Seule." The young pianist performed magnificently both as accompanist and soloist. Throughout the concert Grace was in top form, intensely human, giving of herself unstintingly. Between songs, she announced with deep emotion that when the curtain finally descended on her voice, she would like to be appointed minister to Denmark.

For the last of many encores she sang "One Night of Love," and then, ravishingly, "Ciribiribin." After the last thrilling high note, she sank into a long deep bow. As she arose, the prolonged ovation brought tears to her eyes. She threw her arms wide, flashed them a

A GRACE MOORE BOW. Grace Moore bows to more than 250,000 ecstatic listeners during an open-air concert in Grant Park, Chicago, in September 1940. The radiance and warmth shown here were just as evident in the last bow of her career in Copenhagen in January 1947. *From the Frank McClung Museum, University of Tennessee, Knoxville.*

grateful farewell smile, and made her final exit from any stage. Both star and audience remained for hours in a state of exaltation.

Her colleagues and local friends gathered at the Hotel Angleterre for a late supper party. She ate her favorite Danish delicacies ravenously and washed them down with champagne, much laughter, and bright repartee. The group reminisced about her previous visit, and predicted another triumphant concert in Stockholm on Tuesday evening. Impulsively, she invited Gerda Newman, a noted film star and singer, and her husband Jens Dernow, an impresario-producer, to fly with her to Stockholm. Amid much excited planning and bantering, they accepted. She told them that she was anxious about her husband's health.

When she awoke, around noon on Sunday, 26 January, she sent a cable to Val telling him that the concert was a success, but that without him it was hollow. It had only been a few short hours since they had parted, but already she was terribly unhappy without him.

This is the message, I think, of a wife who loved her husband, who wished he could have come with her, whose concern for him was never far from her mind and heart, no matter where she went or what she did—but who was sometimes, especially on mornings after emotional-hilltop evenings, stricken with pangs of guilt and remorse for possessing so much vitality and zest for song and life when he had so little. Despite a multiplicity of uncommon stresses, they still treasured their love and their marriage as it once had been, as they futilely wished it could be, even as it was. They were still planning to spend their last years together with his health restored and all her passions sated.

A few minutes before the scheduled takeoff time, 3:30 P.M., the Grace Moore party, which included Newman's three-year-old nephew, arrived at the Kastrup Airport. A cold wind had blown away a dark gathering of clouds and some of the snow. Visibility was good. Officials of the airline and reporters followed her almost to the door of the plane. She was one of the last to climb aboard, and the only American.

The ship, a twin-engine, American-made, Douglas DC-3 "Dakota" owned and operated by the Dutch Airlines, KLM, had arrived from Amsterdam at 2:48 P.M. Among the passengers, traveling incognito, was Prince Gustav Adolph of Sweden, student, soldier, sportsman, eldest son of the crown prince of Sweden, and due to his father's illness, regarded as next in line for the throne. With him was his aide, Count A. Stenbock. They were returning to Stockholm from a four-day royal hunt with Prince Bernhard of the Netherlands on Queen Wilhelmina's estate near Amsterdam. In all there were sixteen passengers and a crew of six.

The silver plane, with its blue Flying Dutchman insignia clearly visible, taxied out to the southwestern end of runway Strip 04, warmed up, and took off into a powerful headwind. When airborne, it continued to climb with increasing abnormal steepness, causing anxiety in the control tower, among the airline officials who had come to the airport because of so many distinguished passengers, and among the people who had lingered after saying goodbye to loved ones to watch the takeoff. When the plane reached an altitude of about 225 to 300 feet it went into a sudden stall, shuddered, turned over on its left wing, and, in full view of horror-stricken watchers, fell almost vertically into the first part of a spin, hitting the ground with fierce impact, its nose and portwing downward. One eyewitness said that it fluttered as if a ghost pilot was trying to take over the controls.

Some of the charred bodies were found still strapped in their seats. Some, including that of the one American, had been thrown to the outer edge of the smoking ruins. All the passengers and crew had died instantly. The bodies were taken for identification to the Copenhagen Institute of Medical Jurisprudence.

Grace Moore was identified by her heavy gold bracelet, which was scented with her favorite fragrance, Russian Leather, and bore the inscription "To Grace from Val." The searchers had found her music case, a few slightly burned sheets of music, her diary, and some of her jewels. As late as the following June, the bar pin presented to her in 1936 by King Haakon VII of Norway, and engraved with his initials, was found near the scene of the crash. Also, much later, a sunburst diamond pin, one she adored and wore frequently, was found and returned to Val.

As soon as all identifications had been made, flags in Denmark and Sweden were lowered to half-mast, all light entertainment on radio broadcasts was replaced with hymns and other appropriate music, and word of the tragedy was flashed out to loved ones and news media all over the world.

The last week of January 1947, was considered one of the darkest in commercial aviation history. There were seven aircraft disasters and seventy-two casualties, including a Swedish Prince long regarded as the next king of Sweden, the beloved American Queen of Song, and others of note.

Val received Gracila's cabled message with relief, but the nagging fears still persisted. Another message from Copenhagen soon arrived; it shattered all his hopes, fulfilled his worst premonitions, and sent him staggering to bed.

Among the new friends the Pareras made that summer was an ambitious young girl of Dutch and Italian descent, Anne Vanderwalk, brought to Casa Lauretta and introduced to them by their good friend, Henri Dubonnet, of the famous aperitif family. His young companion was tall and blonde, with blue laughing eyes and full red lips. She had acted in four films in Paris, and was eager to try Hollywood. Grace told Val after that first meeting that this girl was going to be her protégée. She invited Anne Vanderwalk to the villa several times, encouraged her to go to the States to study dramatics and English, and promised to help her get started when she was ready. When she heard of the tragedy, she and playwright Philip Barry rushed from Paris to Casa Lauretta.

It was still morning in Chattanooga. Rich had taken his mother for a drive. Marian was waiting to tell them when they returned to her Riverview Road home. With her tired heart so suddenly and cruelly shattered, Mrs. Moore collapsed and had to be carried to bed. A trans-Atlantic call was put in to Val, but he was so near total collapse he was unable to talk to anyone. The next morning Jim relayed Mrs. Moore's urgent message to him. Grace had expressed a desire to be buried at Forest Hills Cemetery beside her father. Since she was not a Catholic, he must bring her body to Chattanooga for burial a soon as possible. Val reluctantly agreed. This meant weeks of almost unendurable waiting.

The previous May, while in Rome to give a concert, Grace was granted an audience with Pope Pius XII. A rumor immediately spread that she was taking instructions to become a Catholic. She told newsmen on the Vatican steps, before going on for concerts in Milan, Turin, Genoa, Venice, and Bologna, that it would be nice to embrace Catholicism because it was her husband's religion. After her return to the States Clare Booth Luce, another talented achiever and hard worker, invited Grace to lunch at Far Away Meadows, which the Luces had rented for the summer, to meet Monsignor Fulton Sheen. They talked about her audience with the Pope, her search for a closer relationship with God, and the possibility of her becoming a Catholic.

The war had changed Grace Moore; the symbolism and pageantry of a more formal religion now strongly appealed to her. So did the dedication of its members, its pilgrimages, its great contributions to art and music, and the role the Catholic Church had played in preserving the symbols of civilization through the dark ages. Her desire to please her Catholic husband was another strong motive for making the change.

Monsignor Sheen (now Archbishop) had great success converting famous people to his religion. Mrs. Luce was in the process at that time. Although Grace began taking instructions, she shrank from unburdening her heart at a confessional. To Dalrymple she said jokingly one day, "If I should go to confession half the men in New York would have to leave town."

Her Catholic husband, in-laws, and friends were saddened by her procrastination, which resulted in her ineligibility to be given Catholic rites. Her Protestant family and friends were relieved that she would be buried with Protestant rites beside her father, as she had requested.

Letters, telegrams, cables, telephone calls, resolutions, poems, songs, and flowers funneled into Chattanooga by the hundreds, many of them addressed simply "To the Mother of Grace Moore." Other messages were sent to Val, Emily, the three brothers, Lisa Johansson (her maid, who had returned to her home at Sandy Hook only a few days before Christmas) Hans Slusack (caretaker of Far Away Meadows), and to many close friends. Emily Coleman, stunned by the tragedy, received a belated card from Grace, posted in Cannes before her departure for Copenhagen, on which she had written that she would not be coming back (to the states) soon because Val needed her.

The first of several memorial services was held in Newtown, with Luce directing the mourners. In tears, Grace's neighbors and Connecticut friends recalled one unforgettable Memorial Day when she and Gladys Swarthout sang a duet, "America," in front of the soldiers and sailors monument on Main Street. With her usual radiance and patriotic fervor, Grace had led a community sing.

More than twenty-five hundred friends, colleagues, and fans crowded into the beautiful gothic Riverside Church for a formal memorial service arranged by Jane Tibbett and Jean Dalrymple. In recognition of her services to the armed forces, a color guard representing 163 posts of the American Legion, Manhattan District, attended. A longtime member of the church, Grace had sung many solos there, especially during Christmas and Easter celebrations.

Virgil Fox, organist, played "God of Our Fathers," and some of the most poignant strains of Charpentier's *Louise*. Lawrence Tibbett sang "The Lord's Prayer," and Dorothy Kirsten sang Schubert's "Ave Maria." The Riverside Church Choir concluded the musical part of the service with "How Lovely Is Thy Dwelling Place."

The remarkable pastor emeritus, Dr. Harry Emerson Fosdick, delivered the eulogy:

> It is people like Grace Moore, vital, vibrant, loving life and living it to the full, that makes it difficult to believe that death is the end. . . . She was an artist, and that is a beautiful and supremely demanding thing. For an artist, committed soul and body to beauty as Grace Moore was, is carried out of herself by something greater than herself to which she gave herself. She had character. . . . It was her thrilling privilege to bring exhilaration to millions . . . by the beauty of her song. . . . I shall never forget the evening a year ago she stood in this chancel and sang "The Lord's Prayer," set to music Mr. Tibbett sang today. I have often heard glorious singing, but to my dying day, I shall recall those moments as among the most exhilarating of my life.[2]

After the service some of her friends and her brother Jim gathered around a table in a private dining room at the 21 Club, Grace's favorite restaurant. They recalled the hours spent with her as among the most exciting and rewarding of their lives. They marveled not only at her flair for living her life on emotional hilltops and pinnacles, and for intoxicating and inspiring her friends and fans, but also for living a love story as poignant as any of the roles she sang, and for dying as dramatically as had any of the heroines of opera.

For weeks after the crash, every scrap of information that could be gathered about the dynamic prima donna who started so humbly and won world renown and great riches, yet remained as eager as a hungry puppy and as American as Main Street to the final curtain, was used in newspapers, magazines, and on radio programs. The deluge of publicity included feature stories, reminiscences, cartoons, editorials, poems, songs, resolutions, and whole pages of pictures. An aster, a dahlia, a rose, a carnation, a river fall, a tree, a colt, a P-51 fighter plane, a hospital room, a Jenny Lind room, and a niece had been named for her. In London's skimpy newspapers, where wartime conditions still prevailed, she was given an astonishing amount of space and much lavish praise. In Paris, and elsewhere, radio stations dedicated programs to her memory, played her recordings, and recounted the most dramatic incidents of her life.

Monsignor Sheen deeply regretted her sudden exit. George Sloan, a Tennessean, then chairman of the Metropolitan Opera Association, called her one of the loveliest and gayest members of the Metropolitan Opera family with a heart of gold. Tibbett mourned the loss of one of America's truly brilliant singers. General George C. Marshall, secretary of state, offered the family all possible aid. Congress paused to hear eulogies from two members of the House of Representatives from Tennessee, and one from Connecticut. Representative Albert Gore, of Tennessee, said, "Mr. Speaker, a lovely flower has been crushed."[3]

A Dallas reporter wrote, "Most persons either loved or hated her, the latter being the equivalent of wishing she had liked them. Even those who were tormented or financially injured by her temperamental highhandedness forgave her, once the violence died down. She was just too hearty and genuine to be resisted".[4] A *Daily Mirror* reporter wrote of her breathtaking showmanship and called her one of the most fabulous attractions in opera history.

In Copenhagen, an official investigation began immediately into the cause of the disaster. More than a thousand flight cancellations were received during the next few hours. There was mounting evidence that a simple human error—the failure to remove an aluminum elevator lock, a type of clamp or wedge used to lock the aircraft's elevators in a fixed position while on the ground, particularly in windy weather—had caused the crash. Such a wedge, identified as KLM's, was found near the debris.

The experienced pilot, fifty-four-year-old Captain G. J. Geysendorffer of Amsterdam, a senior pilot of the company, had flown more than twenty-five thousand hours. In 1927 he flew the first Dutch commercial airplane to the Netherlands East Indies. During the war he made more than fifty daring flights to the Indies, and on one of them he was missing for weeks. As private pilot to an American multimillionaire, he flew around the world. His employer had left him $50,000, with which the flier had bought a villa in Amsterdam. He met his wife, a Dane, Tofa Spandet, during his early days as a pilot when he made an emergency landing on her father's estate.

KLM officials continued to express utmost confidence in their senior pilot. Some days later, when the final report of the Danish Government Air Inspection Authority was published, it said in part: "It is extremely probable that the crashing of PH-TCR (the

DC-3 'Dakota') was due to the fact that the aircraft had started and made its last flight with the elevator-lock on." It recommended: "that international regulations should be framed to ensure that measures are taken either to prevent aircraft pilots from forgetting to check over their flying controls before starting, or to prevent a start being made at all before all controls are free and ready for normal use."[5]

A memorial service, planned by Dutch authorities, was held in the Naval Church at Copenhagen for all twenty-two victims on the Saturday after the disaster. The three flower-blanketed caskets containing the bodies of Grace Moore, M. Malbac, and M. Peltier, were then flown to Le Bourget Field, Paris. Looking drawn and weak and supported by friends, Val was there to claim his wife's body. He told reporters that he would take her home immediately, that she had always loved Tennessee.

The three caskets were first transferred to an ambulance and taken to the American Cathedral in Paris. More than sixteen hundred of Grace Moore's colleagues and devoted Europan friends gathered there for the third memorial service of organ music and prayers. Among the mourners were U.S. ambassador Jefferson Caffery, the ambassadors to France from many countries, distinguished French officials, leaders of society and the arts and press, directors of the French National Lyric Theaters, the Opéra-Comique, the Paris Opéra, and many international stars.

A few days later, a motor hearse carrying Grace Moore's body in a simple oak casket wended its way from Paris to the port of Cherbourg, where it was placed aboard the U.S.S. *America*. The ship, with Val aboard, docked in New York City in the afternoon of 22 February. Jim was waiting at the dock to meet his brother-in-law and accompany his sister's body aboard a special railroad car. About twenty close friends, including Schang, Dalrymple, Coleman, and Kirsten, made the long trip to Chattanooga.

The train stopped in Maryland to pick up two more mourners. Perhaps the title number-one fan belongs to one of these two, Evelyn White (although a fan in Florida wrote to Grace every day and appointed herself a sort of unofficial clipping bureau). White had written worshipful letters to the prima donna for years, traveled long distances to hear her sing, and sent her extravagant bouquets, some of them containing as many as fifty roses or carnations. After receiving one such expensive floral offering, Grace said worriedly to her concert manager, "Freddie, what should I do about that girl? She shouldn't be spending her time and money on me. How can I repay her?" After investigating, Schang reported that the girl's eyes were crossed, that she was too poor, or too unaware of the advances in eye surgery, to have them straightened. He suggested that Grace arrange an operation. Grace sent her to Constance Hope's husband, Dr. Milton L. Berliner, a famous New York eye surgeon. The operation was successfully performed in only a few moments, enabling the girl to lead a normal life, to find romance and a husband. On the funeral train, she was given a berth in the private car so that she could follow her idol to her last resting place.

At nine o'clock on a dreary Sunday morning, members of the Moore family stood in a sad huddle watching the train rumble slowly into the Chattanooga station. Long before three o'clock, the hour set for the funeral, crowds had gathered outside the First Baptist Church. Relatives, friends, and fans had driven from Slabtown, Del Rio, Newport, Jellico, Murphy, Nashville, Knoxville, and Atlanta disregarding icy roads and the threat of more snow and sleet. Orders for flowers had been received by local florists from all over the world. A group of thirty-two devoted longtime friends in New York sent a magnificent pall of 300 pink camellias. It served as a beautiful cover for the simple oak coffin at the church service, but was replaced by Val's spray of red carnations for the burial. Mrs. Moore had her daughter's grave lined with white cloth, pinned with several hundred clusters of pink roses and smilax, each cluster tied with a pink ribbon. Other members of the family added a pillow of pink roses, tulips, and gardenias.

More than four thousand mourners stood on the wintry church grounds; inside more than two thousand crowded into and around the pews. All the service was broadcast except Dorothy Kirsten's moving rendition of Schubert's "Ave Maria," during which she almost broke down. When, because of her contract, other music had to be used to fill in, radio stations all over the South were inundated with calls of protest.

In his eloquent eulogy, the Reverend Mr. Huff said: "Her golden voice has been heard by thousands in concert halls all over the world, and by millions over the radio. Wherever she has been heard, from the palace of kings to the humble cottage beside the road, human hearts have been blessed by her joyous music."[6]

Only a few friends from Jellico braved the icy roads to attend the funeral, but from the moment the news came in the town was in deep mourning. One Jellicoan said that she had never seen Jellico so upset over anything. Her phone rang almost continually all day and the next day every thirty minutes. A cross of white carnations seven feet tall was sent to Chattanooga, and that afternoon the citizens gathered at the First Baptist Church "to express to the world our love, appreciation and respect for Grace Moore, who began her career in Jellico and sang her first solo in the choir of the First Baptist Church, and who, because of her great ambition and work won the heart of the world with her beautiful voice and personality." Members from all the choirs of Jellico joined in the singing. All day bells tolled from every church steeple.

Part 7
The Magic Quality

It's wonderful to be alive. Best of all is life. I love to
live and to sing.

25 January 1947

Epilogue: The Whole World Grieved

The Lewisohn Stadium was the scene of a Grace Moore Memorial Service in June 1947, at which Dorothy Kirsten sang excerpts from *Louise*. In October a Grace Moore Memorial Exhibition was held at the Museum of the City of New York. It included a replica of the dressing room which Grace used at the Met, and many of her favorite costumes. On one Sunday afternoon alone, more than fifteen hundred people crowded into the museum to say another goodby to her.

Val spent several months going through his late wife's papers, destroying letters, and settling her estate. She left specific items of jewelry and porcelain to her mother; jewelry, furs, and other personal effects to her sister and sisters-in-law; her library to her brothers, James and Richard; and cash to Martin. Her prized set of all-white royal Denmark porcelain and her Bechstein piano were to go eventually to her niece, Grace Moore II. Mementos were to go to other relatives, friends, and employees. The engravings, lithographs, and drawings of Toulouse-Lautrec were to go to George Biddle; many had been gifts from him. The scores and souvenirs of her musical career were to be presented to the Music Department of Ward-Belmont, or to whomever her brother, James, and her husband might designate. She asked her survivors to aid in helping worthy young Americans of outstanding talent as "a gesture of my gratitude for all the blessings and beauty that a voice can give the possessor, as well as a contribution to civilization in general."

The bulk of her estate, estimated at more than half a million dollars, was left to her husband, with her sister, two brothers, and niece as residuary legatees. When the will was probated, the judge

279

ruled out her penciled notations; nevertheless, the widower advised her family and friends that her wishes would be carried out to the letter. On 28 August 1948, he asked the Superior Court in Bridgeport for a ruling on six parts of her will so the estate could be settled and succession and federal taxes paid. While there was no dispute involved, there was much sadness and some hard feelings. Apparently there still are. All the stock that Grace had bought in Loveman's, Inc., with dividends assigned to her sister, was eventually purchased from the widower by members of the family.

Although Grace's grieving friends hoped he would give or sell to them as keepsakes some of the items in the Savoy Plaza apartment, at Casa Lauretta, or at Far Away Meadows, he refused. He sent a few pictures, records, scrapbooks, and furnishings to Jim, gave a few things to others, including a Brazilian-silver letter knife engraved "from Gracila to Valito," which he gave to Francis Robinson. He turned three wigs over to Robinson to give to promising stars, and gave the pretty vicuña rug, now lined and monogramed, to Dalrymple and the "old dog" to Coleman. To pay the stiff inheritance tax, he sold the farm and everything in the home for a fraction of its worth—to Ruth Gordon and Garson Kanin.

After disposing of Casa Lauretta and everything there and undergoing a successful ulcer operation in Paris he married Anne Vanderwalk (who had been acting as his secretary) and brought his bride to the States. Although Grace's friends tried, they could not be genuinely gracious to the couple. To sit across a dinner table from a twenty-years-younger Mrs. Valentin Parera, wearing the diamonds and emeralds Grace had loved and worn with such dash and joy, was too painful. Following this, Val evidently broke off all contact with the Moores and with the United States and took his Dutch bride to Madrid, where they have lived ever since in a fashionable neighborhood. Many letters from this side of the ocean were never answered—if they were received.

During Mrs. Moore's long terminal illness, one leg had to be amputated. She spent her days rereading Grace's letters, destroying them, and carefully pasting the hundreds of eloquent messages of condolence she had received in the last of many scrapbooks. Whether they came from castles, great opera houses, or humble mountain cabins, they filled her heart with pride and gave her something to do after she could no longer move about and tend her garden. She read them so many times she could repeat many of them word for word:

"Thank you for having given her to us; the whole world grieves."

"She reached the heights and pinnacles that every girl dreams about but cannot attain."

"To listen to her golden voice was to feel strengthened."

"My world collapsed. I shall never listen to anyone else sing."

"She was my inspiration. I loved her with all my heart."

"She was one of the great women of our time."

One of the most eloquent of the letters of condolence was written by Emily Coleman:

"I wanted to write to you last week, but it took all I had to keep going. Grace influenced my own growth and career so profoundly that I find it impossible to think of going on without her. But how much we have to remember and be grateful for! Useless words, I know only too well myself, but we who loved her must cling to something, and those memories are rich and full. Nor do we grieve alone; in this the whole world shares our sorrow."[1]

Mrs. Moore died in July 1950, and was buried beside her husband. The bodies of the children who died in Jellico were moved to Forest Hills Cemetery. Jim and Martin are gone, too. Jim's daughter, Grace Elizabeth Moore II, grew up to be a lovely young woman with beauty, talent, and great promise. In 1960 her life, and others, was snuffed out in an automobile accident, somewhere between her school, Briarcliff Manor, and Chapel Hill, where she had gone with a group of friends to attend the dances of the University of North Carolina.

Although Grace Moore's voice was acknowledged by many critics to be the warmest in the lyric-soprano world, and she was the widest known, the most feared, the most hated, and the most loved opera star of her era, some of her severest critics still castigate her for not working harder, for not setting out with grim determination and a one-track mind to scale the heights and live thereafter in the rarefied atmosphere of the great.

Grace had a multitrack mind—and heart. Her definition of the heights, of greatness, was quite different from theirs. She could have reached that rarest of pinnacles if she had dreamed that dream. To ascend any higher would have meant grim dedication to one world, wholesale sacrifices, few friends, and a loveless, funless life-style. She felt sorry for prima donnas who made great sacrifices to reach perfection only to find, when their voices faded, that they had missed out on many of the loves, excitements, and joys of all the other worlds.

"To be made to think in a new and generous way," wrote Lafcadio Hearn, "certain giants must never be judged by their errors but by their strengths."[2]

Grace had magnificent courage, scope, ambition, energy, tenacity, audacity, and eagerness. With these strengths she managed to keep her nightingale soaring on out-stretched wings despite limitations, temptations, and dark forces in her character that constantly demanded first place. The eager striking of the steel of purpose against the flint of obstacle generated the sparks, the power, that propelled her to the top in so many worlds. This was the pattern and the victory of her life.

Eagerness was her greatest strength, her magic ingredient. Eagerness made her tick, touched her heart with fire, her throat with gold. Eagerness to the point of obsession—to be free, to love and be loved, to prove herself, to stretch herself beyond all limitations, to experience, possess and achieve *everything*. Eagerness also to give everything back in overflowing measure, to touch every heart, and to express to everyone everywhere the beauty and ecstasy she found in the many worlds she loved so passionately—in radiant song.

Appendix: Metropolitan Opera Appearances, 1928–1946

Opera and Role	Number of Performances	
	In New York	Outside New York
L'Amore dei Tre Re (Fiora)	3	1
La Boheme (Mimi)	17	6
Carmen (Micaela)	3	2
Contes d'Hoffmann (Giulietta)	2	2
Faust (Marguerite)	2	1
Gianni Schicchi (Lauretta)	2	0
Louise (Louise)	14	5
Manon (Manon)	9	5
Romeo et Juliette (Juliette	7	1
Tosca (Tosca)	13	2
Totals	72	25

Adding to her ninety-seven appearances with the Met, Grace Moore performed many times with the Chicago Opera, one season with the Cincinnati Summer Opera, and with the San Antonio and San Francisco Operas. Her European and South American engagements are noted in the text.

Mrs. John Dewitt Peltz compiled the list above, when she was archivist for the Metropolitan Opera Association. James H. Siler and Bill Park also contributed much helpful data. (For details on performances - places, dates, casts and conductors - refer to Metropolitan Opera Annals by William H. Seltsman, and Opera Caravan by Quaintance Eaton.)

Grace Moore Discography

GRACE MOORE DISCOGRAPHY

The portion of the discography devoted to Grace Moore's commercially recorded discs is listed by company, in the general order that she made them - except that all Victor electrical recordings are listed together in Part V.

Part I details her first recordings made for Victor by the acoustical process. Part II gives the available information on those recordings she made for the Brunswick-Balke-Collender Company. Part III covers the two selections she made for the Brunswick Record Corporation.

Part IV lists those recordings made for Decca - not for Brunswick, as previously thought. The two Brunswick sides (items 10 and 11 in the discography) later became the property of Columbia. Part V catalogs the third and final phase of her recording career: the electrical recordings she made for Victor. Part VI details commercial discs taken from film sound tracks or radio broadcasts. (Broadcast dates printed on record labels are often incomplete or totally incorrect. Where possible, correct data are shown for these selections.) Part VII is a listing of privately issued recordings.

For each discography number in Parts I through V, you will first find the title of the selection, followed by the name of the composer, an initial for the language in which the selection is sung, and the type of accompaniment with the name of the conductor or pianist where known. (Or. denotes that the selection is accompanied by an orchestra; Pf. indicates the selection is sung with piano accompaniment.)

The numbers in column 1 on the line immediately below the title of the recording list the matrix and take numbers. For the Victor recordings, the published take number is underlined. Column 2 carries the recording dates for the takes shown in the first column. Column 3 lists the original 78-rpm catalog numbers; column 4 lists the 45-rpm catalog numbers, and column 5 lists the long playing 33 1/3-rpm catalog numbers. The unpublished numbers were actually recorded but, for any one of several reasons, were not released.

Appreciation is expressed for the information and assistance given by the following: RCA Archives, Bernadette Moore; CBS Archives, Martine McCarthy; MCA Records; and to William Collins; Louis Harrison; William Violi; Mike Polimeni; and Stephen Jabloner.

Athens, Texas   BILL PARK
10 September 1981

GRACE MOORE'S RECORDINGS

Part I: Victor (Acoustic)

1. Tell Me a Bedtime Story - MUSIC BOX REVUE, 1923 (Berlin)(E)(Pf. Moore)
    B---   27 Sept. 1923   Unpublished Test Record

2. Orange Grove in California, An - MUSIC BOX REVUE, 1923 (Berlin)(E)(Pf. Moore)
    B---   27 Sept. 1923   Unpublished Test Record

3. Tell Her in the Springtime - MUSIC BOX REVUE, 1925 (Berlin)(E)   (Or. Bourdon)
    B-31661 -1, 2, 3   19 Jan. 1925   Unpublished   *(Or. Shilkret)
             -4, 5, 6   30 Jan. 1925   Unpublished
             -7, 8, 9, 10*   26 Feb. 1925   19613   -   JJA 19744

4. Listening - MUSIC BOX REVUE, 1925 (Berlin)(E)   (Or. Bourdon; *Shilkret)
    B-31662 -1, 2, 3   19 Jan. 1925   Unpublished
             -4, 5, 6   30 Jan. 1925   Unpublished
             -7, 8, 9*   26 Feb. 1925   19613   -   JJA 19744

5. Rockabye Baby - MUSIC BOX REVUE, 1925 (Berlin)(E)   (Or. Bourdon; *Shilkret)
    B-31663 -1, 2, 3   19 Jan. 1925   Unpublished
             -4, 5, 6   30 Jan. 1925   19668   -   JJA 19744
             -7, 8*   2 Mar. 1925   Unpublished

Part II: Brunswick-Balke-Collender Company

6. LA BOHÈME: Mi chiamano Mimi (Puccini)(I)(Or.)
    Matrix/Take ?   1928   50140A   -   T334
                                              0129 (Eng.)   -   RHA 6018

7. LA BOHÈME: Donde lieta (Addio)(Puccini)(I)(Or.)
    Matrix/Take ?   1928   50140B   -   T334
                                              0129 (Eng.)   -   RHA 6018

8. By the Bend of the River (Edwards)(E)(Or.)
    Matrix/Take ?   1928   15186   -   T334
                                                                -     RHA 6018

9. Pour toi (For You)(Goodman)(F, E)(Or.)
    Matrix/Take ?   1928   15186   -   T334
                                              10277   -   RHA 6018

Part III: Brunswick Record Corporation

10. Ciribiribin (Pestalozza) w. Met. Male Chorus (I)(Or. Pelletier)
    B-16101-A   4 Oct. 1934   6994   -   -
                              (Col.)   35969   -   -
                              (Eng. Col.)   DB 1801   -   -

11. One Night of Love (Kahn-Schertzinger) w. Met. Male Chorus (E)(Or. Pelletier)
    B-16102-A   4 Oct. 1934   6994   -   -
                              (Col.)   35969   -   -
                              (Eng. Col.)   DB 1801

Part IV: Decca

12. The End Begins - THE KING STEPS OUT (Kreisler)(E)(Or. Pasternack)
     60933 B-1   25 Mar. 1936   23000 B   -   DL 9593
                                                    02233 (E. Br.)   -   -

13. Learn How to Lose - THE KING STEPS OUT (Kreisler)(E)(Or. Pasternack)
     60932 A-1   25 Mar. 1936   23001 B   -   DL 9593
                                                    02234 (E. Br.)   -   -

14. Love Me Forever - LOVE ME FOREVER (Kahn-Schertzinger)(E)(Or. Pasternack)
     DLA 285-A   27 Nov. 1935   29000 B   ED 3504   DL 9593
                                                    0130 (E. Br.)   -   -

15. MADAMA BUTTERFLY: Un bel di vedremo (Puccini)(I)(Or. Pasternack)
     DLA 284-C   27 Nov. 1935   29000 A   ED 3504   DL 9593
                                                    0130 (E. Br.)   -   -

16. Our Song - WHEN YOU'RE IN LOVE (Kern)(E)(Or. Young)
     DLA 686 A   10 Feb. 1937   23023 A   -   DL 9593
                                                    02400 (E. Br.)   -   -

17. Serenade (Standchen)(Schubert)(E)(Or. Smallens)
     62119 A   8 Apr. 1937   29010 B   ED 3504   DL 9593
                                                    0136 (E. Br.)   -   -

18. Stars in My Eyes - THE KING STEPS OUT (Kreisler)(E)(Or. Pasternack)
     60921 B   23 Mar. 1936   23001 A   -   DL 9593
                                                    022234 (E. Br.)   -   -

19. TOSCA: Vissi d'arte (Puccini)(I)(Or. Smallens)
     62118 A   8 Apr. 1937   29010 A   ED 3504   DL 9593
                                                    0136 (E. Br.)   -   -

20. What Shall Remain - THE KING STEPS OUT (Kreisler)(E)(Or. Pasternack)
     60920 A   23 Mar. 1936   23000   -   DL 9593
                                                    02233 (E. Br.)   -   -

21. Whistling Boy, The - WHEN YOU'RE IN LOVE (Kern)(E)(Or. Young)
     DLA 687 B   10 Feb. 1937   23023 B   -   DL 9593
                                                    02400 (E. Br.)   -   -

Part V: Victor (Electrical)

     (Note: VIC 1216 was produced in England.)

22. L'Absence - Les Nuits d'Ete. Op. 7 (Berlioz)(F)(Or. Pelletier)
     CS 056451-1   7 Oct. 1940   Unpublished

23. Always (Berlin)(E)(Or. Pilzer)
     D5-RB-94 -1, 1A, 2, 2A   10 Feb. 1945   10-117A   WCT 7004   CAL 519
                                                    -                 449-0167A VIC 1216
                                                    -                 17-0186A   LCT 7004

24. LA BOHÈME: Mi chiamano Mimi (Puccini)(I)(Or. Pelletier)
     CS-047051 -1, 1A, 2, 2A   12 Feb. 1940   17189A   WCT 7004   LCT 7004
                                                    -                 449-01668B -

25. Canto Andalus (Nin)(S)(Pf. Van Grove)
    CS-075218 -1, 1A   20 May 1942   Unpublished

26. Ciribiribin (Pestalozza) w. Chorus (I)(Or. Pilzer)
    D5 RB 97 -1, 1A   10 Feb. 1945   10-1152A   WCT 7005 CAL 519
                                                     -          449-0165A VIC 1216
                                                     -          17-0185A LM 6088
                                                     -             -   LCT 7005

27. Danny Boy (Adapted by Weatherly)(E)(Pf. Van Grove)
    CS-075213 -1, 1A   20 May 1942   Unpublished
               -2, 2A   6 July 1942   Unpublished

28. Dubarry, The - DUBARRY (Millöcker)(E)(Or. Shilkret)
    BS 74709 -1, 2   19 Dec. 1932   1614B   -   CAL 519
                                                  HMV DA 1309   ⌐   VIC 1216
                                                     -             -   JJA 19779

29. Forgotten (Cowles)(E)(Pf. Van Grove)
    CS-075212 -1, 1A   20 May 1942   Unpublished
               -2, 2A, 3, 3A   6 July 1942   Unpublished

30. HÉRODIADE: Il est doux, il est bon (Massenet)(F)(Or. Pelletier)
    CS-075262 -1, 2   5 June 1942   11-8258B   -   CAL 519
                                                  (M918)   -   VIC 1216

31. I Give My Heart - DUBARRY (Millöcker)(E)(Or. Shilkret)
    BS-74708 -1, 2   19 Dec. 1932   1614A   -   CAL 519
                                                  HMV DA 1309   -   VIC 1216
                                                     -             -   JJA 19779

32. Last Rose of Summer, The (Moore)(E)(Pf. Van Grove)
    CS-075219 -1, 1A   20 May 1942   Unpublished

33. LOUISE: Depuis le jour (Charpentier)(F)(Or. Pelletier)
    CS-04752 -1, 2, 3, 4, 4A 12 Feb. 1940   17189B   WC 7004   LCT 7004
                                                     -          449-0165B   -

34. Ma Curly - Headed Babby (sic)(Clutsam)(E)(Pf. Van Grove)
    CS-075214 -1, 1A, 2, 2A   20 May 1942   Unpublished

35. MANON: Adieu, notre petite table (Massenet)(F)(Or. Pelletier)
    CS-056449 -1,1A,2,2A,3,3A 7 Oct. 1940   11-8259A   -   -
                                                  (M918)   -   -

36. MANON: Gavotte-Obéissons, quand leur voix appelle (Massenet)(F)(Or. Pelletier)
    CS-056450 -1, 1A, 2, 2A   7 Oct. 1940   11-8259B   -   -
                                                  (M918)   -   -

37. Old Refrain, The (Kreisler)(F)(Pf. Van Grove)
    CS-075215 -1, 1A   20 May 1942   Unpublished
               -2, 2A, 3, 3A   6 July 1942   Unpublished

38. Old Refrain, The (Kreisler)(E)(Or. Pilzer)
    D5-RB-95 -1, 1A   10 Feb. 1945   10-1152B   WCT 7004 CAL 519
                                                     -          449-0165A VIC 1216
                                                     -          17-0185B LCT 7004

```
39.  Ouvre ton coeur (Bizet)(F)(Or. Pelletier)
     CS-075263  -1, 2              5 June 1942      Unpublished

40.  Phidylé (Duparc)(F)(Pelletier)
     CS-075261  -1               5 June 1942      11-8258A          -      CAL 519
                                                  (M918)            -      VIC 1216

41.  Psyche (Paladilhe)(F)(Or. Pelletier)
     BS-075260  -1               5 June 1942      10-1018A          -      CAL 519
                                                  (M918)            -      VIC 1216

42.  Que deviennent las roses (Paulin)(F)(Or. Pelletier)
     CS-056452  -1, 1A, 2, 2A    7 Oct. 1940      11-8158B     WCT 7004  CAL 519
                                                       -       449-0167B VIC 1216
                                                       -            -    LCT 7004

43.  Red Rosey (sic) Bush (Appalachian Folk Song)(Young)(E)(Pf. Van Grove)
     CS-075211  -1, 1A            20 May 1942      Unpublished
                -2, 2A            6 July 1942      Unpublished

44.  Si mes vers avaient des ailes!  (Hahn)(F)(Or. Pelletier)
     BS-075259  -1, 2             5 June 1942      10-1018B          -      CAL 519
                                                  (M918)            -      VIC 1216

45.  Stars in My Eyes - THE KING STEPS OUT (Kreisler)(E)(Pf. Van Grove)
     CS-075216  -1, 1A            20 May 1942      Unpublished

46.  Toi seule (Tchaikovsky)(F)(Or. Pelletier)
     CS-047053  -1, 1A            12 Feb. 1940     Unpublished

47.  Toi seule (Tchaikovsky)(F)(Or. Pelletier)
     CS-056453  -1, 1A, 2, 2A     7 Oct. 1940      11-8158A     WCT 7004  CAL 519
                                                       -       449-0167A VIC 1216
                                                       -            -    LCT 7004

48.  Valse-Opus 49, No. 5 (Arensky)(F)(Or. Pelletier)
     CS-056454  -1, 1A            7 Oct. 1940      Unpublished

49.  Valse-Opus 49, No. 5 (Arensky)(F)(Pf. Van Grove)
     CS-075217  -1, 1A            20 May 1942      Unpublished
                -2, 2A, 3, 3A     6 July 1942      Unpublished

50.  Without Your Love - DUBARRY) (Millöcker) w. Richard Crooks (E)(Or. Shilkret)
     BS-74707  -1, 2             19 Dec. 1932     1615B       WCT 7004  LCT 7004
                                                  HMV DA 1306  449-0166A JJA 19779

51.  You Are Love - SHOWBOAT (Kern) w. Chorus (E)(Or. Pilzer)
     D5-RB-96  -1, 1A            10 Feb. 1945     10-1171B     WCT 7004  CAL 519
                                                       -       449-0166A VIC 1216
                                                       -       17-0186B  LCT 7004
```

Part VI: Commercial Discs, Primarily from Film Sound Tracks and Radio Broadcasts

```
52.  LA BOHÈME:  Musetta's Waltz Song (Puccini)(I)(Or.)
     C9537-6-1 (film) - LOVE ME FOREVER                       02102A (Eng. Bruns.)

53.  Funiculi, Funicula (Denza)(I)(Or.)
     09539-6-2 (film) - LOVE ME FOREVER              -        02102B (Eng. Bruns.)
```

54. TAP334 GRACE MOORE IN OPERA AND SONG (Rhapsody Records) also RHA 6018

    a. NORMA: Casta Diva (film) A LADY'S MORALS (I)   Also EJS 171
    b. MANON: Gavotte (film)(F)
    c. LA FILLE DU REGIMENT: Chacun le sait (film) A LADY'S MORALS(F) Also EJS 171
    d. MADAMA BUTTERFLY: Bimba non piangera w. Forrest (film)(I)   Also EJS 215
    e. TOSCA: Vissi d'arte (broadcast)(I)
    f. Serenade (Schubert)(film)(E)
    g. Sibony (Lecuona)(film) WHEN YOU'RE IN LOVE (E)
    h. Russian Gypsy Ballad (film) NEW MOON (E)
    i. One Kiss (film) NEW MOON (E)
    j. Lover Come Back to Me (film) NEW MOON (E)
    k. Stars in My Eyes (film) THE KING STEPS OUT (E)
    l. The Old Refrain (film) THE KING STEPS OUT (E)
    m. I'll Take Romance (film)(E)
    n. My Gallant Soldier (film)(E)
    o. Madly in Love (film)(E)
    (Album also contains discography items 6, 7, 8, 9.)

55. STAR-TONE ST 217 GRACE MOORE - THE MEMORABLE RADIO YEARS

    a. One Night of Love (E) Broadcast 1935
    b. Ciribiribin (I) Broadcast 1940
    c. The All American Opera: It Ain't Gonna Rain Grace Moore w. J. Melton and A.
        Templeton (E) Broadcast 1945
    d. Always (E) Broadcast 1945
    e. You Are Love/Why Do I Love You - SHOWBOAT w. J. Melton (E)(Or. Goodman)
        Broadcast 26 Nov. 1944
    f. Through the Years (Younmans)(E) Broadcast 1941
    g. Joy (Cadman)(E)(Or. Voorhees) Broadcast 19 Oct. 1942
    h. None but the Lonely Heart (Tchaikovsky)(E)(Or. Voorhees) Radio 23 Aug. 1943
    i. The Bells of St. Mary's (Furber-Adams)(E) Broadcast 1943
    j. Thine Alone - EILEEN (E) Broadcast 1936
    k. LOUISE: Depuis le jour (F) Broadcast 1937
    l. LA BOHÈME: Mi chiamano Mimi (I)(Or. Voohees) Broadcast 7 Sept. 1942

56. PELICAN RECORDS LP 2020 - NEW MOON - Sound track, Grace Moore's selections are:

    a. Farmer's Daughter (m. by Herbert Stothart)(Same as item 54-h)
    b. Wanting You w. Tibbett
    c. One Kiss (Same as item 54-i)
    d. Dialogue (spoken) w. Tibbett
    e. Lover Come Back to Me (Same as item 54-j)
    f. Lover Come Back to Me/Finale w. Tibbett, Young, Menjou
    (Above musical selections and some dialogue also on Raviola BMPB 1929 -
    Parisian Belle)

57. GRAPHON 15 - ONE NIGHT OF LOVE - Sound track

    a. LA TRAVIATA: Sempre libera (I)
    b. LUCIA: Chi mi frena
    c. Ciribiribin (I)
    d. CARMEN: Habanera (F)
    e. MADAMA BUTTERFLY: Ancora un passo (I)
    f. MADAMA BUTTERFLY: Un bel di vedremo (I)
    Some of the above selections have introductory dialogue. Album also contains
    discography items 55-h and 59-1.)

58. LP-801 EMPIRE RECORDS PRESENTS GRACE MOORE
   This album contains discography items numbered:
   10, 11, 17, 19, 23, 33, 37, 45, 51, 56-c, 56-e, and 59-m.

59. MDP-027 GRACE MOORE - LIVE! LP (Mono)(MDP Collector' Limited Edition)

   a. Will You Remember - MAYTIME w. Bentonelli (E) Broadcast 1936
   b. ROMÉO ET JULIETTE: Non, ce n'est par le jour w. Tauber (F)(Or. Rapee)
       Broadcase 24 Oct. 1937
   c. LOUISE: Depuis le jour (F)(Or. Rapee) Broadcast 24 Oct. 1937
   d. MANON: Gavotte (F)(Or. Rapee) Broadcast 24 Oct. 1937
   e. PAGLIACCI: Ballatella (I)(Or. Rapee) Broadcast 24 Oct. 1937
   f. MADAMA BUTTERFLY: Un bel di vedremo (I)(Or. Rapee) Broadcast 7 Nov. 1937
   g. TOSCA: Vissi d'arte (I)(Or. Rapee) Broadcast 7 Nov. 1937
   h. Who Will Buy My Lavender (German)(E)(Or. Rapee) Broadcast 24 Oct. 1937
   i. Serenade (Schubert) w. Tauber (E)(Or. Rapee) Broadcast 24 Oct. 1937
   j. Ouvre ton coeur (F)(Or. Kostelanetz) Broadcast 1938
   k. Ciribirin (I) (Or. Voorhees) Broadcast 19) Oct. 1942.
   l. Indian Love Call - ROSE MARIE (E)(Or. Voorhees) Broadcast 25 Oct. 1943.
   m. I'll Take Romance (E)(Or. Voorhees) 31 May 1943
       (Also on Star-Tone ST 211 OPERA GOES TO HOLLYWOOD)
       (Album also contains discography items 55-h and 55-l.)

60. MDP-019 JOSEPH SCHMIDT - LIVE PERFORMANCE. Grace Moore selections included:

   a. LA BOHÈME: Mi chiamano Mimi (I)(Or. Rapee) Broadcast 7 Nov. 1937
   b. LA BOHÈME: O soave fanciulla w. Schmidt (I)(Or. Rapee) Same date
   c. MADAMA BUTTERFLY: Bemba non piangera w. Schmidt (I)(Or. Rapee) Same date

Part VII: Private Releases

61. L'AMORE DEI TRE RE (complete opera) w. Kullman, Pinza, Bonelli (I)
   (Or. Montezzi) 15 Feb. 1941, Metropolitan Opera   EJS 112   ME 102-2 (E.)

62. LA BOHÈME (excerpts) w. Landi, Pinza, Tagliabue (I)(Or. Papi)
   15 Jan. 1938, Metropolitan Opera   EJS 509

63. LA BOHÈME: Act 3, w. Jagel, Valentino (I)(Or. Sadero)
   12 Dec. 1942, Metropolitan Opera   EJS 220

64. LOUISE (excerpts from film) w. Thill and Pernet (F)('39) EJS 456A
   Disc also contains:

   a. MADAMA BUTTERFLY: Un bel di vedremo (I)(Or. Mengleberg) Broadcast Amsterdam,
       June 1936
   b. Ciribiribin (I) Broadcast, Amsterdam, June 1936

65. LOUISE (complete opera) w. Jobin, Pinza (F)(Or. Beecham)
   20 Feb. 1943, Metropolitan Opera   EJS 164   MOP-1

66. MANON (10 min. excerpts) w. Gigli, De Luca, Rothier (F)
   (Or. Hasselmans) 5 Mar. 1932, Metropolitan Opera   EJS 111B   ANNA 1032

67. MANON (complete opera) w. Crooks, Brownlee (F)
   (Or. Pelletier) 13 Jan. 1940, Metropolitan Opera   EJS 148

68. TOSCA: Act 3 w. Jagel (I)(Or. Panizza) 1 Dec. 1941, Chicago Opera   EJS 220

69. TOSCA (complete opera) w. Jagel, Sved (I)(Or. Panizza)
     7 Feb. 1942, Metropolitan Opera   UORC 214

70. TOSCA (complete opera) w. Kullman, Sved (I)(Or. Sadero)
     8 Apr. 1944, Metropolitan Opera   UORC 287

71. TOSCA (excerpts, Act 2) w. Tibbett (I)(Metropolitan Opera,
     9 Feb. 1946)   EJS 456A

72. Potpourri 6 - Contains discography items 54-a and 54-c   EJS 171

73. Potpourri 10 - TOSCA: Mario! Mario! Mario! (Act 1 duet)
     w. Kullman (I) 8 Apr. 1944, Metropolitan Opera   EJS 186

74. Potpourri 13 - Contains discography item 54-d   EJS 215

75. Potpourri 17 - Contains selections from sound track of
     ONE NIGHT OF LOVE: discography items 57-a, b, c, d, e, f;
     plus "Last Rose of Summer" (E)   EJS 263

76. Potpourri 20 - Contains discography items 59-c, d, e, f, g, h;
     60-a, b, c   EJS 418

77. Richard Tauber - Contains discography items 59-b and 59-i   EJS 440

Titles of Album Collections

Titles of album collections numbered in Parts I through V of this discography are:

M918 (Victor) SONGS AND OPERA ARIAS (78-rpm)
DA 165 (Decca) GRACE MOORE, SOUVENIR ALBUM (One 10, and two 12-in. 78-rpm
    records) 1940
DL 9593 (Decca) GRACE MOORE SINGS. Also issued as ED 3504 (Decca)
LCT 7004 (Victor) & WCT 7004 (Victor) GRACE MOORE IN OPERA AND SONG
CAL (Camden) THE ART OF GRACE MOORE. Also issued as VIC 1216 (Decca, England)
T334 (TAP Records) GRACE MOORE IN OPERA AND SONG; RHA 6018 (Rhapsody Records, Eng.)
JJA-19744 (Music Master Record) IRVING BERLIN, 1909-1939
JJA-19779 (Music Master Record) THE MUSIC OF BROADWAY, 1932.

Notes

Chapter 2

1. Grace Moore, *You're Only Human Once* (New York: Doubleday, 1944), p. 19 (hereinafter to be referred to as *YOHO*).

Chapter 4

1. Moore, *YOHO, p. 26.*
2. *Ibid., p. 30.*

Chapter 5

1. Arthur Mizener, Book Review of *Zelda,* Nancy Milford, *Life,* 1970.
2. Grace Moore, "Life Has Been Exciting," *Woman's Home Companion,* July 1936, p. 8.
3. Moore, *YOHO,* p. 38.
4. Ibid., p. 39.
5. Romain Rolland, *Jean Christophe,* trans. Gilbert Cannon (New York: Henry Holt, 1927), p. 83.
6. André Maurois, "My Debt to Romain Rolland," *Saturday Review,* 16 December 1967.
7. Moore, *YOHO,* p. 41.
8. Ibid, p. 50.

Chapter 6

1. Moore, *YOHO,* p. 52.
2. Walter H. Pater, *The Renaissance* (New York: Random, Modern Library, 1919), p. 197.
3. Moore, *YOHO,* p. 61.
4. *Baltimore Evening Star,* September 1921.
5. Franklin P. Adams, "The Conning Tower," *New York World,* 16 December 1922.
6. Ibid., 9 January 1923.
7. Grace Moore, "Life Has Been Exciting," *Woman's Home Companion,* July 1936, p. 9.

Chapter 7

1. Cole, Lesley, *Remembered Laughter* (New York: Knopf, 1976), p. 238.
2. Moore, *YOHO,* p. 73.
3. James Huneker, *Bedouins* (New York: AMS Press, 1920), p. 10.
4. Ibid., p. 17.
5. Unsigned, combined edition representing *New York Herald, Journal of Commerce,*

New York Daily News, New York Morning Telegraph, New York Times, New York Tribune, New York World, 24 September 1923.

    6. Alexander Woollcott, *New York Times,* 28 September 1923.

    7. James Craig, *New York Evening Mail,* 28 September 1923.

    8. Moore, *YOHO,* p. 88.

Chapter 8

    1. Mary Jane Matz, *The Many Lives of Otto Kahn* (New York: Macmillan, 1963), p. 89.

    2. Moore, *YOHO,* p. 92.

Chapter 9

    1. Moore, *YOHO,* p. 111.

    2. Ibid., p. 114.

    3. Ibid., p. 110.

Chapter 10

    1. Samuel Chotzinoff, *New York World,* 8 February 1928.

    2. Leonard Liebling, *New York American,* 8 February 1928.

    3. W. J. Henderson, *New York Sun,* 8 February 1928.

    4. Olin Downes, *New York Times,* 8 February 1928.

Chapter 11

    1. Moore, *YOHO,* p. 146.

    2. Ibid., p. 146.

    3. Ibid., p. 150.

    4. Ibid., p. 150.

    5. Ibid., p. 148.

Chapter 13

    1. Moore, *YOHO,* p. 181.

Chapter 14

    1. Nancy Milford, *Zelda* (New York: Harper and Row, 1970), p. 317.

    2. Constance Hope, *Publicity Is Broccoli* (Indianapolis, Ind.: Bobbs-Merrill, 1941).

Chapter 15

    1. Moore, *YOHO,* p. 201.

    2. Grace Moore, "Life Has Been Exciting," *(Woman's Home Companion),* August 1936, p. 68.

    3. Glenn Dillard Gunn, *Chicago Herald Examiner,* 10 December 1934.

Chapter 16

    1. Moore, *YOHO,* p. 208.

    2. Ibid., p. 209.

Chapter 18

    1. Bob Thomas, *King Cohn, The Life and Times of Harry Cohn* (New York: Putnam, 1967). See page opposite dedication.

2. Phoebe McDonald, "I Saw Grace Moore Make a Movie," *Chattanooga Sunday Times,* 29 November 1936.

Chapter 19
1. Moore, *YOHO,* p. 228.
2. Ibid., p. 230.
3. Ibid., p. 229.
4. Ibid., p. 228.

Chapter 20
1. Bob Thomas, *Thalberg, Life and Legend* (Garden City, N.Y.: Doubleday, 1969), p. 196.

Chapter 21
1. Olin Downes, *New York Times,* 16 January 1938.
2. Moore, *YOHO,* p. 252.
3. Ibid., p. 253.
4. Olin Downes, *New York Times,* 28 January 1939.
5. Moore, *YOHO,* pp. 256–57.

Chapter 22
1. Grace Moore, "Life Has Been Exciting," *Woman's Home Companion,* August 1936, p. 68.
2. Frederick C. Schang, *Grace Moore* (unpublished Ms, Musical Library, Lincoln Center).

Chapter 23
1. Virgil Thomson, *New York Herald Tribune,* 29 January 1941.

Chapter 24
1. Jean Dalrymple, *September Child* (New York: Dodd, 1962), p. 204.
2. Moore, *YOHO,* p. 267.
3. Dalrymple, *SC,* p. 209.
4. Virgil Thomson, "The Grace Moore Case," *New York Herald Tribune,* 22 February 1942.
5. Ibid., *Virgil Thomson* (New York: Knopf, 1966), p. 168.
6. Claudia Cassidy, *Chicago Tribune,* 6 November 1945.

Chapter 25
1. James Huneker, *Bedouins* (New York: AMS Press, 1920), p. 58.

Chapter 26
1. "Minnie," "Music and Rain," *New York Times Magazine,* 16 July 1961.
2. Jean Dalrymple, *September Child* (New York: Dodd, 1963), p. 198.

Chapter 27
1. Jean Dalrymple, *September Child* (New York: Dodd, 1962), p. 237.
2. Thomas Brahan, *Chattanooga Daily News,* 31 January 1947.

3. Chattanooga Daily Times, 28 January 1947.

4. John Rosenfield, *Dallas Morning News,* 31 January 1947.

5. A. Stenver, Directorate of Civil Aviation, Copenhagen, Denmark, to author, 3 March 1970.

6. Funeral Service Program, First Baptist Church, Chattanooga, 23 February 1947.

Epilogue

1. Emily Coleman to Mrs. Richard L. Moore, January 1947.

2. Lafcadio Hearn, *Talks to Writers* (New York: Dodd, 1927), p. 158.

Bibliography

Adler, Bill, ed. *The Wit and Wisdom of Bishop Fulton J. Sheen.* Garden City, N.Y.: Doubleday, 1968.

Aherne, Brian. *A Proper Job.* Boston: Houghton Mifflin, 1969.

Alda, Frances. *Men, Women and Tenors.* New York: AMS Press, 1937.

Auden, W. H. *The Dyer's Hand and Other Essays.* New York: Random House, 1948.

Baruch, Bernard. *My Own Story.* New York: Holt, Rinehart and Winston, 1957.

Beatty, Shirley MacLaine. *Don't Fall off the Mountain.* New York: W. W. Norton, 1970.

De Beauvoir, Simone. *The Prime of Life.* New York: Harper and Row, 1962.

Belasco, David. *Theatre through its Stage Door.* New York: Arno, 1919.

Bennett, Joan, and Kibbie, Lois. *The Bennett Playbill.* New York: Holt, Rinehart and Winston, 1970.

Biddle, George. *Artist at War.* New York: Viking Press, 1944.

————. *The American Artist's Story.* Boston: Little, Brown and Co., 1939.

Bowen, Catherine Drinker. *Beloved Friend.* New York: Random House, 1937.

Briggs, John. *Requiem for a Yellow Brick Brewery.* Boston: Little, Brown and Co., 1969.

Brown, John Mason. *The Worlds of Robert E. Sherwood.* New York: Harper and Row, 1962.

Buck, Dr. Percy C. *Psychology for Musicians.* Oxford: Oxford University Press, 1944.

Buxton, Frank, and Owen, Bill. *Radio's Golden Age.* New York: Avon, 1966.

Cather, Willa. *The Song of the Lark.* Boston: Houghton Mifflin, 1915.

Chase, Ilka. *Past Imperfect*. Garden City, N.Y.: Doubleday, 1942.

Cornell, Katharine. *I Wanted to Be an Actress*. As Told to Ruth Woodbury Sedgewick. New York: Random House, 1938.

Coward, Noel. *A Talent to Amuse*. Garden City, N.Y.: Doubleday, 1969.

Crowther, Bosley. *Hollywood Rajah: The Life and Times of Louis B. Mayer*. New York: Holt, 1960.

Cushing, Mary Watkins. *The Rainbow Bridge*. New York: Arno, 1965.

Dalrymple, Jean. *September Child*. New York: Dodd, 1963.

Davenport, Marcia. *Too Strong for Fantasy*. New York: Scribner, 1967.

Day, Beth. *This Was Hollywood*. Garden City, N.Y.: Doubleday, 1960.

Dodge, Raymond, and Kohn, Eugene. *The Craving for Superiority*. New Haven, Conn.: Yale University Press, 1931.

Dykeman, Wilma. *The French Broad*. Knoxville: University of Tennessee Press, 1955.

Eaton, Quaintance. *Opera Production: A Handbook*. New York: Da Capo, 1961.

———. *The Miracle of the Met*. Westport, Conn.: Greenwood, 1968.

Edwards, H. Sutherland. *The Prima Donna: Her History from the Seventeenth to Nineteenth Centuries*. 2 vols. New York: Da Capo, 1888.

Ewen, David. *George Gershwin: His Journey to Greatness*. Englewood Cliffs, N.J.: Prentice-Hall, 1970.

———. *The Story of America's Musical Theatre*. Philadelphia: Chilton, 1968.

Ewing, David. *The Story of Irving Berlin*. New York: Holt, 1950.

Farrar, Geraldine. *Such Sweet Compulsion*. New York: Arno, 1938.

Fitzgerald, Gerald; Freeman, John W.; Merkling, Frank; and Salin, Arthur. *The Golden Horseshoe*. New York: Viking Press, 1965.

Finck, H. T. *My Adventures in the Golden Age of Music*. New York: Arno, 1926.

Freel, Margaret Walker. *Our Heritage: The People of Cherokee County, N.C.* Asheville, N.C.: Miller Printing Co., 1956.

Friedan, Betty. *The Feminine Mystique*. New York: W. W. Norton, 1963.

Friendly, Fred W. *Due to Circumstances beyond My Control*. New York: Random House, 1967.

Gallo, Fortune T. *Lucky Rooster: The Autobiography of an Impresario*. New York: Exposition, 1967.

Garden, Mary, and Bioncalle, Louis. *Mary Garden's Story*. New York: Simon and Schuster, 1951.

Gerber, Aime, and Highbut, Rose. *Backstage at the Opera*. New York: Arno, 1937.

Goldovsky, Boris. *Bringing Opera to Life*. Englewood Cliffs, N.J.: Prentice-Hall, 1968.

Goodman, Ezra. *The Fifty Year Decline and Fall of Hollywood*. New York: Simon and Schuster, 1961.

Gould, Jean. *The Poet and Her Book: A Biography of Edna St. Vincent Millay*. New York: Dodd, 1969.

Graham, Sheilah, and Frank, Gerold. *Beloved Infidel*. New York: Holt, 1958.

Gatti-Casazza, Giulio. *Memories of the Opera*. New York: Vienna House, 1941.

Gutman, Robert W. *Richard Wagner: The Man, His Mind and His Music*. New York: Harcourt, Brace and World, 1968.

Hale, Nancy. *Mary Cassatt*. Garden City, N.Y.: Doubleday, 1975.

Hayes, Helen. *A Gift of Joy*. Philadelphia: Lippincott, 1965.

Harriman, Margaret Core. *The Vicious Circle*. New York: Rinehart, 1951.

Henderson, W. J. *The Art of Singing*. New York: Da Capo, 1906.

Hope, Constance. *Publicity Is Broccoli*. Indianapolis, Ind.: Bobbs-Merrill, 1941.

Hopper, Hedda. *The Whole Truth and Nothing but the Truth*. Garden City, N.Y.: Doubleday, 1963.

Huneker, James. *Bedouins*. New York: AMS Press, 1920.

Jacobs, Lewis. *The Rise of the American Film*. New York: Teachers College Press, 1939.

Johnson, Guy B., and Odum, Harold W. *The Negro and His Songs*. Halboro, Pa.; Folklore Associates, Inc., 1964.

Kanin, Garson. *Hollywood*. New York: Viking Press, 1967.

Katov, Norman. *The Fabulous Fanny*. New York: Knopf, 1952.

Keats, John. *You Might as Well Live: The Life and Times of Dorothy Parker*. New York: Simon and Schuster, 1970.

Kellner, Bruce. *Carl Van Vechten and the Irreverent Decades*. Norman: University of Oklahoma Press, 1968.

Klein, Joseph, and Schjeide, Ole A. *Singing Technique*. Princeton, N.J.: Van Nostrand, 1967.

Kolodin, Irving. *The Metropolitan Opera*. New York: Knopf, 1940.

Lesley, Cole. *Remembered Laughter*. New York: Knopf, 1976.

Likeness, George C. *The Oscar People*. Mendola, Ill.: Wayside, 1966.

Loos, Anita. *A Girl like I.* New York: Viking Press, 1966.

Lyons, Eugene. *David Sarnoff.* New York: Harper and Row, 1966.

Marafioti, Dr. P. Mario. *Caruso Method of Voice Production.* New York: D. Appleton, 1922.

Marafioti, Dr. P. Mario. *The New Vocal Art.* New York: Boni and Liveright, 1925.

Martin, Ralph G. *Jennie: The Life of Lady Randolph Churchill.* Englewood Cliffs, N.J.: Prentice-Hall, 1969.

Mason, Daniel Gregory. *The Dilemma of American Music.* New York: Macmillan, 1929.

Mattfeld, Julius. *Variety Music Cavalcade.* Englewood Cliffs, N.J.: Prentice-Hall, 1952.

Matz, Mary Jane. *Opera, Grand and Not So Grand.* New York: Morrow, 1966.

Matz, Mary Jane. *The Many Lives of Otto Kahn.* New York: Macmillan, 1963.

Maxwell, Elsa. *The Celebrity Circus.* New York: Appleton-Century, 1963.

Meredith, Scott. *George S. Kaufman and His Friends.* Garden City, N.Y.: Doubleday, 1974.

Michener, James A. *Iberia.* New York: Random House, 1968.

Milford, Nancy. *Zelda: A Biography.* New York: Harper and Row, 1970.

Moore, Grace. *You're Only Human Once.* New York: Arno, 1944.

O'Connell, Charles. *The Other Side of the Record.* Westport, Conn.: Greenwood, 1947.

Odell, Ruth Webb. *Over the Misty Blue Hills.* Nashville, Tenn.: By the author, 1951.

Overstreet, Bonaro, and Overstreet, Harry. *The Mind Goes Forth.* New York: W. W. Norton, 1956.

Pater, Walter H. *The Renaissance.* New York: Random, Modern Library, 1919.

Rasponi, Lanfranco. *The International Nomads.* New York: Putnam's, 1966.

———. *The Golden Oasis.* New York: Putnam's, 1968.

Robinson, Francis. *Caruso: His Life in Pictures.* New York: Studio Publications, 1957.

Rolland, Romain. *Jean Christophe.* Translated by Carmin Gilbert. New York: Henry Holt, 1927.

Rosenthal, Harold D. *Two Centuries of Opera at Covent Garden.* St. Clair Shores, Minn.: Scholarly, 1958.

Sablosky, Irving L. *American Music.* Chicago: University of Chicago Press, 1969.

Sanford, Nevitt. *Self and Society.* New York: Atherton Press, 1966.

Scott, Anne. *The American Woman, Who Was She?* Englewood Cliffs, N.J.: Prentice-Hall, 1971.

Seashore, Carl E. *Psychology of Music.* New York: McGraw, 1938.

Shaw, George B. *Shaw: An Autobiography.* New York: Weybright, 1969.

Shipman, David. *The Great Movie Stars.* New York: St. Martin's, 1952.

Shirer, William. *Twentieth Century Journey.* New York: Simon and Schuster, 1976.

Skinner, Cornelia Otis. *Madame Sarah.* Boston: Houghton Mifflin, 1966.

Stone, Irving. *The Passions of the Mind.* Garden City, N.Y.: Doubleday, 1971.

Stowe, Leland. *While Time Remains.* New York: Knopf, 1946.

Taubman, Howard. *Music for My Beat.* Westport, Conn.: Greenwood, 1943.

Talese, Gay. *The Kingdom and the Power.* Garden City, N.Y.: Doubleday, 1966.

Thomas, Bob. *King Cohn: The Life and Times of Harry Cohn.* New York: Putnam, 1967.

Thomas, Bob. *Thalberg, Life and Legend.* Garden City, N.Y.: Doubleday, 1969.

Thompson, Oscar. *The American Singer.* New York: Johnson Reprints, 1937.

Thomson, Virgil. *Virgil Thomson.* New York: Da Capo, 1966.

Time-Life, Inc. *This Fabulous Century.* Vols. I to VI. Boston: Time-Life, 1969–71.

Walter, Bruno. *Theme and Variation.* New York: Knopf, 1946.

Warner, Jack Leonard. *My First Hundred Years in Hollywood.* New York: Random House, 1965.

Weinberg, Herman. *The Lubitsch Touch.* New York: Dutton, 1968.

All available Grace Moore papers.

The American Musician, The Etude, Good Housekeeping, Ladies' Home Journal, McCall's, The Musical Courier, Newsweek, The New Yorker, Opera News, Psychology Today, Radio Guide, Reader's Digest, Stereo Review, Vanity Fair, Variety, Vogue, Woman's Home Companion (all issues of these magazines published between 1898 and 1947). Also clippings from dozens of newspapers published in the United States and several foreign countries during the first half of the twentieth century, from the *Jellico Journal* to the *New York Times.*

Index

Aber, Myrtle, 156
Academy of Music (Philadelphia), 131, 132
Adams, Franklin P. (F.P.A.), 81, 82
Alda, Frances, 130
Algonquin Round Table, 81, 82
American Embassy, Buenos Aires, 240
Amsterdam, Holland, 74, 193, 267, 268, 272
Anderson, John Murray, 96
Antibes (French Riviera), 102–4, 138
Aranda, Dr. Oswaldo (Brazil), 239
Arlen, Michael, and wife, 149
Armour, Ambassador Norman, and wife, 240
Armstrong, Zella (music critic), 114
Arnstein, Nicky and Fanny Brice, 96
Arrowhead Springs, Calif., 139
Askin, Rena (G. M. secretary), 198
Atkinson, Brooks (music critic), 153
Atlanta (Ga.) *Constitution*, 36, 156, 274
Austria, 212, 265

Baker, Edythe (pianist), 79
Baltimore (Md.) *Evening Star*, 79
Balsom, Col. and Mrs. Jacques (Consuelo Vanderbilt), 188
Bamboscheck, Giuseppe, 105, 109
Bampton, Rose, 153, 162
Bankers Club (New York City), 109
Baragwanath, Jack, 89. See McMein, Neysa
Barry, Philip, 269
Bathelmess, Richard, and wife, 156, 167
Barthelemy, Richard, 101, 102, 104
Baruch, Bernard, 80
Bass, Warner (pianist), 254

Beaulieu, France, 101, 104
Beecham, Sir Thomas, 169
Belasco, David, 66, 114
Belgian Order of Leopold, 213
Bellezza, Maestro, 111, 112, 169
Bellini, Vincenzo, 139
Benchley, Robert, 80, 81, 90, 92
Berlin, Irving, 71, 81, 92, 96
Berlin, Ellin Mackay (Mrs. Irving), 98
Berliner, Constance Hope (Mrs. Milton), 145–47
Berliner, Dr. Milton, 274
Bernard (prince of the Netherlands), 228, 268
Bernstein, Eugene, 145
Beverly Hills, Calif., 166, 194, 195
Biddle, Ambassador Anthony Drexel, 190
Biddle, George, 120, 279
Bierce, Ambrose, 15
Bizet, Georges, 265
Black Cat Café, 66, 69
Bodanzky, Artur, 94, 97–98, 106, 109, 111, 114, 130
Bogard, Jane Marston (Mrs. Lawrence Tibbett), 141, 150
Bohème, La (Puccini), 104; Mimi, 120–21, 131, 169, 171, 184, 210–11, 242, 257. *See* Discography Appendix
Bologna, Italy, 269
Bonelli, Richard, 153, 162
Bori, Lucrezia, 141, 216
Brazil, 239
Brice, Fanny (Mrs. Nicky Arnstein), 96
Bridgeport, Conn., 193; *Post*, 209
Briskin, Samuel, 158
Broadmoor Hotel (Colorado Springs), 252
Brown, John Mason, 153

Brunswick Recording Co., 98, 162, 288
Butler, Frank (screenwriter), 140
Buzzi-Peccia, Arturo, 264

Caffery, Jefferson (ambassador to France), 273
Callas, Maria, 15
Calloway, Cab, 194
Calvé, Emma, 93, 98, 129, 186
Campbell, Orme, 68
Canada, 108, 203, 243; Montreal, 260; Toronto, 163; Winnipeg, 151, 234
Cannes, France, 102, 109; Grand Hotel, 218; Martinez Hotel, 148, 174; opera house, 200, 211, 219, 255, 270
Carillo, Leo, 176
Carl (prince of Sweden), 192
Carmen (Bizet), 55, 95, 283
Carminati, Tulio, 158
Carré, Albert, 104, 122
Caruso, Enrico, 54, 56, 67, 112, 127, 129
Casa Lauretta, 147, 149, 155, 189, 190, 200, 211–12, 218, 219, 222, 228, 260, 269, 280
Case, Margaret, 82, 83
Cassidy, Claudia, 243
"Casta Diva" (Bellini's Norma), 139
Castle, Irene (Mrs. Vernon), 83–84
Certificate of Merit, New York City, 257
Chapel Hill, N.C., 281
Chapman, Frank, 149
Chapman, Gladys Swarthout (Mrs. Frank), 16, 130, 149, 179, 186, 270
Charpentier, Gustave, 88, 95, 122, 212, 222, 265, 271
Chattanooga, Tenn., 107, 124, 162; parents moved to, 163, 169, 176, 185, 207, 252; visit to, 258, 269, 273–74
Chattanooga Times, 114, 115
Chatterton, Ruth, 141, 142, 143, 225
Cherbourg, France, 273
Chevalier, Maurice, 16, 160, 181
Chevalier, French Legion of Honor, 216, 256
Chicago, Ill., 81, 98; Blackstone Hotel,

101, 164, 210, 222–23, 242; Civic Opera, 54, 89, 93, 197, 243; Herald and Examiner, 164; Lyric Opera, 257; Tribune (Paris edition), 120
Chotzinoff, Pauline (Mrs. Samuel), 75
Chotzinoff, Samuel, 75, 115–16, 131, 147, 149
Christian (king of Denmark), command performances, 190
Churchill, Winston, 87, 150, 228
"Ciribiribin" (Pestalozza), 149, 158, 160, 162, 166, 193, 265
Cocke County, Tenn., 30
Coffee House Club (New York City), 83
Cohan, George M., 114; Theater, 152
Cohn, Harry, 156, 157, 159, 167, 181; threatened to sue G.M., 182; 185–88
Colbert, Claudette (Mrs. Joel Pressman), 157, 167, 178
Coleman, Emily, 104, 200, 202, 216, 225, 254, 259, 272, 280; letter of condolence, 281
Collier's Magazine, 81
Colman, Ronald, 145, 151
Columbia Pictures, 156–57, 180, 182, 185, 187, 231, 250
Concerts (selected), 117, 230, 239, 256, 260, 265
Connecticut, 207, 210, 225, 263
Contes d'Hoffmann, Les (Offenbach), 149
Copenhagen, Denmark, 190, 263, 265; Hotel Angleterre, 267, 269–70, 272; Institute of Medical Jurisprudence, 268
Cooley Plaza Hotel (Boston), 72
Countess de Montgomery (editor, Magazine Marie-Claire), 219
Covent Garden, 169, 170–71, 193
Coward, Noel, 86, 104, 149, 167, 193
Craig, James (music critic), 92
Crosby, Bing, 165
Crowninshield, Frank, 82, 83, 85
Cunard, Lady Emerald, 169, 170–71, 193, 260
Czechoslovakia, 212

Dallas, Texas, 163, 272
Dalrymple, Jean, 16, 232, 234, 236;

September Child, 239, 240, 241, 252, 264, 270, 273, 280

Daniels, Josephus, (ambassador to Mexico), and wife, 235

Danish Government Air Inspection Authority: final report on fatal crash of airplane killing 22 persons, including G.M., 272. *See also* Douglas DC-3 "Dakota"

Davis, Norman H. (State Department), 109

Deauville, France, 120, 260

Debussy, Claude, 119, 265

Del Rio, Tenn., 27, 29, 39, 40, 163, 274

De Luca, Giuseppe, 127

"Depuis le jour" *(Louise),* 89, 105, 125, 216

Dernow, Jens (impresario-producer), 267

Detroit, Mich.: *Up in the Clouds,* 80; "Ford Sunday Evening Hour," 163

Dillingham, Charles, 72, 80, 82

Doe, Doris, 16, 216, 242

Donizetti, Gaetano, 139

Douglas DC-3 "Dakota," 267

Douglas, Melvyn, 198

Doulens, Humphrey (G.M. tour manager), 207, 232; Army Air Force, 248

Downes, Olin, 115, 116, 211, 216

Doyle, Dinty (columnist), 228

DuBarry, The, 152, 153, 155, 156

Duke and duchess of Windsor (Wallis Warfield Simpson), 200, 211

Duffy, Father Francis Patrick, 81

Duparc, Marie Eugène, 119, 265

Eames, Emma, 98, 242

Eaton, Quaintance, 15

École du Cordon Bleu, 122

Eddy, Nelson, 181, 202

Eisenhower, Gen. Dwight David, 256

Elizaga, Lorenzo ("Chato"), 103, 105, 106, 235

Elliott, Maxine, 150

Emerson, John, 103

Etude, The, 41

Eugenia (princess of Greece), 172

Fairbanks, Douglas, 218

Falstaff (Verdi), 127

Far Away Meadows, 207, 209, 210; housewarming and reunion, 223, 236, 241, 247, 260, 269–80

Fargo, N. Dak., 234

Farmer, Michael, 149

Farrar, Geraldine, 15, 83, 87, 95, 109, 112, 119, 120, 127, 184, 216, 242

Fauré, Gabriel, 87

Faust (Gounod), 107, 131, 154, 155

First Baptist Church (Chattanooga), 229, 253, 274

Fitzgerald, F. Scott, 63, 103, 144

Fitzgerald, Zelda (Mrs. F. Scott), 63, 103, 144

Flagstad, Kirsten, 184, 192

"Ford Sunday Evening Hour," 155, 163

Fosdick, Dr. Harry Emerson (eulogy), 271

Fox, Virgil, 271

France, 211, 219; Fouquet's, 220, 228, 238; prisoners of war, 256; liberated citizens, 256, 259

Francis, Kay, 141, 143

Franklin, Sidney, 139

Freed, Arthur (songwriter), 139

Fremstad, Olive, 242

French Riviera, 79, 80, 86; Grand Corniche, 103; Maritime Alps, 105, 108, 147, 169, 197, 200; Villa de Cedres, 102, 211, 213, 216, 218, 255, 263

Frog Pond, N. C., 36

Ft. Worth, Texas, 84

Galli-Curci, Amelita, 129, 130, 193

Garber, Goldie, 39, 57, 107

Garden, Mary, 13, 69, 79, 83, 89, 93, 98; becomes G.M's mentor, 101, 104, 122, 126, 160, 164, 179, 186; G. M. pinnacle, 214–16, 223

Gatti-Casazza, Giulio, 94–95, 105, 109, 114, 116, 120, 130, 184

Genoa, Italy, 269

George V (king of England) and Queen Mary 169; command performances, 172, 192

Geri, Ruth (Hollywood reporter), 17

Germany, 108, 174, 219, 221, 228; occupation of France, 255, 265

Gershwin, George, 72; "Rhapsody in Blue," 81

Gest, Morris, 66, 112, 114
Geysendorffer, Capt. G. J. (pilot), 272.
    See also KLM Dutch Airlines
Gianni Schicchi (Puccini), 283
Gigli, Beniamino, 127
Gilbert, John, 129, 143, 145, 151, 157
Gimbel, Bernard, 234, 236
"General Electric Hour," 155
"General Motors Hour," 125
Glendale, Calif., 159
Gluck, Alma, 75, 87
Gluck, Christoph Willibald von, 118
Goldbeck, Ruth Obre (Mrs. W. D.),
    103. *See also* Obre, Ruth
Goldbeck, Walter Dean, 66
Goldwyn, Samuel, 127, 167
Goodman, Lillian Rosedale ("Cherie,
    je t'aime"), 98, 104
"Goodyear Tire and Rubber Hour,"
    155
Gore, Representative Albert (Tenn.),
    272
Gower, Constance and William, 149
Goulding, Edmund, 137, 149, 156
Grace Moore School of Singing, 228–32
Graham, Marion (G.M. secretary), 241
Granada, Spain, 146
Grand Duchy of Luxembourg, 218, 228
Grand Ole Opry (Nashville), 119, 230
Grant, Cary, 194
Greene, Kate Wilson (Mrs. Thomas
    E.), 53–56
Greene, Thomas Evans, 54
Griffis, Stanton, 234, 236, 240
Grove, Isaac Van, 228, 234, 235
Gunn, Glenn Dillard (music critic), 164
Gustav (king of Sweden), Medal of
    Honor to G.M., 193
Gustav Adolph (prince of Sweden),
    267–68

Haakon (king of Norway) and Queen
    Maud, 192, 268
Haber, Joseph (violinist), 254
Hageman, Richard, 230
Hahn, Reynaldo, 119; "Si Mes vers
    avaient des Ailes," 265
Hammerstein, Oscar, 140
Harkness, David, 14
Harris, Sam, 90, 96

Harrison, Jessie, 78, 79, 109, 111
Hartford, Conn., 234
Haydn, Josef, 118
Hayesville, N. C, 36
Hearn, Lafcadio, 282
Heidelberg, Germany, 259
Heifetz, Jascha, 64, 75, 87, 117, 147
Heldy, Fanny, 88
Helena (princess of Rumania), 172
Hempel, Frieda, 193
Henderson, W. J., 115
Herbert, Julia Robards (composer),
    230
Heuningen-Huene, George, 159
Herman, Edward, 89, 105
Hindrum, Mrs. John A., 14, 16, 17
Hitchcock, Raymond, 72, 76
Hitler, Adolf, 174, 212, 213, 216,
    218, 219, 220, 254, 259
Hollywood, Calif., 127–28; G. M. ar-
    rival, 135–37, 142–47, 153–56; big hit
    movie, 159, 160, 165, 167, 175, 177;
    fight with studio, 180–86, 194, 196–
    97, 202; purchase contract, 203, 207,
    209; Hollywood Bowl, 230, 242, 269
Hope, Constance (Mrs. Milton L. Ber-
    liner), 145, 146; *Publicity Is Broccoli*,
    147
Hopkins, Miriam, 143, 167, 210
Horne, Marilyn, 237
Horthy, Adm. Niklos (Hungary), 190
Horton, Gov. Henry H. (Tenn.), 117
Huff, Reverend John A., 229, 253;
    G. M. eulogy, 274
Huff, Helen (G. M. protégée), 229
Huff, Laura (G.M's favorite aunt), 31,
    46
Hull, Cordell (secretary of state), 39,
    185, 235, 240
Huneker, James *(Bedouins)*, 89, 247

Ile de France (steamship), 145–46, 150,
    169
Italy, 108

Jagel, Frederick, 156, 239
Jellico, Tenn., 34–38, 41, 44, 52–53;
    G. M. at home again, 55, 57, 79, 119;
    Emily's wedding, 125–26, 152, 185;
    grief stricken town, 274–75

Jenny Lind Society and Museum, 142, 192
Jeritza, Maria, 242
Johnson, Betty Lawson, 171
Johnson, Edward, 108, 114, 153, 162, 210, 251
Jolson, Al, 127
Jones, Jesse H. (U.S. statesman), 109
Just a Minute (John Cort), 72

Kahn, Alexander (tour arranger), 121
Kahn, Gus, 159
Kahn, Otto, 94, 97, 105, 108, 111, 114, 116, 127, 152, 184
Kastrup Airport (Copenhagen), 265, 267
Kaufman, Louis (banker) and Daisy, 102
Kern, Jerome, 71, 72
Kiepura, Jan, 130, 210
Kilpatrick, Reed, 234, 236
Kirsten, Dorothy (G. M. protégée), 16, 228, 229, 271, 273–74, 279
KLM Dutch Airlines, 267; fatal accident January 27, 1947, 272
Knoxville, Tenn., 34, 107, 125, 163, 274; *Tribune*, 30
Koveman, Ida (L. B. Mayer's secretary), 143
Kullman, Charles, 242

Lachman, Harry (director), 194
La Guardia, Mayor Fiorello (New York City), 176, 257
L'Amore dei Tre Re (Montemezzi), 93, 230, 234, 283
Laurens, S. K. (songwriter), 157
Lawrence, Marjorie, 200
LeGarde, Blanche, 54, 56, 70, 198
Le Havre, France, 219–21
Lehar, Franz, 157
Leopold (king of Belgium), Order of Leopold to G.M., 213
Levitski, Mischa, 75
Lewisohn Stadium, 267, 260; memorial service, 279
Liebling, Leonard, 115
Lifar, Serge, 218
Life Magazine, 80
Lilac Domino, The, 65
Lillie, Beatrice (Lady Peel of London),

81, 96, 104, 135, 136, 143, 149, 164
Lima, Peru, 241
Lind, Jenny, 137, 139, 142; Jenny Lind Room, 270
Little Rock, Ark., 135
Litvak, Anatol, 167
London, 152; Claridge's and Victoria Station, 169–72, 174, 193; Philharmonic orchestra, 198, 213, 260, 264, 270; *Daily Herald, Daily Sketch, Daily Telegraph, Morning Post*, 171
Los Angeles, Calif., 151, 155
Louisville, Ky., 80
Loos, Anita (Mrs. John Emerson), 103
Louise (Charpentier), 88, 89, 95, 105, 122, 198, 212, 213–14; debut at Met, 216; film version, 220; G. M. clash with the Maestro, 222, 223, 232, 251, 262–63, 265, 271; played at G.M. memorial service, 279, 283
Lubitsch, Ernst, 157, 167
Luce, Clare Booth, 269–70
Lynchburg, Va., 107
Lyons, France, 263

McAlister, Gov. Hill (Tenn.), 163
McCall's Magazine, 81
MacArthur, Charles, 103, 140
MacDonald, Jeanette, 157, 181, 202
McDonald, Phoebe (reporter), 185
Mackay, Ellin (Mrs. Irving Berlin), 98
MacKenna, Kenneth, 103
McLean, Evelyn Walsh, 259
McMein, Neysa (Mrs. Jack Baragwanath), 81–83, 87
McSween, Mabel (high school teacher), 42
Madama Butterfly (Puccini), 192; "Un bel dí," 158, 257, 265
Madrid, Spain, 146, 150, 280
Mahan, Thomas Seth, 124, 139, 163
Maison, René, 216
Malibu Beach, Calif., 139, 166
Malone, Dudley Field, 87–88
Manon (Massenet), 102, 105, 121–22; Gavotte, 147, 239, 283
Mantle, Burns, 153
Marafioti, Clara (Mrs. P. Mario), 69, 129
Marafioti, Dr. P. Mario, 67, 69, 93, 104, 111, 129, 136, 143, 158, 165

Maranzoni, Roberto, 93
Marshall, Gen. George C. (secretary of state), 272
Martinelli, Giovanni, 56, 127
Martini, Nino, 130, 254
Mary (queen of England), 169, 172, 213
Massenet, Jules Emile, 102
Matz, Mary Jane, 94
Matthews, Helen Ruth (G. M.'s last secretary), 263
Maud (queen of Norway), 192, 268
Maugham, Somerset, 104, 150
Maurois, André, 68
Maxwell, Elsa, 72, 85–86, 104, 147, 188, 218–21, 230, 242
Mayer, Louis B., 128, 136, 156–57, 187
Medal of Honor of Mexico City, 236
Mediterranean Sea, 79, 103, 218
Melba, Nellie, 98, 112, 171, 193
Melchior, Lauritz, 130
Mendle, Lady Charles (Elsie de Wolfe), 83, 84, 104
Menjou, Adolph, 140, 158
Merola, Gaetano, 156
Mesta, Perle, 218
Metro-Goldwyn-Mayer, 127, 128, 135–37, 141, 146, 155, 157, 165, 181, 202
Metropolitan Opera Co. (Met), 54, 65, 83, 87, 94; G.M's first audition, 95, 96, 97, 108; G. M. debut, 111–14, 127, 128; reaction to Hollywood, 130, 184, 196, 203, 210–11; *Louise*, 216; *Tosca*, 242, 251, 257, 279. See also Appendix: G.M.'s Metropolitan Opera Appearances
Metropolitan Opera Quintet, The, 153–54, 162
Mexico City, 105, 234–36
Miami Beach, Fla., 248
Milan, Italy: La Scala, 93; Teatro Lirico, 105, 108, 109, 269
Millay, Edna St. Vincent, 63, 64
Millöcker, Carl, 152
Milwaukee, Wisc., 197
Minneapolis Symphony Orchestra, 234
Missouri, 108
Molyneux, Capt. Edward H. (Eddie), 86, 88, 104, 119, 149–50, 220
Monte Carlo, 101; casino, 102, 104, 263

Montemezzi, Italo, 93, 94, 230
Moore, Anna Catherine (sister), 39
Moore, Emily Huff (sister), 37, 45, 47, 102, 105, 106, 108, 114; first marriage, to Thomas Seth Mahan, 124–26, 139, 152, 163, 223, 258. See also Wright, Mrs. Kenneth M.
Moore, Estel Carver (brother), 37, 39
Moore, Grace: adolescence and schooling, 41–48, 49–52, 53–55, 56–57; appearance (physical), 44, 128, 129, 159, 227; auditions (Met), 94, 97, 105, 136; autobiography *You're Only Human Once*, 252, 253; birth, 27; character traits inherited, 15–17, 40, 42, 43, 45–46; free spirit, 212, 282; lucky, 96, 102; magic ingredient, eagerness, 54, 75, 88; childhood, 28–33; death, 268, 272; debuts at Covent Garden, 170; as Good-Will Singing Ambassadress, 234–36, 238–41; in Hollywood, 142; at Met, 111, 112; in musical comedy, 90–92; at the Opéra-Comique, 120; earnings, 54, 66, 93, 106, 196, 197; health hazards of dieting, 144, 178, 193, 199, 227, 232, 236, 260, 263; worry about husband's illnesses, 231–32, 263; homes: Casa Lauretta, 165, 174, 188; Far Away Meadows, 207, 222–27; honors: 117, 163, 190, 213, 216, 236, 257; marble plaque at Opéra-Comique, 122; Society of Arts and Sciences award, 167–69 passim; hobbies, 188, 190, 194; legal entanglements, 162, 194–97, 203, 258; loves at first sight, 41, 54–57, 78, 146, 207; marriage, 146–47, 150–51, 160, 211, 238; memorial services, 107, 270, 272–74; messages of condolence, 270, 281; moral code, 247; movies, 140, 142, 145, 166, 176, 187, 194, 208; *Louise*, 220–22, *One Night of Love*, 81, 159–61, 167, 181, 192, 202, 213; Pathé News, 111; parents, 27; radio broadcasts, 119, 125, 155, 165, 172, 199, 250; recordings, 92, 98, 213, 214, 264; repertory, 283; religious affiliations, 46–48, 54, 93, 119, 269, 270; romances, 17, 56–58, 66, 74–75,

78–79, 93, 95–96, 100, 103, 105, 120, 143; scholarship funds, 207, 230; School of Singing, G.M., 228–32; siblings, 28, 37, 45, 47, 55; sports, 42, 51, 145; staff, 177; stage fright, 56, 239; tempestuous prima donna, 121, 124, 258; traumatic experiences, 37, 47, 50, 67, 119, 144, 162, 170, 203; voice, 51, 164, 203, 237; will, 279, 280; world wars, 86, 175, 213, 220, 248, 254

Moore, Grace Elizabeth II (niece), 271, 281

Moore, Herbert Briscoe (brother), 28, 37

Moore, James Leslie (brother), 39, 47, 107, 135, 151, 163, 193, 207, 223, 258, 269, 271, 273, .281

Moore, Marian Volkhardt (Mrs. James L.), 193, 223, 258, 268

Moore, Martin Stokely (brother), 28, 47, 55, 107, 151, 163, 223, 270, 281

Moore, Nancy (Mrs. Richard L. Jr.), 13, 223, 258

Moore, Richard L. Jr. (brother), 39, 47, 107, 108, 139, 151, 163, 223, 258, 270

Moore, Col. Richard Lawson (father), 27, 32, 34, 36, 38, 44, 47, 53–55, 57, 58, 76–77, 93, 107, 108, 109, 151, 163, 169, 175, 186, 253

Moore, Tessie Jane Stokely (Mrs. Richard Lawson mother), 14, 27, 31, 32, 34, 39, 40, 47, 49, 53, 58, 92, 118, 139, 151, 152, 163, 169, 175, 253, 258, 269, 274, 280

Moranzoni, Maestro, 105

Mozart, Wolfgang Amadeus, 214

Murphy, N. C., 31, 36, 176, 274

Murphy, Gerald, 103

Murphy, Sara (Mrs. Gerald), 103

Music Box Revue, 90–93, 96

Mussolini, Benito, 156, 157

Naff, Mrs. L. C. (manager, Ryman Auditorium), 117

Nashville, Tenn.: American, 30, 31, 49, 77; Andrew Jackson Hotel, 119; Centennial Club, 118; Lion's Club, 17, 119; Ryman Auditorium and Union Station, 117; War Memorial Auditorium, 230

Nast, Condé, 82, 83, 85, 102, 160

National Decoration of the Mexican Order of Aztec Eagle, 236

National Service Fellowship Medal, 167

Newman, Gerda (film star and singer), 267

Newport, Tenn., 42, 274

Newton, Ivor (pianist), 264

Newtown, Conn., 207, 270

New York, 50, 58, 63, 64, 71, 90; Capital Theater, 142, 153; Daily Mirror, 272; Daily News, 91, 153; Evening Mail, 92; Evening Post, 153; Fifth Avenue apartment, 124, 151; Herald (Paris edition), 120; Herald Tribune, 232, 242; Journal American, 220; Journal of Commerce, 292, 102, 107, 109, 124, 136, 141; Little Carnegie Playhouse, 223; Manhattan Opera House, 89; Martha Washington Hotel, 58, 152–53, 156, 162, 180; Morning Telegraph, 92, 181, 182, 199, 200, 203, 210, 213; Park Avenue apartment, 115–16, 153, 222, 234, 240, 241; Radio City Music Hall, 160; Ritz Carlton Hotel, 169; Roxy Theater, 251; Savoy Plaza apartment, 247, 252, 256, 274, 281; Sun, 115, Times, 92, 115–16, 153, (Paris staff), 122; 21 Club, 27; World, 82, 92, 115, 253, 263, 270, 273

North Carolina, University of, 281

Obre, Ruth (Mrs. Walter Dean Goldbeck, later Countess de Vallombrosa, still later, Mrs. André Dubonnet), 65, 69, 102

Ochs, Adolph S., 115, 116

O'Donnell, Robert, 234, 236

Oklahoma City, Okla., 151

Omaha, Nebr., 162

"One Night of Love" (song), 158, 160, 167, 192, 265

Opéra-Comique, 87–89, 95, 104, 120, 122, 124, 145, 147, 172, 214, 220, 256, 262, 273; G. M. plaque, 122

Order Ingenio et Arte, 190

Orsatti, Frank (agent), 155, 182

Oslo, Norway, Concert Hall, 192

Owen, Ambassador Ruth Bryan, 190

Packard Agency, 58, 65
Padilla, Exequiel (Mexican Minister of Foreign Affairs), 235, 236
Palace Theater (New York City), 70, 98, 105
Palm Beach, Fla., 97
Palm Springs, Calif., 179
Paramount Pictures, 127, 141; Paris studios, 212
Parera, Valentin: 146, 147, 150, 151; balance wheel, 152–59; Hollywood, 166, 194–203, journeys abroad, 169–93; life in Conn., 209–10; life on Riviera, 211–19, 222–30; overcome by illness, 231–34, 236–38, 240–42; partial recovery, 251–52, 260, 263; tragic blow, 269, 270, 273–274, 279; weds again, 280
Parera, Anne Vanderwalk (second Mrs. Valentin), 280
Paris, France, 79, 84, 87; Ciro's, 90, 95, 102; Bourget Airport, Le, 105, 273; Hotel Astoria, 120; Lyric Theater, 273; Maxim's, 220, 122, 146–47, 164, 181, 190; Montmartre, 122, 213; Paris Opéra, 88, 120, 256, 271; Theater Trocadera, 255
Parker, Dorothy, 81, 82
Parsons, Louella, 136, 143, 185, 203
Pater, Walter, 75–76, 147
Peltier, Jean Loup (pianist), 265, 273
Peru, 241
Pescia, Ustalgo, 228, 229
Pestalozza, Alberto, 149
Philadelphia, Pa., 131, 186, 232, 260
Pickford, Mary, 42, 81, 218
Pinza, Ezio, 216, 234
Pittsburgh, Pa., 80
Pons, Lily, 16, 130, 149, 186, 193
Ponselle, Rosa, 109, 114, 186
Power, Tyrone, 209
Porter, Cole, 87, 103
Porter, Linda (Mrs. Cole), 87, 103
Portland, Ore., 151
Pressman, Dr. Joel, 178, 179, 182
Previn, Andre, 242
Puccini, Giacomo, 107, 112, 172, 242, 243, 257

Quesada, Ernesto de, 234, 235
Quincy, Ill., 81
Quito, Ecuador, 240

Raleigh News and Observer, 36
Rand, Frank C., 109
Randolph-Macon Woman's College, 105, 108, 124
Reeves, Mary Watkins, 67
Reuben, Arnold, 71, 114
Rigoletto, (Verdi), 108
Rio de Janeiro, 239, 241
Rheims, France, 254
Richmond, Va., 258
Riskin, Robert (director), 194
"Ritorna Vincitor" (Aida), 56
Robertson, T. Markoe (Tommy), 74, 75
Robinson, Francis, 12, 14, 16, 280
Rockefeller, John D., 121, 160
Rockefeller, Nelson, 235
Rodeheaver, Homer, 46
Rolland, Romain (Jean-Christophe), 68, 147
Romberg, Sigmund, 140
Rome, Italy, 157, 229, 269
Roméo et Juliette (Gounod), 104, 105, 109, 117, 120, 131, 260, 283; play, 66
Roosevelt, Pres. Franklin D., 39, 223
Rose Marie, 181
Ross, Harold, 81, 82
Rouen, France, 120, 121
Rubin, J. Robert (MGM official), 128
Rye, Gov. Tom C. (Tenn.), 39

Sacramento, Calif., 151
Saint Quinta, Count René de (French Ambassador to U.S.), 216
Salzburg, Austria, 193, 259
Salt Lake City, Utah, 164
San Antonio, Texas, 200
Sanderson, Julia, 72, 74
Sandy Hook, Conn., 207
San Francisco: Opera, 74, 151; Symphony Orchestra, 198
Santa Barbara, Calif., 159
Santiago, Chile, 239
Saranac Lake, N.Y., 231–32, 234, 236, 240–41
Sardou, Victorien, 242–43

Satoris, Cècile (music critic), 89
Saturday Evening Post, 81
Savannah, Ga., 167
Scarlatti, Alessandro, 118
Schang, Frederick C., 16, 150, 152, 154, 160, 180, 196–98, 229; in USAAF, 273–74
Schertzinger, Victor, 158, 167
Schlee, George, 149, 220, 235
Schlee, Valentina (Mrs. George), 149, 220, 235
Schenk, Nicholas (president MGM), 128
Schneider, Louise (music critic), 120
Schumann-Heink, Ernestine, 117, 127
Scotti, Antonio, 83, 242
Seattle, Wash., 164
Sheen, Monsignor Fulton (now Archbishop), 269, 270, 272
Serafin, Tullio (conductor), 105
Sevareid, Eric, 17
Shaw, George Bernard, 87, 184
Shaw, Oscar, 96
Sheean, Vincent, 16
Shearer, Norma (Mrs. Irving Thalberg), 129, 136, 167, 194
Short, Hassard (stage director), 90
"Sign of the Southern Cross," 239
Simpson, Wallis Warfield (Mrs. Ernest), 171. *See also* Duke and duchess of Windsor
Slabtown, Tenn. (Nough), 27, 34, 274
Sloan, George (Met Chairman), 272
Smart Set, 86
Sofia, Bulgaria, 214
Sorel, Cècile, 86, 87
South Africa, 263, 265
South American tour, 108, 235, 238, 240, 247
Spain, 108, 174; Barcelona, 150; Civil War, 218; San Sebastian, 150
St. Leger, Frank, 251
Steel, John, 91, 93
Stenbock, Count A., 267
Sternberg, Josef Von, 180, 182
Stevens, Risë, 130
Stockholm, Sweden, 192, 193, 267, 268
Stokely, Emma Huff (Mrs. William Russell, maternal grandmother), 29, 31, 35

Stokely, Estel (uncle), 32
Stokely, William Russell (maternal grandfather), 30, 35
Stothart, Herbert (songwriter), 139
Stowe, Leland, 207
Stroheim, Eric Von, 157
Strok, A. (Far East booking agent), 256, 257
Suite Sixteen, 70, 114
Sved, Alexander, 239
Swanson, Gloria, 137, 149
Swarthout, Gladys (Mrs. Frank Chapman), 16, 130, 149, 179, 186, 270
Sweden, 192–93, 263, 265, 267–68
Switzerland, 108; St. Moritz, 263; Swiss Alps, 169, 193

Talley, Marion, 108, 127
Taylor, Deems, 223
"Telephone Hour" (Famous Artists series), 250
Tennessee, 30, 34, 64, 108–9, 113–14, 185, 259, 272–73; University of, 55, 207
Ternina, Milka, 242
Tetrazzini, Luisa, 193
Thaïs (Massenet), 89, 127, 179
Thalberg, Irving, 136, 141–43, 156–57, 167, 181, 194, 195
Thalberg, Norma Shearer (Mrs. Irving), 136, 167, 194
Thalberg, Sylvia (screenwriter), 140
Thill, Georges, 120–21, 124, 212
Thiral, Roger, 87
This Week, 89
Thomas, Bob (Cohn's biographer), 182
Thomas, Mrs. Joseph B., 232
Thomas, Jane (Nette), 72, 95
Thomson, Virgil, 16, 232, 242–43
Tibbett, Jane Bogard (second Mrs. Lawrence), 270
Tibbett, Lawrence, 109, 127–28, 140–43, 149–50, 164, 270–72
"Toi Seule" (Tchaikovsky), 265
Toledo Blade, 36
Tosca, (Puccini), 232, 234, 238–39; "Vissi d'arte," 243, 251, 258–60
Toscanini, Arturo, 169, 193
Town Gossip, 79
Toye, Geoffrey, 169–71
Trabadello, M., 87

Tramell, Herman, 35
Tramell, Mabel, 45
Turin, Italy, 269
Tucson, Ariz., 197
Twentieth-Century Fox, 143, 159, 160

Ulbeck, Madame Sylvia, 137
United States, 165, 174, 235, 238
Up in the Clouds (Gates), 80
U.S. Good-Will Singing Ambas-
  sadress, 235–36, 238, 240–41
USO, 141, 247, 151, 254, 256
U. S. Treasury war-bond drives, 248,
  250
U.S.S. *America*, 273
"Un bel di" *(Madama Butterfly)*, 158,
  257, 265

Valentina (Mrs. George Schlee), 149,
  220, 235
Vallee, Rudy, 160
Vanderbilt, Consuelo (Mrs. Jacques
  Balsan), 188
Vanderbilt University, 119
Vanderbilt, Commodore Cornelius,
  119
Vanderwalk, Anne (second Mrs. Valen-
  tin Parera), 269, 280
Vanity Fair, 82
Verese, Italy, 105
Venice, Italy, 95, 102, 149, 169, 193,
  269
Vienna, Austria, 149, 152, 190, 193,
  211, 260
Verdi, Giuseppe, 116, 127
Victor Chemical Co., 165
Victoria (princess of England), 172
Victor records, 213–214, 250. *See also*
  G. M. Discography
Victor Symphony Orchestra, 250
Vincent, Dr. George E., 109
Vitaphone, 127
Vogue, 82
Volkhardt, Marian (Mrs. James L.
  Moore, Jr.), 193, 207
Vorhees, Donald, 125

Wagner, Richard, 78, 130, 149, 218
Wagner, Charles L., 56, 111
Waldo, Mr. and Mrs. George, 209
Walker, Joe (expert movie cameraman),
  158
Walter, Bruno, 105
Ward-Belmont School for Girls, 49–52,
  81, 111, 118, 230. *See also* Moore,
  Grace
Warren, Robert Penn, 225
Warren, Whitney, Jr., 74
Warren, Whitney, Sr., 74
Washington, D. C., 53, 58, 107, 141–
  42, 185–86, 258
Warsaw, Poland, 214, 221
Washburn, Professor Charles Camp-
  bell, 51–52
Webb, Clifton, 65, 86, 103, 149, 197,
  202
White, Evelyn (ardent fan), 273
White, George, 71
Whiteman, Paul, 81, 130
Whitney, F. C., 70, 71
Wilhelmina (queen of the Netherlands),
  268
Williams, Tudor, 156
Williamsburg, Ky., 46
Winchell, Walter, 203
Wiseman, Sir William, 94
Wolfe, Elsie de (Lady Charles Mendle),
  83, 86, 104
Woman's Home Companion, 81
Woman's Suffrage Movement, 50, 77
Woods, Henry (songwriter), 139
Woollcott, Alexander, 81–82, 92, 103
Wright, Emily Moore (Mrs. Kenneth
  M.), 48, 102. *See also* Moore, Emily
  Huff; Mahan, Mrs. Thomas Seth

York, Cpl. Alvin C., 64

Ziegfeld, Florenz, 96, 159
Ziegler, Edward, 94, 97, 196, 210
Zirato, Bruno, 105–6
Zimbalist, Efrem, 75